CROSS

MY

HEART

by Frank Scully

New York

GREENBERG : Publisher

To the Memory of
Carolyn Patten Swett
February 2, 1870–June 14, 1944

For this body at best
Is a bundle of aches
Longing for rest.

Introduction

•

"This is a book I want from you," said a publisher who knew me like a book. He wrote "This Is My Faith" on the back of an envelope. "I don't want the wisecracking Scully. I have known him for twenty years and he was a doomed man. I want you to unlock the secret that kept the other Scully from sinking into oblivion all these years."

That was in 1933.

In the summer of 1953, while making kneelers for a chapel we had built on our ranch on the Mojave Desert, and padding them with rubber to comply with the demands of Air Foam Christianity, I got to thinking about that conversation of twenty years before. I asked the publisher if he still wanted that confession of faith. He said he did.

Cross my heart, this is it.

Desert Springs
California

FRANK SCULLY

Contents

1

Thunder and Enlightenment

•

God made you an individualist, Frank, and for once you sure cooperated!"

It was a remark lightly tossed off by Edward F. Murphy, S.S.J., author of, among other works, *The Scarlet Lily* and *The Yankee Priest*. He was standing at the door of Bedside Manor, our Hollywood hilltop home, which those of our children who have been to college say looks like a merger of a religious goods store and a miniature of Grand Central Station.

The chaos that passed for order was not wholly of our making. For years, when things got too disorderly we used to say by way of warning: "And then the Cardinal came!"

This ran back to a time when James Francis Cardinal Mc-Intyre, the first Prince of the Church to be elected to the College of Cardinals from Los Angeles, wrote us that he understood because of poor health I didn't get around much and if it were convenient he would like to pay a visit some afternoon.

The afternoon His Eminence picked Bedside Manor couldn't have looked worse if bandits had just raided it. It had been a hot night and some of our children and neighbors' children had slept on the terrace which opened from the living room and looked over all Hollywood. Their bedding was still on the terrace, we being the determined sort of parents who insist children shall clean up their own messes. The whole place looked

1

like Margaret Kennedy's description of the Sanger Circus in
The Constant Nymph. But the Cardinal treated it as if it were
as orderly as High Mass.

The place was neater, though, the day Father Murphy called.
He had come up from New Orleans, where he is on the faculty
of Xavier University. We had a holy and hilarious time at
breakfast and afterward, until he had to leave for a studio appointment. I, who write with the hope of being interrupted,
was reluctant to see him go, particularly after that remark,
which I felt unlocked the door to a mystery that must have
puzzled many people, myself included.

On the surface I belonged to a large group whose day-to-day
behavior is a mosaic of contradictions—the sort who want
peace and will fight at the drop of a glove for it, who favor a
superstate like the United Nations provided we don't have to
give up one inch of local autonomy, who think that nationalism
and large standing armies have just about ruined Europe but
that universal military training in America constitutes a horse
of a decidedly different color, who think churches are good to
see but a bore to spend much time in, who join anything that
comes along but rarely put their shoulders to the wheel afterward.

I suspect my inconsistencies over the years have exceeded
even those of the general run of fellow Americans. I was a confirmed bachelor for thirty-eight years; I then married and fathered five children. I was a non-joiner and then proceeded to
preside over everything from a chamber of commerce to a foundation to find a cure for muscular dystrophy. I grew up in a
big city and then spent my adult years as a cure-chasing escapologist in desert hamlets. I thought politics was for the birds
and then proceeded to become so active politically I nearly got
my head blown off and actually had to be heaved out of office
by some lawless goons at the controls. I wrote hardboiled stories,

controversial and belligerent best sellers, and then veered off in the blue and spent a year cleaning up and adding holy humor to nursery rhymes.

My ideal seemed to be neither left-wing, nor right-wing, but, like the angels, all wings. To be on the side of the angels never was easy but seemed particularly difficult in the modern world where material progress had practically become deified. I had to go back two thousand years to find the sort of people whose views I shared. And most of them came to ignominious ends. They were hanged, thrown to the lions, or condemned to a dismal existence in catacombs. But, secretly, I loved them and prayed to be like the bravest of them.

I became a grief commissioner without portfolio and liked nothing better than helping people far better off than myself solve their troubles. I told them my secret was to take everything but life seriously. At least that made them laugh and restored a sense of proportion. I was a gypsy who had traveled over half the world and at the same time hated to move across a room. Scratch me anywhere and as in Alexander the Great the ichor of a rebel seemed to flow. My heroes were men like St. Jerome who defied his superiors and then retreated to the desert to translate the Bible in the Vulgate version used to this day. My heroines were women like St. Thérèse who said she was going to spend her Heaven doing good on earth. I was, in the phrase of the day, just one more crazy mixed-up kid, though by the time of this conversation with Father Murphy I was a white-haired grandfather of sixty, delicately supported by one lung, one leg, and about one idea.

I had been blessed with the happiest marriage since the Feast of Cana, despite the fact that we lived for twenty years in an area of America where there were four divorces for every three marriages.

At home all was harmony, love, and understanding. But all

around us holy wedlock seemed in shreds, civic virtue seemed lower than the Dead Sea, and all over the world people with different political and economic ideologies seemed to be fighting for the same material ends. They made and unmade alliances with the debased practicality of Hollywood marriages. They didn't so much believe they were good as that their neighbors were bad.

It was difficult to follow them or stay with them as they shuttled back and forth. It became increasingly clear to me that I had one soul to save and that was my own. If by precept and example this could inspire others to do likewise, we would all be saved and more than likely the world would be saved from reaping the seeds of its own wilful destruction. By living as if we really believed our kingdom was not of this earth we would bring the Garden of Eden back to this world. To the modern world I knew this sort of bias seemed like another variety of chauvinism, so I kept such articles of faith more or less to myself.

This would have been my answer to Father Murphy's sally, but because it would not have been news to him I didn't give it. Instead I remarked that his clerical black outlined against the red of our front door made him look like an anointed *réclame* of Monte Carlo. We embraced amid laughter and said good-by.

I watched him walk up the brick walk, wondering why I never in my life thought of being a priest, since I loved priests so much.

Here was one who was born in Salem, Massachusetts, and knew the story of the slave trade so well, he vowed when he grew up to join a religious order which was devoting itself to the reparation of injustices that whites had visited on blacks. He found what he wanted in the Order of St. Joseph.

Once having been rewarded with a trip to Europe, he met

a Negro architect in New York who pined for just such a cultural experience. Father Murphy had a first-class ticket. He turned it in for *two* third-class tickets and gave one to the architect. They shared a cabin below deck.

Why had I feared I never would have been able to stand the discipline of holy orders? Because such obedience and humility narrowed one's development? Who could have had more freedom than Father Murphy, as this one illustration shows? He wrote as he pleased and this gave pleasure to a lot of readers. He had plenty of liberty. He didn't want more.

What was there about being an individualist in a day when even the rich and the poor hunted in packs? The mother who, watching the troops marching by said "They're all out of step but Jim" would have made me proud if she had been my mother. I was all for Jim. But why? Because he was out of step, or because he was out of step with the regimentation of the world? It's important to know which.

To those who thought I was a mixed-up modern Don Quixote, would it matter to them if they knew I was not trying to tilt windmills by hand but striving to rope them with a rosary?

The more I thought of Father Murphy's parting remark, the more it struck me as the truest summary one man ever made as to what motivated the life of another. The most comforting thing about his time capsule was that he said God had a hand in making me what I was.

One cannot write a personal confession without seeming to some readers—some bigger than himself, others smaller—to have developed chronic I-trouble. God does not share this view. He holds each of us personally accountable for our acts. No penitent says, "Through *somebody's* fault." He says, "Through *my* fault."

Some writers get around this difficulty by using such phrases as "the writer" or "this reporter" or by simply putting down a highly personal opinion as if it were dug from some ruins on Mount Sinai by an automatic shovel. This is a style peculiar to editorial writers who specialize in big type.

But isn't it fairer in a personal confession of one's beliefs to use the first personal singular, not as an exaltation of one's ego but simply as an identification tag? I have one leg and one lung, but I have a draft card that says: *"Identifying Marks: Wears glasses."*

Can you imagine an FBI man on the hunt for an aging author whose only identifying mark was that he wore glasses? Actually I was flattered by this tag, because I have never thought of myself as a cripple, either. However, it would have pleased me even more if the draft board had said: *"Identifying Marks: Wears a scapular and a cord of the Third Order of St. Francis."*

Well, we can make it clear at the beginning that the first person singular, though it stands up like a self-raised obelisk to oneself, is really nothing more than an outstanding proof of the limitations of the English language.

This then is the story of my body. God gave it a soul. Many times I lost sight of their unity. Many times I thought the body's perfection was everything. It took more than half my life to realize which came first. In the forty-odd years I spent as a health-seeker over half the uncivilized world, I took time out now and then to find out what made me tick the way I ticked. I had examined my conscience hundreds of times and had found so many things wrong with me that I despaired of ever finding the right answer to myself or anything else. The trouble was I was more rebellious than I was religious.

The only positive and constant things in my life were pain and good humor. Though I had been crippled since I was seventeen, I never thought of myself as permanently crippled. Generally speaking, I presented a picture of a cheerful invalid. I literally had fun in bed, and this in the sense the phrase was used in the half-dozen convalescent handbooks I edited. I often thought more of others than I did of myself. Surrounded by fellow sufferers, I often tried to right situations which made others suffer unnecessarily. I was not cowed or awed by authority, nor did I deify specialists. They were human and they erred, and I was charitable toward them when they failed. But I couldn't stand self-centered ignorance.

It is of course a common Irish characteristic to be "agin the govamint" chiefly because the Irish had been misruled for centuries. Unlike my Saviour, I wouldn't trust a Caesar with even his half of a coin.

Thus I got in the habit of rarely thinking the best of superiors in any field and was delighted when someone high and mighty was getting his. Every time I read how Christ heaved the money-changers out of the temple I almost cheered, not so much because they were sacrilegious as because they were bankers.

On the other hand when He brushed off worldly honors by reminding His followers and His critics that His kingdom was not of this earth, I wished on many occasions I could have said the same. In my heart I felt that what the world had to offer any place any time was worth dying for about as much as a counterfeit three-dollar bill.

Whenever I succumbed to the world's temptations, decorations, allurements, or honors, which I often did, I inwardly felt ashamed at being so weak as to enjoy these things. It wasn't that I didn't think I deserved them. I didn't think anybody deserved them, certainly not the ones who were usually awarded them.

As the world viewed success I had had more than a fair share. As it viewed failure I had had plenty. The difference between them when viewed in terms of eternity wasn't the thickness of a fingernail. Men have ruled other men by that thickness, it is true. All I can say is they have not ruled me by it. At least not with my consent.

To me the free world and the slave world are political distinctions, not necessarily as clear-cut as black and white. I have taught our children that in this world we are all slaves. We either give ourselves orders or others give us orders. There is no escaping slavery, not even in the free world. He who is his own master is therefore his own slave. Even a tramp is not free to go where he likes. There are all sorts of ordinances which he will have to obey or land in jail. The same goes for a freewheeling capitalist.

In areas where the Church has been allowed to function without political interference it has frequently expressed its gratitude and repaid the kindness by blunting the sharp edges of the evils inherent in any and all political and economic systems. Where it has been hampered or persecuted, it has answered with martyrdom.

The Scullys may have supplied some of these (for there are many anonymous saints), but the best I can say of us is that none ever completely strayed from the fold. We did not supply any priests or nuns, but we never had a divorce either.

We were a large family, ten children in all, though only Tom and I lived beyond our twenties. Irish families of that size usually have one child inspired by a call to Holy Orders, the one who is supposed to do all the praying for the rest of them. Such good fortune did not befall us.

Unlike our own children, who were born in cathedral cities like Paris, New York and Los Angeles, I was born in a town that didn't even have a Catholic church. It was Steinway, a minor note in the symphony of Greater New York and named after "the instrument of the immortals". I was born on April 28, 1892, the day Chauncey Olcott was writing from London to Lillian Russell for a job as the tenor in her Broadway company.

I went to a brand new school, called P.S. 84. In order not to annoy any sect the principal read from the Old Testament at the beginning of assembly each day. Nobody apparently took issue with the Old Testament. His name was Dr. John Melville. He had a Ph.D., which was quite a distinction in those days, and read in a soft mellow voice, which was certainly not an authentic reading of the thunder of the Old Testament.

To hear the thunder we had to go several miles from home to Mount Carmel Catholic Church, which was in Astoria, the next town. We had to go anyway, thunder or no thunder, because we were Roman Catholics and had to attend Mass every Sunday and every holy day of obligation on reaching the age of reason, which was seven.

The parish priest was Irish and when he talked he became increasingly angry with the perfidities of the world and the transgressions of his flock, especially those who spent Saturday night at North Beach, a junior grade summer resort in the Coney Island syndrome. Every now and then he would come to a halt in his denunciations of the place, and get himself under control. He would then continue in a lower key for a while and work himself up to a *crescendo* again. He certainly put the fear of God into us.

This sort of inflamed oratory has passed away in the main, though you still run into it now and then in pulpits and on political platforms. When the sermons became really thunderous I was comforted to see our principal in the congregation. I would glance at him and gain solace from the calm way he faced these denunciations of the evils in our midst. It soothed me to see that none of this thunder rubbed off on him when he read the Bible to us at assembly the next day.

Our parish priest talked with a brogue and his assistant was an Italian with as little command of English as a Venetian gondolier. It was hard to understand either of them, but there was no mistaking their moral indignation. My father told me this failure was not important. "In Shakespeare," he explained, "the play's the thing. In church the miracle of Mass is everything. Sermons are secondary. Those who go to early Masses get short sermons. It's the late Masses that get the long sermons and being mainly attended by lazybones they need them more."

We were a big family and lived in the two ground-floor apartments of a six family house my father had built. It was one of the few privately-owned places in what was otherwise the company town of Steinway. The Steinways escaped from a turbulent Europe shortly after the Revolution of 1848 and set up making pianos in America as they had in the old country. Three of the family served in the Civil War but had recovered sufficiently by 1866 to open Steinway Hall on 14th Street, the predecessor to the one now on West 57th Street. New York was their show window but the real work of making these instruments was at the far end of Long Island City on Bowery Bay. The family had a large estate there. It adjoined the amusement park known as North Beach, now a part of La Guardia Field.

A fairly law-abiding citizen, I hadn't as a boy, and haven't now, an awe or even a fear of cops. Several of our gang were sons of cops. One cop advanced to become Police Lieut. Becker, executed for his part in the Rosenthal murder at the Hotel Metropole years later. Most of the cops were fat and if taunted into hot pursuit were soon out-distanced. Today of course they would shoot kids like us in the back on failing to obey their command to "Halt!"

In 1900 five boroughs were consolidated into the City of Greater New York. But in my childhood Steinway, now a part of the Borough of Queens, was run by a handful of Irish politicians who congregated around the Long Island shore of the 34th Street ferry. These politicians had small use for the Germans who were our neighbors, and once when the election returns seemed to indicate the Germans had voted against Mayor Paddy Gleason, he cut off their water supply in reprisal.

My father took a day off and journeyed to the mayor's office and demanded the water be turned on again. He reminded Gleason that the Germans might thrive very well on beer, but there were some Irish who needed water with their whiskey and they would not stand for his high-handed nonsense. Though my father was inclined to appeal to the courts for redress, he assured His Honor that others favored bashing in the mayor's head with alley apples, as cobblestones were called in that set. His Honor relented and invites us all, Germans included, to a chowder party and boat ride to Connelly's Grove, College Point —all at the mayor's expense.

My father came to Steinway in a roundabout way. He was an engineer and, on arriving from Ireland, worked on the caissons of the Brooklyn Bridge. Then he was called to Hartford to share in the perfecting of the Gatling gun in Colt's Armory. He then swung over to Brooklyn and worked on the change from brown sugar to white sugar at Havemeyer's refinery. That done, he was asked to head up a dye manufacturing plant in Steinway. It adjoined the Steinway piano plant.

He met my mother when he was working at Havemeyer's. They were married by her parish priest in Brooklyn. She was of Irish descent but a more fiery sort than my father. He was a well-nourished middle-aged man when I was born, with masses of black curly hair, and the finest set of teeth I've ever seen. He didn't have a filling or an extraction till he died at 59. He could have doubled in appearance for Theodore Roosevelt. They had a lot in common, too, being both high-tariff Republicans. But T.R. was a member of the Dutch Reformed Church while my father was as Catholic as Saint Patrick. He was not, however, of the sort of Irish who are so proud of it they remind you of green porcupines. He took everything calmly, even being Irish.

His favorite newspaper was Charles A. Dana's sardonic *Sun*.
It became mine in time, too. He was a beautiful mixture of the
poet and the practical man, which was not surprising for he was
of the Clan O'Scholaidhe, which is Gael for 'scholar.' His vo-
cation was engineering; his avocation, a minstrel boy. He didn't
smoke or drink, but he sang. He wrote his own ballads, folk
songs and travel ditties, and taught us the choruses so we could
all join in. I remember some of the titles. *Take a Peek at Scully's
Landing Where McGarry Downward Flew, Burke's Wooden
Castle on Berrian's Isle* and *The One-Armed Buccaneer Who
Wound the Car-Barn Clock* were some.

My mother was the sort who would light blessed candles and
huddle in a darkened room during thunder storms. My father,
on the other hand, would sit by an open window, and revel in
the thunder and lightning. To my mother such a storm was proof
that God was angry with us. My father rather favored the theory
that He thought we needed some rain and was drawing our
attention to the wisdom of preparing for it. Our roof, my father
explained to my mother, was in good condition. We had nothing
to fear.

We didn't either. He was a good provider and though he
worked hard all week, he would get up for early Mass on Sunday and walk the several miles to and from church. (Apparently
the trolley cars were too tired after the Saturday night revels at
North Beach to move.) After Mass he would have a whopping
big breakfast, featuring steaks or chops, and then change to his
work-clothes. The rest of the day he would spend making re-
pairs on one of the three houses he owned.

He could do anything with his hands. His carpentry was of
cabinet-making caliber. He could wipe a joint as well as the best
plumbers. I loved to work beside him. I would fetch and carry
tools for him, and was constantly amazed at his skill. He gave
me the happiest childhood a boy ever had.

Most of this repair work, according to our parish priest, might have come under "unnecessary servile work", but my father thought it necessary and in any event he felt there was nothing servile about it. It wasn't the sort of work he did weekdays and he took as much pleasure in it as other executives take today in gardening or golf. He taught me that all work in the sight of God is equally dignified and should be arranged to make people happy, not weary, disheartened and bitter. I never saw him come home from work except smiling, and I loved to meet his trolley and take his grip from his hand, earn a pat on the head, get a rough male kiss, and bask in that heavenly smile of his.

I never heard him take issue with his faith, except once in the matter of hell and damnation. He treated hell-fire rather as he treated lightning. He once confessed as much to his father-confessor who then asked him if he doubted he would have to make some retribution for his trespasses against God's laws. He said he did not doubt this at all and was truly sorry for ever having offended God in any way. His father-confessor assured him it was more important to be sorry for having offended God, who loved us all, than to be frightened into reforming, gave him absolution, blessed him, and told him to go and sin no more.

Since that time I have observed more and more the Church's emphasis on contrition for the offense rather than dread of the pains of hell and I have been heartened by it. I, too, like to do kind things because I like to do them, not because of fear of what will happen if I don't.

Besides, obeying God's commandments is like swimming with the tide. It's easier that way.

2

A Rosary for Remembrance

•

TODAY Catholic children receive instructions in preparation for their First Holy Communion when they are seven, but in my childhood the awesome experience was postponed till several years later. The children are supposed to be well versed—letter perfect, in fact—in the Baltimore Catechism, a book of questions and answers that runs 130 pages.

They are examined by the parish priest and those who pass are permitted to quake through their first soul-washing experience in the Sacrament of Penance (confession) on Saturday, and then the next morning, dressed all in white, they are invited to share in the mystical body, a holy ecstasy that, however often repeated, never quite wears off through life. After their First Communion, if in a state of grace, they may share in this feast all days of the year, barring Good Friday.

After my first confession I didn't have the awesome solace of holy communion the next day because I didn't make my First Communion until I was twelve. I was confirmed, however, when I was ten. This was because the Bishop of Brooklyn, who presided over all confirmations on Long Island, came to our church in Astoria only once every three to five years.

To make the instructions easier, I was transferred from P.S. 84 to Mount Carmel School and thus had to add a six-mile hike each day to the normal mileage a boy piles up in doing nothing in particular.

To reach Mount Carmel School I had to pass through an area of young hoodlums called the Ninth Avenue Gang. Some I knew at P.S. 84, and I was not in the least afraid of them there, but passing through their neighborhood singlehanded took lots more courage than facing up to them in the schoolyard, which was at our end of town, not theirs.

All my life I have got on easily with underworld characters as well as those in higher callings. I am simply not afraid of one, nor awed by the other. This compassion is as easy for anti-social characters to sense as their hostility to the law-enforcement arm is for us to see.

Once I had arrived in the parochial school yard I felt much better. And I felt best of all when we entered the classroom and I could see our teacher. She was a beautiful, rosy-cheeked, slender nun of the Order of St. Joseph. Her name was Sister Frances Geraldine. She was the first one to teach me that it is better to work hard and get a thing done so you can play with nothing on your conscience. Thus you might excel in sports as well as in studies. "Work when you work, play when you play," she used to say. "But don't spoil your fun by mixing them up."

In public school I soon found out that teachers would not keep you for more than a half-hour after school, because they had appointments elsewhere and a home life which they favored far more than the ordeal of the class room. So I would outsit them until with a sigh they would say: "You may go home now."

But at Mount Carmel that didn't happen. After even an hour the Sister never said anything of the sort. She ordered us back to our seats and told us to study the lesson for another half-hour when she would question us again.

This went on till as late as six o'clock, and then one day she explained to us there was plenty of menial work for her to do in the convent and if we insisted on not learning our lessons she much preferred the quiet of the classroom, where she could read undisturbed, to the drudgery of housework in the convent. The logic of this floored me. It was my first lesson in free will and the wisdom of gaining freedom by a self-imposed temporary enslavement.

I loved to play football. We had a great team called The Comet Mascots. This was in an era before floodlights. Thus if we didn't get our practice and our play in before dark—no football. So I decided I simply would have to buckle down, as they say in Winsocki, and get a little ahead of the lesson of the day rather than drag so far behind it. It worked out beautifully and I still thank Sister Frances Geraldine, who must have long ago passed to her heavenly reward, for effecting this change in my life.

Unfortunately, after two years at Mount Carmel school, I developed a sort of rheumatic fever and the six-mile hike became too much for me; so I returned to P.S. 84. By this time I was so far ahead of my contemporaries who had stayed in P.S. 84 that I began coasting again till they could catch up. They didn't catch up until we were graduated, and thus I fell back into an old habit of understudying rather than overstudying.

In my childhood the Church's view was that if they were able to educate a child till he or she reached high school they wouldn't have to worry about the child's soul thereafter. In my case their policy has been vindicated in the main. Though I went to a public high school and a non-Catholic university and after that into an unbelieving world, or at least many areas of it, I stuck fairly well to what I had been taught under those nuns at old Mount Carmel.

In fact on one occasion when I was in London I was invited to take a trip to Russia, all expenses paid, and when I found out that there would be precious few places where I could attend Mass, only one in fact (in Moscow) in the whole country,

I said, "No thanks, not for me." So I have never seen Russia and because I have never seen the place I have not damned it, either. As instructed by Our Lady of Fatima, I pray for the Russians, figuring that there are more than enough people cursing them as it is.

3

The Wounded Eagle

•

LIKE most boys who found themselves handed a surprise package which, when opened, turned out to be the twentieth century, I carried an interest in sports and adventure almost to the verge of a fixation. The year I was born—1892—Charles A. Dana of the *Sun* was seventy-two years old, Charles E. Duryea was trying out his first horseless buggy, the Pinkertons were shooting down the Homestead strikers, the Australians were introducing their famous ballot, and Charlie Hogan drove Engine 999 (the Empire State Express) in excess of a hundred miles per hour—the fastest any human had ever traveled up to that time.

The four hundredth anniversary of the discovery of America fell in that same year, but it was not actually celebrated until 1893 with a World's Fair in Chicago. A fifty-cent piece known as the Columbus half-dollar was struck by the mint. One was placed in my tiny hand to celebrate the coincidence. I treasured it for years but lost it about the time it would have become a collector's item.

By the time I was old enough to talk back to my elders, the Olympic Games were being revived in Athens and my imagination was fired by the success of American athletes. A little later the exploits of Teddy Roosevelt and his Rough Riders in the Spanish American War were emulated by us kids in Stein-

way, and I had my head split open by a rock while leading a
charge up our own particular San Juan Hill. It was thrown by
a member of our rear guard who didn't have quite the strength
to reach the enemy. He probably grew up to shoot officers in
the back. I bled profusely for my country on that occasion.

When T. R. became President, the old Greek ideal of a
sound mind in a sound body got a lively renaissance. Presumably that accomplished, the soul would take care of itself. He
believed in the strenuous life and welcomed athletes to the
White House. I was all for it. Besides, he was my father's hero.
I thought Charles Dana Gibson's sketch of a lot of hero-
worshiping kids trailing popeyed behind a strutting heavy-
weight champion was a greater work of art than anything in
the Metropolitan Museum.

From the time I was ten I played, even overplayed, every
sport I ever heard of. I scrounged around for material and improvised much of the athletic equipment needed to play. We
had no Boy's Club, no Boy Scouts or Big Brothers to give us
equipment. We cut hockey sticks from the roots of shrubs. Our
disks were bashed-in tin cans. We took two discarded Christmas
trees, cut the branches in close, and used the denuded trees for
high jump standards. We made our own pole for vaulting, dug
our own pits and runway. I found a platter-shaped rock weighing about four pounds and used it for discus-throwing. I
watched great all-around athletes like Martin Sheridan practice
at Celtic Park, now an apartment house development but then
the home of the Irish American Athletic Club. I had an uncle
who was a trolley car motorman. His old gloves served for playing baseball, the left one for right-handers, the right one for
left-handers. Our balls were taped when the stitches broke. The
black tape made the ball sting but it was better than nothing.

The sport in which we excelled was football. Our equipment
was strictly sandlot, as was our playing field. Helmets were

made by our mothers out of rags sewn like a fat sausage skin and then stuffed with cotton from old bustles. Sometimes we used to stuff the football with rags, too, when we had no money for a pneumatic inner bladder. Skinned faces, elbows, and shins were more or less ignored. A veneer of spit took the place of iodine. Bloody noses were stopped by the hand of time.

In the fall we would run miles in cross-country races. Or an older bunch, armed with rubber hoses, would give us a head start in a game of cops and robbers. Once they almost caught us, but all of us were stopped in our tracks by real cops who had been shooting it out all night with a bandit hidden in a cornfield. One of the cops was blinded for life by the bandit's buckshot. He turned out to be my cousin.

I was big for my age and usually competed against boys several years my senior. I didn't know what fatigue or fear was. I had none of the childhood diseases, either. I even boxed with sparring partners of professional fighters rather than with kids. I got my nose broken twice, once by one of these palookas and once on a missed flying tackle. Otherwise my body seemed singularly elastic.

It remained elastic until I was seventeen, at which time I was five feet ten and weighed 150 pounds. Then one day in a football game while carrying the ball through the line I got my right leg caught in a mixup. I fell across a rock. Friends and foes alike piled on me.

The least I should have come out with was a broken leg. It would have been better that way, as it turned out. But instead of breaking the thigh bone, I sprung it, and some fibres inside the bone broke off and floated around in the marrow. They had no outlet.

The injury didn't seem to bother me particularly at the time. In fact, I kept right on overdoing in sports. Months after the injury, I played as many as three basketball games in one day.

Then on the night of February 11, 1911, I started home after
a hard session of practice with a semi-professional basketball
team. It was snowing and I began to limp from pain. The next
day, Lincoln's birthday, was a holiday. But not for me. I
couldn't get out of bed.

It was thought that rest would ease the pain. It didn't. It got
worse. Doctors were consulted. They in turn consulted specialists. (They were cheap in those days.) The next thing I knew I
was being shipped to St. Elizabeth's Hospital, now on Washington Heights, but in those days on West 53rd Street. I was transported in a horse-drawn cab, the kind usually reserved for fu-
nerals. It cost my family five dollars. Everything at the hospital,
private room and board included, cost twenty dollars a week.

X-rays revealed that those free-wheeling fibres had developed
an abscess inside the bone and there was no way to get them
out save by chiseling into the bone. I had developed a condition
known as osteomyelitis, a disease that attained some gilt-by-
association years later by killing young Calvin Coolidge when
his father was President. But the disease was little known in
my time.

Thus began a horizontal career that during the next forty
years was to carry me into thirty hospitals in seven countries
in search of a cure. Each operation would put me in drydock
for several months, and then I would get up and around—first
on crutches, then with a cane—till another attack made surgery
again imperative. Many times I was near death and was surprised, as a minor poet once wrote, "that one so grim should
think of me who rarely thought of him."

The nuns who ran St. Elizabeth Hospital were Franciscans
—that is to say, of the Order of St. Francis of Assisi. Today I
belong to the Third Order of this religious rule, but in those
days I knew very little about them, my patron saint being St.
Francis Xavier, a Jesuit. They saw that I received Extreme Unc-

tion before the operation. Instead of scaring me, this made me singularly calm. I was in a state of grace. That meant I was one of the lucky ones.

The surgeons joked with me while preparing for the operation. They dug up a wire splint which had been used on a Civil War major and told me they were giving it to me free. Then they put the ether cone over my doubly fractured nose. That velvet glove began choking me into unconsciousness. I didn't fight it, but I tried not to pass out. I had never fainted in my life. I felt it was a sissy thing to do. But suddenly I felt my consciousness getting smaller and smaller. Then the final atom exploded and I was unconscious.

Eight hours later I came to. I was in agony. That chopped and chiseled bone was crying with pain. It cried all night. But the next day the pain eased.

I didn't get up for three weeks. And the first time I did, I fainted. I felt disgraced. But the nuns and nurses assured me it was nothing to be ashamed of. Grown men did it. Nevertheless, I felt like a sissy for the first time in my life and blamed the anesthetic. Ether became my *bête noire*—the mortal enemy, the terror to a courage I thought could never be weakened.

Two rooms down from mine was the mother of Harry Thaw, the murderer who gained a lot of notoriety and escaped execution by claiming temporary insanity. He had murdered Stanford White, a noted architect who had designed the buildings of Columbia University, among other well-known projects. In his off hours White was a high-class rake, but Thaw could match him in this field.

Thaw's mother, however, was a sweet woman and she was most kind to me, a kid going through his first operation to relieve an abscess which was about to burst through the femur. A contestant on a Groucho Marx show won four hundred dollars for knowing where this bone was located, but it cost my family only 150 dollars to find out about it the first time.

The nuns, who obviously knew what a sad future I had ahead of me, would come in and cheer me up. Sometimes they would sing duets with me and even stop in their busy work to listen to what I thought in my feeble condition was a good joke. For instance: What's the best light in New York harbor? Statue of Liberty? No. Give up? Daylight! The sort of thing which, incidentally, killed vaudeville.

I left the hospital on crutches and was transported home in the same funeral coach which had brought me to the hospital. Spring was in the air and it felt good to be alive. My days as an athlete were over.

Carolyn Patten Swett, head of the biology department of Bryant High, arranged to have my lessons brought home to me each day. Even so, I fell behind my class. My teachers gave me every break. The most beautiful girl in the school tutored me in math. We held hands, of course, but we studied too. Anyway, she pulled me through the Regents' examinations.

The fall term was interrupted by another operation, not nearly as painful as the first, though the curetting procedure was the same. Even bones, it seems, get used to hacking. The same teachers and particularly my classmate, Miss Waspwaist, tutored me while I was in the hospital and later when I was sent home.

I managed to attend school fairly regularly in the spring term on crutches, and because I could no longer participate in sports, I sublimated the hunger by writing for the school paper about the feats of others.

Thus began a writing career that was to be my means of livelihood for the rest of my days. Where before I dreamed of being Dick Merriwell at Yale or Christy Mathewson at the

Polo Grounds, I now began to imagine myself as Grantland Rice and having all the great athletes look up to me as the Homer of their brilliant performances.

I got a lot of pleasure out of this sort of daydreaming. In time the wish was fulfilled.

4

Sublimation and *The Sun*

•

Oᴜʀ school was no cradle of celebrities. It was named Bryant High School after William Cullen Bryant, the poet and former editor of the old *New York Post*. Winifred Lenihan, an eminent Theatre Guild actress, had gone there in my time and later Eddie Bracken, Paul Berlenbach, Ethel Merman, and Milton Sperling were among its students.

It had the air of a private preparatory school, like Erasmus Hall in Brooklyn and Morris High in the Bronx. Its teachers were mostly Smith, Vassar, Bryn Mawr, Wellesley, and Radcliffe graduates, interspersed here and there by a Tammany illiterate with fewer qualifications than a hod carrier.

By the time I was ready to be graduated from Bryant, our family of ten children had been decimated to two. In my senior year I had lost my father, a sister who was twenty-two, and another who was twenty-six.

Indeed, while I was cramming through nine finals, my sister Jennie was dying of tuberculosis. I recall how she embraced me on learning I had passed the finals.

The next day while I was at school preparing to make a commencement address (for I was a popular kid, president of this and head of that), word came that she had died. She was the third sister I had lost from pulmonary t.b. between my thirteenth and nineteenth years, an age when joys and sorrows

25

cut deepest in your memory. Doctors suspected that my number might be coming up next, but I had a keen sense of survival.

Ever since I was thirteen I had always believed that if my oldest sister Marguerite, a beautiful girl with auburn hair, perfect teeth, fair complexion, trim figure, and a gay, charming disposition, had steeled herself to stay in the Adirondacks she would have conquered the disease and spared the rest of us from infection.

But she was engaged to be married and when winter came, Shelley to the contrary, she doubted that spring was far behind. To her, a year in exile seemed like an eternity. So she came home when the snow began to fall. She looked the picture of health. She felt it too. In fact she felt it so much that one night she slipped off her warm clothing, dressed in a dancing frock, and sneaked off with her beau to a ball.

That was the last fling she ever had. Within a few days she was down with a hemorrhage of the lungs and within three months had wasted away to nothing. A priest came to administer the last rites and as beautiful a girl as ever lived was soon on her way to a cold Calvary cemetery. All of us followed behind in horse-drawn carriages. The horses were black, the carriages were black, and we, all in mourning, quietly wept behind drawn black curtains.

Not many weeks after this loss I went down with a whooping cough that took months to shake off. On one occasion the neighborhood grocer ordered some of my gang away from his corner. He was a fat German and a great bowler. I was sunning myself on a cellar door across the street. I told my pals to pay no attention to the old Dutch bastard. He came tearing across the street, swearing a blue streak at me. I got up and waited for him. As he swung a roundhouse punch, I ducked. He knocked my hat off. I planted a right in his solar plexus and he went

The entire Scully circus.

The author's mother, Mary Ann Scully. She gave birth to ten children; saw only two live beyond their teens and twenties.

Scully as a patient at Saranac Lake where the temperature sometimes went to 50° below zero.

As a high school student (seated, left end, second row

down as if felled by a mallet. He weighed two hundred pounds, I perhaps 120.

Not waiting for him to recover his breath, I turned and ran up the street. I heard a cobblestone galloping at my heels. I turned a corner and the "alley apple" galloped on. If it had caught up with me it would have broken my ankle for sure.

Scarcely had I turned the corner when a seizure came upon me. I wheezed and gasped for air. I fell in the gutter, coughing and struggling. As frightening as those seizures can become, mine was terror piled on terror while I listened for the grocer's footsteps. If he found me lying there, I hadn't the slightest doubt he would have kicked me to death.

But apparently he was too spent, what with the blow in the belly and the heaving of the pavement stone, to give any further chase.

Minutes later the coughing ceased and I dragged myself home over a roundabout route. The next day our family doctor checked me over and was baffled by certain rales in my chest. Years later buckshots of scar tissue confirmed that what I had had was an incipient case of t.b. under the guise of whooping cough, which in time I seemingly had conquered, permitting me to go on and try to wreck myself by overdoing in athletics until mercifully the injury to my right leg took me out of all athletic competition.

The only regret I had at the time was that I could no longer become a great athlete and a lawyer like Jerry Mahoney, since I would be unable to stand up before juries and hold them spellbound by my eloquence as counsel for the defendant. (I could never imagine myself, even then, as prosecuting anybody.)

I would have to choose another profession. I might have gone into medicine or engineering but here, too, I realized that a sound body was as important as a sound mind. (I didn't know then about Trudeau, Steinmetz, and other great men of science whose healthy minds had triumphed over diseased bodies.)

My father's death destroyed all ambition to follow in his footsteps, especially since my step was now more like Long John Silver's than an engineer's. He had never been sick in his life till one day about a month after my sister Annamae, twenty-two, had died of pulmonary t.b. My dad was nearing sixty at the time. He came home from work with a pain in the pit of his stomach that later shifted to his right side.

The doctors dithered around for two weeks before deciding to operate. The thing that misled them was that he had practically no fever and, being a smiling stoic, rarely complained about the pains he was suffering.

When they operated they discovered he not only had a ruptured appendix, but in the two weeks' delay (theirs, certainly, not ours or his) he had developed peritonitis. Such complications were touch-and-go in those days and soon it was obvious he was going.

We were all called to his bedside. I leaned over to kiss him. Though he was barely conscious, he waved me away. The nurse, a nun, explained that he had been vomiting straight poison and obviously was fearful that if I got too close I too would become infected.

This seemed to crush all control out of me. It was such a Christlike act, so much like the doctrine of vicarious sacrifice we had been taught to practise, that all the love I had had for him seemed to flood over me like a giant wave. I wept like a child. It was all I could do to gain control of myself again when a priest and several nuns came in with lighted candles and all of us knelt down to say the prayers for the dying. He soon breathed his last, and every time I recall him to this day I feel my breathing getting labored and something in me dies too.

All that happened in 1911 and nothing that has happened since has eased the loss in the least. Time may heal most wounds, but it has never healed that one. Whenever I have done anything since, which pleased me or others, the edge has been dulled by the fact that my father was not around to share in the pleasure.

When he died I was a crippled kid, not likely to get better ever. Indeed, there was a substantial fear that I might go the way of my sisters. I had a Dutch uncle who had a big farm in Pennsylvania, across the Delaware River from Narrowsburg, Sullivan County, New York. I had worked one summer for him, ten hours a day, six days a week, for five dollars a *month*.

The family thought he would not begrudge me a corner of a field—it was lying fallow anyway, in which I could put up a tent and perhaps build myself up. I had a classmate who offered to go with me and share the expenses. We had just been graduated together. We bought a tent for five dollars and stocked supplies, including a ham and a bacon. The supplies set us back twenty-eight dollars. The railroad fare was another ten dollars.

We picked a slope that led down to a lake surrounded by huckleberry bushes. The lake itself contained plenty of catfish and pike. We pitched the tent against a stone wall, along which grew all sorts of berries. We built beds out of dry hay and covered them with oat bags. We had a lantern to read by. I did the cooking on an open fire and my pal fetched water and milk from a nearby farmer.

After two weeks he tired of the simple life. We had a fight. He lost and blew for home. I decided I had to stick it out or I might just as well fold up and die. It was dreadfully lonely but I made friends with a frog that lived in an abandoned spring house where I hung my bacon. The bacon began to get moldy. I scraped the mold off as best I could and ate it even so. It tasted sweet. For all I know I may have been the first guinea pig to use penicillin.

I stayed all summer (ten weeks), gained twenty pounds more than I had ever weighed in my life, and grew taller. I sold the tent for four dollars to hunters before returning home. Brown as a berry, I checked in to our family doctor and he was amazed to see how I had improved. I weighed 170 pounds and was now five feet eleven inches tall. But I still had that draining osteomyelitis of the right femur and I still needed a crutch to get around.

Because my credits were too skimpy for a first-class college, I decided to return to high school for some post-graduate courses. My teachers decided that the Pulitzer School of Journalism, which had fluttered between Harvard and Columbia and had finally settled on Morningside Heights, had possibilities. It was obvious to them that any profession that didn't give me much chance to sit down was out. Maybe I could become an editor!

What appealed to me about the school of journalism was that it had no math courses. Without Miss Waspwaist I doubted I could get through calculus, and she was not going to college. I realized even then that in math nothing is *nearly* right. It is either right or wrong. You can't bull your way through math as you can through politics, say.

While we were computing my credits to see if I would have enough by spring to get into Columbia, George Smith, son of the managing editor of *The Evening Sun*, was commissioned to pick some schoolboys to write for the *Sun's* sports page. He had been writing the stuff himself, but he was now in medical school and study was taking all his time. He picked one lad for Manhattan and the Bronx, one for Brooklyn, and one for Queens. I guess my stories in the school paper made him feel that I would be a likely prospect. We were each to get fifteen dollars a week and expenses. We were to work after school hours and turn in our copy by eight each night.

The idea behind this experiment was to see if *The Sun* could pick up readers among the parents of high school students. I was doubly anxious to make good because my father had been a *Sun* reader. It saddened me that he was not alive to enjoy this turn of affairs.

I was told to appear at the *Sun* office the following evening at six to be interviewed by Harry Cashman, the sports editor.

Perhaps it was an intimation that I had the makings of a newspaperman—anyway I felt ashamed to come even to my first interview empty-handed. On the way down to Park Row on the Third Avenue Elevated I began writing little squibs about schoolboy doings in Queens. I had got off about half a column of them by the time the El reached Brooklyn Bridge.

The *Sun* building was a little old fugitive from a slum clearance sandwiched between the golden dome of the *World* building and the "skyscraper" which housed the New York *Tribune*. All three faced City Hall.

By all odds the *Sun*, though housed in the lowest building, had the highest standing. The *Tribune* had never quite recovered its standing under Horace Greeley, while the *Sun* under Edward P. Mitchell still held the preferred position it enjoyed under Charles Anderson Dana. It was still "the newspaperman's newspaper." It's slogan was: "If you read it in the *Sun* it's so," and the staff view was that until you read it in the *Sun* it wasn't even news!

It had suffered lean years because it had refused to join the Associated Press when the syndicated service was started. The *Sun* was convinced that syndication would destroy the individuality of newspapers.

In this its publisher was unquestionably right, but his decision meant that the *Sun* had to have correspondents in almost every hamlet in the world, and time proved it could not compete alone against a combination of thirteen hundred mutually helpful papers.

Nevertheless up to 1912, the *Sun* was the best payer of any paper in town. It paid its reporters eight dollars a column. Among its staff men were Frank Ward O'Malley, Edwin C. Hill, Thoreau Cronin, Sam Wood, Joe Vila, Si Evans, Chick Divine, and Paul Palmer. The managing editor was Chester Lord and his son Kenneth was the city editor.

The *Sun* building had been originally occupied by Tammany Hall when that had been a charitable institution, founded for the express purpose of relieving the starving Irish who were in the throes of a potato famine. By the time the *Sun* acquired the building it had slumped down like a man who had carried the *World* (and the *Tribune* as well) on his back for too many years.

Actually the *Sun* building was five stories high. The *Sun* city room was on the third floor, the *Evening Sun* on the fourth, and the composing and makeup room on the fifth. On the main floor and just above were the business offices wherein most reporters never entered except for their pay or blue slips. The presses were in the basement.

From the main floor two long flights of stairs ran straight up without a single turn. Once up there, and well out of breath, you turned into the *Sun's* city room. It was one big room. The sports department operated nearest the entrance, the city editor and his copy desk nearest the windows which faced City Hall Park.

As I looked up those long two flights of stairs I wondered if I could make it *once*, let alone day after day. I had come downtown supported by only one crutch. I used the rail for the other and took a long rest at the top of the first flight of stairs.

When I reached the entrance to the city room, I didn't dare walk in supported by a crutch. After all, I was applying for a job as a legman and I had hardly a leg to stand on. I could walk perhaps ten feet without pain. So I hid the crutch behind a door and walked as erect as I could to the sport editor's desk.

Fortunately Harry Cashman was busy reading copy and writing headlines. I was at his side before he looked up. I told him who I was and he was pleased to see that I had arrived promptly at six o'clock. He told me to sit down and then began discussing what the job was about. He told me that it would not last more than nine months—if, of course, I were not fired before then.

As he was talking, my leg began to ache and quite unconsciously I raised it and put it on the rung of his chair. When I realized what I had done I took it off immediately, explaining I had suffered an injury and the leg still hurt when I put too much pressure on it.

When everything was settled I asked him when I would be expected to start? "Tomorrow," he said, "unless you ran into something big on the way downtown." He smiled, but I played it straight. I told him I could start that night because while riding downtown on the El I had jotted down some notes which I thought would fulfill what he considered a day's quota.

He was quite pleased with this and motioned me to a desk. I sat down and began writing those modest little squibs, realizing from the first that names make news and that human interest in any field makes the name even better news.

When I was through and handed him the sheets, he read them through very rapidly, corrected them here and there, put a head on them, and seemed quite pleased. I was through for the night.

I didn't want to leave right away. It was like exploring a

musty old fairyland. Except for low-hanging lights over the battered old desks, the place was almost dark. In the right-hand corner against the wall sat the managing editor, hidden behind a rolltop desk with his back to the city lights coming through the windows behind him.

Reporters were writing all over the place. There were two partially private rooms for groups of them who worked type-writers. This was in 1912, an era when many still wrote long-hand. But more and more were swinging over to typewriters and a few of them were two-fingered marvels who seemed to type with the speed of light.

Using the back of chairs for support I walked around a corner to the files of other papers. They had been placed, with a touch of satire, along with the back files and bound copies of the *Sun* itself, next to the toilets.

The editor in chief had a room to himself off at the far side of the city room. It was Charles A. Dana's old study. When I came on the paper the editor, Edward P. Mitchell, was about eighty. A small frail man, he wore pince-nez glasses and had a kind and gentle air about him. Indeed there was none of the roaring nonsense of fiction or Chicago about the *Sun*. The star reporters, editors, and everybody else were just grand to us cubs.

To ease ahead of my story a little, after I had been on the paper about a month I went to see Mitchell about my entering the Columbia School of Journalism the next term. I had dis-covered he was a member of the board of trustees and felt none could give me better advice. But he turned out to be what would now be described as a subversive character, and were he alive today, he might possibly be subpenaed, cross-examined, and subject to deportation to Vermont, where he came from.

As I told him of my dreams, he listened, smiled, and then leaned over to me and whispered, "Don't go up there. You're in the best school of journalism right here!"

Of course he was right. That first night I couldn't imagine anything on earth that could match the *Sun* as a school—of experience or anything else. I didn't want to go home. But it would be four hours before what I had written would reach the magic of print.

In all the years I was with the *Sun* I never enjoyed leaving when my job was done, even if it were to go to a theater or a dinner party. But that night, after a few hours, I quietly picked up my crutch behind the outer door and slowly descended the long flights of steps into Park Row. I reached home by midnight and was up at dawn to buy a paper. There it all was, bringing me back to a magic world I never wanted to leave.

Naturally I couldn't conceal my infirmity forever and one day while crossing City Hall Park I ran into my editor. He was surprised to see that my injury hadn't healed yet.

By that time I not only was doing my work well but often got extra night assignments. In fact on Saturday nights after my own stint was finished I was assigned to help out reading copy on less important football games and other sports. Thus it was rare that I didn't make twenty-five dollars a week. Out of this I saved fifteen dollars a week for my college fund, for I was determined to go to Columbia the next fall.

At the end of the school year when we were expected to be laid off, the editor told me there might be assignments for me if I would call in each day. He explained why he had made this decision. He recalled a cold and snowy Saturday the previous November when I had been assigned to cover a football game at Ebbett's Field in Brooklyn. The game was to have been between Adelphi and Poly Tech, two great rivals.

When I got there, the only soul around the snow-covered field was a tall handsome man who turned out to be George Beaver, an All-American end from West Point. He was to have refereed the game. It had apparently been called off and everyone had been informed except him and me.

We got to fanning about games played under adverse weather conditions and he said he couldn't recall a game ever having been called off at West Point because of rain, snow, sleet, or excessive heat. It sounded to me like the familiar postman's slogan. Beaver was inclined to think kids were getting soft. We rode back to Manhattan from Flatbush and by the time I said good-by to him at Park Row we were fast friends.

When I reached the sports desk, none of the staff had arrived, but there were notes from several of my fellow scribes saying simply: "No Game. Snow." The press despatches bore the same melancholy tale. But I simply couldn't write those words. Instead, I sat down and wrote an interview with George Beaver on "Hothouse Athletes." It ran long—certainly twice as long as the story of the game would have run had it been played. It got a featured spot on the sport page the next morning.

"That settled in my mind," said the editor, "that you were a newspaperman first and a reporter of scheduled sports events second. So I have decided to keep you on for the summer."

I told him that I wanted to enter Columbia in the fall and asked him if there were any chance of being the paper's correspondent up there? He said he couldn't speak for the city side, but he would give me the sports section. It developed that Columbia had a tightly knit press group, small and self-perpetuating, and that I was to be the first to establish a breakthrough.

In time our school of journalism gang clipped many papers off the closed corporation's string, and though I couldn't get the city desk to let me work both sides of the street, I averaged twenty-five dollars a week on space in sports, paid all my college expenses, and indeed ended with a favorable bank balance of three hundred and fifty dollars, this despite several operations and doctors' fees and treatments, which of course were nothing like today's charges.

5

Dear Old Columbia

•

DURING the summer of 1913 I decided to try another operation. I wanted to enter Columbia at least *looking* sound in mind and limb, not like a cross between a bad copy of a Stuart portrait of Washington and Long John Silver. Expected to kill or cure, this operation, like the others, ended by doing neither. I even tried new surgeons and a new hospital. This time it was St. Luke's on Morningside Heights.

The surgeons, however, followed the old procedure of curetting the bone, scraping it clean and hoping finally to get rid of that low-grade bug which seemed to hold on in spite of a lot of spite. I read all the medical literature on osteomyelitis I could get my hands on. I felt that perhaps I might stumble on a cure or a treatment that the surgeons had missed. I suspect I was the best-informed layman on the disease. But between us we got nowhere.

All that resulted from the internal sculpture of my latest surgery was a larger bone cavity, which of course was not what the doctors were trying to accomplish at all. They had hoped the muscle tissue would fall into the cleaned-out bone cavity, thus closing it. But it didn't work out that way.

After six weeks I was back where I was before I entered the hospital, first walking on two crutches, then on one, and finally concealing my infirmity behind a stout Irish blackthorn cane. By the time college opened I could bend my right knee halfway, despite the suppurating sinus in the lower third of the femur. Indeed I suffered more from people kicking my outstretched foot in trolleys and subways than I did from walking on it.

At Columbia I was fortunate enough to find accommodations in a new dormitory which formed an L with the new school of journalism. Thus I was spared much walking, which may be a healthy exercise for most folk but was a pain-producer for me. The arrangements had an added advantage in that the 116th Street subway stop was right outside the door and this subway ran directly to Park Row without a change. Altogether, my guardian angel was doing the best he (or she) could to cut down my painful mileage.

It has frequently been observed that an unusual group of students were at Columbia at that time, especially in the school of journalism. This could be explained in great measure by the fact that a new school in an old and highly regarded university attracted the most adventurous students from all parts of the country. It was a sort of self-screening operation.

Wanting the new school to make good (since an additional million dollars would soon be forthcoming from the Pulitzer estate if it did) the university lavished its teaching genius on us. *Professors*, not instructors, mind you, taught first-year men. Our dean was the famous Talcott Williams, and among our teachers were Walter B. Pitkin, Franklin (Boss) Mathews, Brander Matthews, Robert MacAlarney, Albert W. Atwood, Charles Austin Beard, Carlton Hayes, Edwin E. Slosson, and Dr. John Cunliffe. We had the pick of professors anywhere on the campus if we wanted to take special courses for extra credits.

We were the first guinea pigs to be used in the Thorndike I.Q. tests. We had a lot of fun making our own tests. We asked how high was the North Pole and if so, why not?

We were pediculous with writers of light verse and ad-libbing wisecrackers. Of the poets, Howard Dietz, Morrie Ryskind, and Irwin Edman were the best. Of those possessed of spontaneous humor, Si Seadler produced the best classroom laughs. George E. Sokolsky was best at lecturing the professors. Max Schuster (who entered the school in short pants), Merryle Rukeyser, and George Hough were our best students. They were generous with their notes to those of us who had other things to do than study. They led all-night skull sessions at exam time.

Among the first graduates were Carl Ackerman, later dean, Fred Van de Water, J. W. Greenberg, Bo McAnney, and Freddie Schang. But our class of 1917 was the first to open the new school as freshmen. Today many of them are better known than their professors. Among those I remember are:
Tom Black, Joe Bowles, Jim Danahy, Howard Dietz, Irwin Edman, Max Felshin, George Anthony Hough Jr., Oliver Hoyem, Fenton Johnson, Clarence E. (Ike) Lovejoy, James Marshall, Freddie Pitts, Ilo Orleans, George Bassett Roberts (our first banker), Abe Rothman, Merryle Stanley Rukeyser, Morrie Ryskind, Elliott M. Sanger, M. Lincoln Schuster, Silas F. Seadler, Palmer Smith, George E. Sokolsky, Donald McGregor Stern (our first millionaire), Lee West Sellers (our first hero to die in combat), and Wayne Wellman. Over on the Barnard side (to join us later in their junior year) were Phyllis Perlman, Alice Fox, Mildred Meyers, Maria Sermolino, and Esther Norton.

The college end of the class of '17 contained Oscar Hammerstein II, Jim Harrison, Herman J. Mankiewicz, Henry William Hanemann, Harold Lamb, Ray Perkins, Milt Winn, Manny Littauer, Howard Miller, and Edward Meade Earle. Senator

Paul Douglas was of our group, but I believe he was in law school. Lorenz Hart, Henry Hough, Al Seadler, and Morrie Werner were in the class behind us.

At first there was a great deal of feuding between the college and journalism sections of the class. The college men had Alexander Hamilton's statue outside their hall; we had Thomas Jefferson's. They were traditionalists; we were idol-smashers. We barred hazing, had no class distinctions, attended formal dinners in soft white shirts and yellow ties (because we were called "yellow journalists"), and threatened to move the Wobblies (who were making a flophouse out of John D. Rockefeller's church) to Morningside Heights if the college men tried to carry their Piltdown nonsense to our end of the campus. If you looked north, ours was at the left end, which was a convenient way to remember it, because we were radicals in the main and the college men were conservatives.

Though we had an imposing chapel on the campus, a chaplain, and a Newman Club, and were founded as King's College, which officially made the college Episcopalian after the Revolution, agnosticism was the most fashionable religion on Morningside Heights when our class entered. The atheists were the arch-priests of this religion. It turned out to be the narrowest sect in the world because they couldn't believe anything.

George Sokolsky was called Sok. The son of a rabbi, he was the most radical dissenter of all. He was an anarchist and an agnostic, if not an atheist. We were great friends (still are), but politically we were on opposite sides of the fence (still are). He used to have a lot of fun at my expense in religious matters. I was, I believe, the only practicing Catholic in the class. Most of the others were Jews, but few were practicing their faith. One of them, however, Max Felshin, later became a rabbi.

Years later, when Sok became the eminent capitalist agitator, he swung so far to the right that I often wondered why he didn't go past me on wings and pitch for a place in the communion of saints. Notre Dame even awarded him an LL.D.

In undergraduate days, Frazer's *The Golden Bough* and Sumner's *Folkways* were the new Bibles of these amiable doubters. Marx's *Das Kapital* and, more popularly, his *Communist Manifesto* were the material proof that this was a world best understood and best run by pragmatists who had got rid of the good old religion, "the opiate of the peasants."

Most of the scientists of the era had knocked good-natured holes in the old-time religion, and any student who went through their bottlenecks with his faith unimpaired was proof that miracles still happened. If he came out with any of his early beliefs in God's creation of the world, the Ten Commandments, or the divinity of the Author of the Sermon on the Mount, he really deserved a medal.

As I look back after forty years I see that I was one of those minor miracles. I would come out of classes and all around me I would see fellow students reeling under the impact of what the professors, especially those specializing in the sciences, had done to their beliefs.

Even geologists had been among the wrecking crews. "How can you possibly believe all the old stuff about the creation of the world," students would argue, "when the prof just proved that strata of rock would indicate this earth was not thousands of years old, as the Bible indicates, but *millions?*"

"That is not what I am believing," I said at the time. "I'm believing that Almighty God created everything seen and unseen and if He were *all mighty* it would be no task at all for Him to dress up this silly little planet with layers and layers of rock in time too rapid to calculate. He could have done it a second before that professor was born and the professor, being in love with his own little guesses and believing only what he personally could measure, would imagine it had been done millions of years before. Or He could have done it *billions* of years ago and the professor, not being able to count that high, would have stopped at a smaller boxcar figure."

This, most agreed, was an argument too naive for even a college sophomore, and certainly unworthy of a journalism first-year man. So they, in the main, went the way of agnosticism while I went nowhere at all, being quite happy to stay where I was.

In forty years I have seen many of them go full-circle and come back to where they began. I have seen others become so reactionary that it is hard to believe they ever had a liberal thought. In time I began to think I was the only radical in the bunch because I had not changed. I had not changed, I believe, for the simple reason that my roots went down too far to be pulled up.

My job downtown on the *Sun* helped me keep a sense of balance between what seemed important on the campus and what was considered important in the outside world. I often got night assignments to add to my string. One snowy, slushy evening a few days before Christmas I was asked by the city desk if I would go to East Orange and help cover a big fire. The Edison plant was in flames and the local men were not equal to it.

I was being sent with Frank Ward O'Malley, the *Sun's* star reporter at the time. It was said of O'Malley that he was the cause of the itemized expense account. It seems that he once covered a national political convention in Chicago and then stopped off at Pittsburgh to gather some material for articles on the steel industry.

The swindle sheet he handed in was so staggering he was

ordered to itemize it. He doubled and tripled everything and still couldn't effect a balance. So in desperation he added: "For Laundry in Pittsburgh. One week, $100."

He was a brilliant, kindly, free-drinking, and funny writer. But he could also write a straight story that could bring tears to a Viking's statue. When we reached East Orange we found the fire surrounded by what looked like Keystone Cops. They would not honor our New York police passes. So O'Malley said he'd go around to the bars and talk to those firemen who had been relieved for refreshments. He suggested I try Edison's home in the hills.

When I got there, I found the place dark. The fire had burned out the power lines of the inventor of the electric light. While groping around, I ran into an old butler who was carrying two baskets of food toward an Edison electric. He explained he was taking it to the inventor who was holed up in the storage battery building, having retreated there when his laboratory caught fire.

I offered to carry one of the baskets of food and climbed in the Edison electric at his side. We had no trouble passing the cordon of cops, and in fact drove right up to the storage battery building. It was across the street from the rest of the plant, which was in flames.

I held on to my basket and kept a step behind the Edison butler. We finally got to the sixth floor and to Edison himself. Mrs. Edison was scolding him for not taking time out to eat. It seems he had been busy from early morning with plans for rebuilding. As soon as the fire got out of control, he telegraphed all his associates and began planning what to do as soon as the ruins cooled. They, gathered there in the room, kept looking out the window at their money going up in smoke, paying little attention to him. He quoted Kipling's *If* with the hope of bringing them back to the business at hand. I thought it was a magnificent example of courage in the face of a personal catastrophe, for the plant represented a five-million-dollar loss and had practically no outside insurance.

I got out of the building as fast as I could and hunted for O'Malley. Not finding him, I filed my story, suggesting that the lines from Kipling's *If* could be got out of the morgue.

Then I went back to hunting out O'Malley. I found him drinking and conversing with smokeaters. He had filed what he had. I told him of my rich treasure. We decided to go back there for more. Being now known to the cops around the storage battery building, we entered as if we were very busy executives of the company.

There wasn't much to pick up on this second trip except that an official had brought the Old Man a copy of a photograph of himself which had been rescued from his laboratory. It was burned around the edges. "You see," he said to those around him, "it never touched me."

When we got back to Park Row it was three in the morning and the paper was on the streets. In the office we learned of a funny twist in the *If* poem. It seems no copy of it could be found around the *Sun* office and a man on long wait was sent to the Press Club around the corner. He couldn't find it there either. But on the way back he ran into a *World* man, and when he explained what he was looking for, the *World* reporter said, "I carry that with me all the time!" He took a dog-eared clipping out of his wallet and handed it over to our bird dog. "You can give it back to me tomorrow," he added.

It was the finest example of cooperation I had seen on Park Row. Perhaps too fine, because the *Sun* had it as part of the great Edison fire and the *World* didn't.

Adventures like this naturally made it hard for me to take my courses at Columbia as seriously as I should have. It explained, too, why I was not a joiner of campus activities. It was an era when your church and your paper were considered enough things for a reporter to belong to. Stories were to be written objectively, and if you had opinions it was suggested that you write them to the Letters-to-the-Editor column.

Even sports were written that way. Commentator journalism was confined to the editorial page. Today, of course, slanting has become more important than the news itself. There is hardly a paper that is free of it. But forty years ago straightforward news-reporting was a *must*, except of course for the yellow rags like the Hearst press.

The only campus journalism I took part in was editing a weekly called *The Dorms*. It was, I believe, the only publication of its kind in any American college. The Dorms was in the main a journal of opinion. Sok was one of my columnists, and if you would reverse everything he says now in his syndicated column you would approximate what he wrote for *The Dorms*.

Howard Dietz corresponded for the *New York American*, Merryle Rukeyser for the *Herald*, Max Schuster for the Boston *Transcript*, and George Hough for The New Bedford *Standard*. My dormitory room in Furnald Hall was the press room.

Years later, Merryle Rukeyser, whose undergraduate ambition was to be financial editor of the New York *Tribune* (he made it by the time he was twenty-one) said I was a better reporter from a dormitory window than most legmen who covered things as eyewitnesses, and he learned more from me than in most of our classes.

Others of our class wrote for *The Spectator*, the daily newspaper, or *Jester*, the comic monthly. In fact Morrie Ryskind wrote so freely for *Jester* that his punctuation slipped. He kept referring to "Nicholas Murray, Butler of Columbia." The misplaced comma ultimately got him "canned" from the university. He went back later to accept a Pulitzer Prize for his part in writing "Of Thee I Sing." In those days he was an emotional socialist and pacifist. Later he turned into an emotional Red-baiter and rightwing radical.

It was our class in the main that published *Challenge*, a revolutionary journal of opinion that caused quite a stir. I wrote in the *Sun* of its first issue: "*Challenge* is out today and judging from the excitement on the campus the editors will be out tomorrow."

H. J. Mankiewicz tried to offset *Challenge* by bringing out a satire from the college end of the campus. He called his publication *Dynamite*. It didn't quite come off. Wet fuse, probably, because even then Mank, God rest his soul, could drink like a fish.

In Furnald Hall we had a lot of graduate law students. They came from all parts of the country, most of them from the South. I found myself frequently in arguments with them, especially on the Negro problem.

Naturally the Southerners thought I knew nothing about the problem, couldn't possibly know anything about it, and would soon retreat from my broad understanding of it if I had to face it on the level of everyday living. All these discussions took place less than a mile from Harlem where there were more Negroes, I suspect, than in any Southern city. Still, it was true that I knew personally only one Negro, a classmate named Fenton Johnson. He was a quiet, well-dressed poet.

The arguments with the Southerners, of course, would soon drop to the level of "body odors." I took the view that odors for the most part were a matter of hard work, poverty, and a lack of soap and water. This was true anywhere in the world.

But it didn't help matters to tell this to my Southern friends, or to explain that while they came from fine families, the sort that washed the most and worked the least, the Negroes they employed were forced to live in slum areas under economic conditions not much better than those of the slaves who had been their ancestors. Thus soap and water remained the core of the odor issue.

Now this was long before the country was inundated with products and radio commercials for the alleviation of halitosis, body odors, and other aryan by-products caused by hard work. But any locker room where white athletes gathered after a hard workout would have vindicated my position. On one occasion I remember letting my emotions get the better of me, because I shouted to these Southern gentlemen, "Well, in my book you stink too!"

As a clincher they sought to decimate me with the old favorite: "Would you like your sister to marry a Negro?"

"There are a lot of people I wouldn't like her to marry. You're one of them!" I would shout. "But what she does eventually with her biological urges is her own particular racial, religious, and emotional problem."

Besides, by then I had no sisters. All six of them were dead.

I could not have talked this way if far down in my mystical Irish roots something of great religious significance was not still alive. Christianity did not begin in Ireland. It began among people who were a good deal closer to Negroes and the poor— notably Galilean fishermen—than they were to the Irish who today seem to have the snobbery of royalty because they are convinced that they all have descended from kings.

But the Founder of Christianity had told His fishermen to become fishers of men. "Go forth," He said, "and teach all nations." He didn't say "some nations." He didn't say "nations with a lighter skin than we have along the Mediterranean." He said all nations. There are black Madonnas in art and even paintings of a black Christ, which show how much His teachings affected His followers. Anyone who takes exception to this may be something else, but I don't think he ought to call himself a Christian.

This impeachment would fall like a shadow on many Catholics, too, for I have heard Father George Dunne tell them, "If a Negro came into this church and you would resent it and wouldn't move over, I'm telling you, you may get up and leave right now. You don't belong here." Father George Dunne never referred to them as "colored people." He said they were "colorful," and whites, obviously, were "colorless."

God knows the Negro has reason to resent the intolerance, discrimination, and prejudice he has suffered for generations. But if he is to become a good Christian, he must learn to forgive those of us who have injured him. Otherwise he is only giving lip service to the Lord's Prayer.

In a little mountain chapel, I once heard an Irish priest tell his congregation, "Don't ask for justice. You might get it. Ask for mercy."

I point this out to show that it is not wise to tar everybody with the same stick. There are bad Irishmen and good Irishmen and the two priests I am referring to here were both Irish, but they had not lost their way, nor had they become so yeasty with power that they fed on the destruction of other people's liberties.

Like *nouveau riche*, second and third generation Irish (*lace-curtain* Irish, many people call them) frequently forget the eight hundred years of tyranny and suppression which their forebears suffered—tyranny which forced them to immigrate to a freer America with nothing in their purses except a rosary, the finest symbol of their faith.

6
Peace, It's No Fun
•

ONE of the melancholy things about youth maturing into manhood is that they so often believe they have accomplished the whole miracle of life single-handed. Not until much later, when their faculties begin to wither and die, are they likely to conclude that they themselves contributed only a small part to whatever success they enjoyed. Then they often call on a God they long ignored to help them. He never fails to forgive them.

It is hard to convince young people that a divinity is shaping their destinies and that all the skill acquired from older men or from observation or education is as nothing compared to what God has breathed into each soul. College is a difficult place to deflate an ego or even to scale one down to its proper place within the scheme of things. This may be less true of denominational colleges than state universities, but it is measurably true of all of them.

Few men believe that John Bunyon's "But for the grace of God there go I" applies to them. The hand of destiny separated them from the mass of mankind, they believe, for one reason only: because there was an obvious superiority in their genes. They are certain that the reason they did not land on Skid Row was because they *thought* their way to the top. The others were free to follow suit, but they landed in the gutter because they were too lethargic or too stupid to lift themselves up. The slough of despond they fell into was obviously of their own making.

This sort of Nietzschean nonsense and Darwinian droppings was quite common in my youth. It was a rare scholar indeed who would acclaim his good fortune as strictly a gift from God and give thanks daily for it in his prayers.

I was no different from the rest. I paid only a small measure of gratitude to the Creator who had made my good fortune possible.

Voluntary chapel was held each noon at St. Paul's on the campus. Few attended. For Catholics like myself there was a chapel at Notre Dame a few blocks away and another at Corpus Christi on 121st Street. Few attended those either.

The university chaplain was Raymond C. Knox, an Episcopalian. I got to know him around the boathouse where we would take out shells. He was a charming man, but considering the religious origin of Columbia University, his status was certainly obscure. Bishops Manning and Greer were on the board of trustees, but Chaplain Knox was lucky to get his picture included with the officers of the YMCA, and even there he got no billing.

I was surprised recently to discover that I had been a member of the Newman Club for at least three years while at Columbia and that a friend of mine from the Journalism class of 1916, Warren Leary, had been president. Jeff Healey, captain of the first football team after the sport had been revived in 1915 (he subsequently attained the rank of captain and died in combat), had been president of the Newman Club in 1915. Dr. John Fowler was a good track athlete. I knew him well, but only recently in looking through a class yearbook did

I discover that he too had been a member of the Newman Club. I didn't even remember that he had been a Catholic.

Such was the vague character of religious life on Morningside Heights in our day.

Fraternities at Columbia were not on the campus and their activities were not very visible, but they bored from within and without and made it a point to put their fraternity brothers in key positions everywhere.

Before I had come to Columbia I had read Owen Johnson's *Stover At Yale* and as a result disliked the fraternity idea intensely. Woodrow Wilson had recently abolished them at Princeton. Secrecy in any field found me hostile, and still does. I can't believe that any other citizen should know things which, "for my good," are kept from me. Neither do I believe that any other citizen is capable of absorbing shocks which would fell me if revealed. In that lies the seed of second-class citizenship. Any group which has anything good of itself should not hoard it but should announce it from the rooftops. If it's secret, it's shady and suspect. At least it is in my book. That was my opinion then and the years have not altered it much.

In my second year at Columbia I was approached on this subject of fraternities and had it pointed out to me that the Jews were in such an overwhelming majority in the class they could be held at bay only by the concerted activity of the fraternities. I was so hostile to the whole fraternity idea anyway that almost anything they said would have set me against them, and this appeal to racial and religious bias was all I needed to revolt. I discovered they had control of practically every activity down to class officers. Even on our side of the campus, in the shadow of the statue of Thomas Jefferson, they ran everything. When I found out what they were up to, far from supporting them as a sympathetic aryan, I set up a ticket against them. As a result

they got only eight votes for every office. We got the overwhelming majority. It turned out there were only eight fraternity men in the class.

That Columbia University was not wholly barren of religious
growth, or even of change, I learned on meeting Carlton Hunt-
ley Hayes, who was the faculty representative of the Newman
Club. He was one of our professors of history and a more entertaining teacher would be hard to find. He would act out the
main characters in European history in three dimensions. He
made the study of history as painless as visual education would
have been under the great clown Grock.

Possessed of a great sense of humor and a warmth and ca-
maraderie toward his students, he successfully bucked the tide
which was fast going out in matters of faith in those days. The
day after he was graduated from Columbia in 1904 he became a
Catholic convert. His position was unique on that faculty of agnostics, but it did not impede his progress or promotion in the
least.

Not having known him before this great event took place in
his life, I cannot say whether it effected much change. But certainly the Hayes we knew reflected such good cheer that the
change in any event could not have been for the worse. When
people talk of humorless converts, they can't be talking of G.
K. Chesterton or Carlton Hayes.

Later as ambassador to Spain at a time when Franco was a
painful subject on the political plane, Carlton Hayes acquitted
himself admirably. He must have been a Gibraltar of faith in
those days when all around him in the State Department was a
morass of doubt.

Aside from Carlton Hayes, I remember only two who did
something positive about the agnostics of Columbia. One became
a Jesuit priest, and the other became a rabbi.

Though Nicholas Murray Butler, exponent of the International Mind and a pacifist of sorts, veered away from the Kaiser's concept of *Deutschland Uber Alles* and rather favored England's cause in World War I, his faculty remained antimilitarist. The Wall Street sort of support that gave a measure of solvency to the university was all on the side of England, and in time it was generally admitted that J. P. Morgan helped push us into the First World War to get back their enormous loans to the British Empire.

I recall that after the *Lusitania* was sunk I had to interview such diverse personalities as Dr. Butler, Rabbi Stephen Wise, and Rev. John Haynes Holmes, a former Unitarian minister and in 1915 pastor of the Community Church in midtown Manhattan.

I caught Dr. Butler and his daughter Sara coming from services at St. Paul's on the campus. I managed to catch Dr. Holmes on his way to take a train out of town. Rabbi Wise, too, was leaving for the day. All of them were visibly shocked men and their pacifist convictions were shaken to the roots. It was a benumbed set of interviews, though Dr. Holmes was obviously more deeply convinced than the others that "there's no such thing as a good war."

On the Columbia campus the point of view changed so much that by 1917 the pacifist president was heaving pacifist instructors into the Hudson. Leon Fraser, an S. of J. graduate and instructor in history, managed to escape his wrath, grew to head the International Bank in Geneva, and subsequently committed suicide. But others were liquidated early. One was an English instructor, Henry Wadsworth Longfellow Dana, a descendant of both the famous poet and the famous editor. This dismissal so incensed Charles Austin Beard that he resigned his chair as Professor of History and issued such a blistering blast against Butler that its memory still shakes me more than the atomic explosions in nearby Frenchman's Flat, Nevada.

In those days, some of the biggest faculty members and outstanding students belonged to such things as the Intercollegiate Anti-Militarism League and backed such quixotic projects as the Ford Peace Ship—the *Oscar II*—which sailed from New York for Stockholm with the avowed intention of getting all troops out of the trenches by Christmas. Paul Douglas, who later became Democratic United States Senator from Illinois, was active in this movement; so was Karl Karsten, who later became a big wheel in advertising.

I received an invitation to join the Ford Peace Ship, but after giving it some thought I turned the invitation down. In fact I gave my credentials to another student. I was still on the *Sun* and must have had a large bump of caution. Unless I could combine business with idealism I was not enamored by a trip to Europe with a boatload of beautiful dreamers.

I seem to have been well grounded in self-preservation as well as economic survival. I tried to hold a middle course between the Prussianized way of life and those who believed in the doctrine of non-resistance. Among the latter was Dorothy Day of nearby Barnard College, now editor of *The Catholic Worker*. Freda Kirchwey, editor of the *Nation,* was another Barnard rebel.

A third Barnard girl in this steaming syndrome was Eleanore Parker. She and two male students on our side of the campus got themselves badly messed up in an anti-conscription campaign in 1917. One of these was Owen Cattell, son of a professor; the other was Charles Phillips, to whom I had given my invitation to the Ford Peace Ship pilgrimage. When Phillips returned to America, he, Eleanore Parker, Dorothy Day and other avowed pacifists started a campaign to resist the draft. They were arrested, given a stiff lecture by the judge, and dismissed.

Phillips, however, was over twenty-one; so his draft number was destined to come up soon. When it did, he was yanked off to Camp Upton on Long Island where he continued his policy of passive resistance. The military gave him the works but couldn't budge him.

Finally the commanding officer had Phillips brought before him and, with all the rookies looking on, told Charlie he was a felon and as such unworthy to wear the uniform of the United States Army. Whereupon he proceeded to rip the buttons off Phillips' uniform and then had him tossed off the reservation.

This was in a fine old tradition of volunteer armies, but it soon became evident to the brass in Washington that this sort of thing could well result in having no army at all. The Upton commanding officer therefore was ordered to get Phillips back in uniform at all costs and not to repeat such romantic nonsense in the future or he would find himself stripped of his buttons himself.

By this time friends had got Phillips out of the country and into Mexico. He changed his name and rose to a position of eminence in the changing political scene south of the border. In time he visited the United States as a highly honored foreigner.

Subsequently he switched billings again, settled down in New York, and divided his time between teaching Marxism nights and working days as a financial expert for one of the more conservative metropolitan dailies. He was quite skilled and conscientious in both fields.

He was something of an exception in that he clung to what he believed in. Most of the others were salon socialists until they had to support salons of their own. Then they transformed them into places of repose, or, as in a few instances, reversed their fields entirely and used them to denounce politically what they had previously acclaimed.

In our undergraduate days, George E. Sokolsky was an outstanding example of this sort of change. Sok was the son of a rabbi who housed his large family of diverse talents in a tenement flat in the Bronx. In the fall of the year, Sok used to stump for the Republicans to get enough funds to stay in college. He campaigned from the top of taxicabs even for women's suffrage.

Once I was invited to Sok's home to share in a Jewish feast at which wine was drunk and hymns were sung. I joined in the singing, as the music seemed familiar. It was, too, for young Jewish song-writers had been filching from these chants and making Hawaiian melodies out of them.

The rabbi was quite touched by my efforts and patted me on the head. One of Sok's sisters, however, a beautiful girl, suspected my ear for the old and melancholy music was not quite that good and smiled in a way that indicated she knew my ear for music stemmed from Tin Pan Alley, not the Talmud.

Sok showed flashes of personal courage that even his enemies, who were many, had to admire. One night returning from Greenwich Village to Morningside Heights a bunch of us were riding atop a Fifth Avenue bus. We were noisy and full of wine. As we reached Riverside Drive around 90th Street, we remembered that John Purroy Mitchel, the then Mayor of New York, was a Columbia man. We let out several college cheers for him.

Within a minute a cop was climbing up the steps of the bus and reading us a riot act. We all took it sitting down—all except Sok. He informed the cop that we were cheering Mayor Mitchel, the chief law enforcement officer of the city. "You'd look pretty silly putting that charge on the police blotter, wouldn't you?" The cop mumbled something about disturbing the peace, backed down the steps, and got off the bus.

At that time a small, frail youth with a wild mop of curly hair and fine teeth, in contrast to the close-cropped, well-nourished character of later years, Sok treated the faculty from the very beginning as if they were the students and he was the professor. He would contradict them in class and quote names most of us had never heard of as his authorities. Professors Pitkin and Hayes were his particular targets in these classroom tilts.

He became such a thorn in the side of the faculty that a few days before graduation they trumped up charges against him and heaved him off the campus. To make sure he wouldn't be more trouble off the campus than on it, they fixed a job for him to represent the *New Republic* News Bureau in Russia. He rather liked the idea of being paid to be exiled. He saw himself as the Mark Hanna behind Kerensky, pulling the strings and effecting a successful peace maneuver that would paralyze the military on all fronts by its daring and thus stop the war.

But he met with some delay in Stockholm and by the time he reached Russia, the tide was already turning in favor of Lenin and Trotsky. Sok began to fight them in print. There couldn't be two representatives of the Bronx in the Soviet and Trotsky was there first, so Sok had to get out or be liquidated.

He moved into capitalist circles with amazing dispatch. One day I received a letter from the Shanghai Chamber of Commerce. There were scores of Chinese names down the left margin and at the bottom I read: "George E. Sokolsky, Chairman."

In the letter he told me he was about to marry a beautiful Chinese girl. Her name was Rosalind Phang. He admonished me not to say anything about it "because the laws of Judea are

OLD FRIENDS, *from top left to right*

Howard "Freckles" Dietz, famous lyric writer and now one of MGM's big-shots.

Si Seadler, who still uses Central Park as his lunch club.

George Sokolsky as a tycoon in Shanghai, in 1921.

J. P. McEvoy at the Victorville rodeo in 1937.

Jack Keevan before the Japanese marched him to death at Bataan.

Recent portrait of Dorothy Day, stormy petrel, lovable woman, great soul.

Old pic of Merryl Rukeyser and his lovely bride, Bernice.

Most of the male members of the Class of 1917 J, Columbia, when Scully presided:

Left to right, front row: George E. Sokolsky, Merryl S. Rukeyser, M. Lincoln Schuster, James Danahy. *Second row:* James Marshall, Elliott Sanger, Howard Dietz, Silas F. Seadler, Ralph Dibble, George A. Hough, Joe Risely III, Louis R. Mann, Harry Rove, George B. Roberts. *Third row:* Thos. E. Black, Alan Temple, George Robinson, Donald M. Stern, Frederic G. Pitts, Joseph S. Kavanaugh. *Back row:* Morrie Ryskind, Fenton Johnson, Palmer Smith, Wayne Wellman, George Wickersham, Ben Heyman, Clarence E. (Ike) Lovejoy, Ralph B. Smith.

hard and the laws of Judea are about to be transgressed."

I wrote him that such news was too good to keep and I had rushed it to all our friends. He wrote back that it was all right because he was making her a Chinese Jewess.

He returned to New York in the depression and then set himself up as the economist of the capitalists on a twenty-thousand-dollar-a-year retainer. He began writing for the *New York Herald-Tribune* and later for *The Sun*. Ultimately he joined King Features, a Hearst subsidy.

He told me that his affinity for Hearst dated back to when Hearst ran for mayor of New York on the ticket of the Municipal Ownership League. Sok stumped for him. It is generally agreed that Hearst won that election, but Tammany threw three thousand ballot boxes into the East River, thereby saving the day for their man.

This soured Hearst on social reform. It was the turning point of his career, as Sok's subsequent tilt with the Bolsheviki in Leningrad was to be the turning point in his. Hearst remembered Sok's earlier forensics and was pleased to note that his point of view and conclusions ran parallel to Hearst's own social and political convictions.

Several times Sok rallied to my defense when some crackpot denounced me as a communist. Sok knew me better than most, and when his writings began to show a gold thread of the good old religion, he had more reason than ever to claim that his knowledge of what made me tick was superior to latter-day appraisers of my character. He was the first newspaper columnist to combine religion and readability. Before his time religion was considered poison in the field of syndication.

Sok has followed the normal life-curve from youth to old age, which arches from radicalism to conservatism. Such is the course of those whose radicalism did not go down very deep.

Authentic reformers, those destined for sainthood, don't change this way. In fact they intensify their zeal. Why not? . . . Isn't the time getting shorter?

7

The *Sun* Goes Down

•

THERE is an old saying: "Revenge is best when served cold." From
the Christian point of view, it is of course better when not
served at all. But to harbor no resentment for an injustice
suffered is to be found only among those soon destined for
sainthood. If the injustice is against many, perhaps one's personal resentment will more easily find forgiveness in God's eyes.

In 1935 I became a founder-member of the Los Angeles
Newspaper Guild and put up the small sum needed for its
charter. I played a part in the first strike of reporters in Hollywood and stayed with it until it was won. This was years after
I had ceased to be an active newspaperman.

The reason for it dated back to New York in 1916 when I
was among the victims of the first merger of newspapers. The
merger was consummated by the late Frank Munsey, a bachelor who when he died left twenty million dollars to the Metropolitan Museum of Art (where he had never been in his life)
but practically nothing to working newspaper men.

After he consolidated the *Sun* and the *Press,* he went on a
rampage, knocking out one good newspaper after another until
he tried to merge the *New York Tribune* and the *New York
Herald* and got his *Herald* swallowed up by Ogden Reid instead.

Munsey was one of those self-made men who are exceedingly

proud of their maker. He owned a chain of grocery stores and any store that didn't show a hundred-dollar profit for the week on Saturday night was closed the following Monday. This meant that the clerks to hold their jobs often had, as they say in football, "to eat the ball." He also owned some magazines and was a glorified pawnbroker on the side.

Then he bought the *New York Press* to use as a house organ for Teddy Roosevelt and the Bull Moose Party, which, armed with a platform filched mainly from the Socialist Party, was expected to bury Woodrow Wilson and William Howard Taft in an avalanche of votes. The movement failed to put T.R. back in the White House, but it did elect Woodrow Wilson, the first man I ever voted for. This Roosevelt defeat soured Munsey on progressive political movements as a road to a greater personal fortune. He decided to become a highly respected conservative bachelor on a diet of dining off his betters.

As far as prestige went, his *Press* was at the bottom of the heap. The *Sun* was still at the top. He figured it would take too much time and talent to earn what the *Sun* had, which by then was a sort of cynical idealism that left the door wide open for the healthier idealism of the *New Republic*. Being a banker of sorts, Munsey figured it would be easier to buy what the *Sun* had.

The *Sun*, sticking to its earlier decision not to join the Associated Press, was having a hard time keeping its head above water. By the time it might have acquiesced, it was too late to get in the swim.

The staff was loyal to its ideal. But its bankers, the House of Morgan, were not so sentimental about newspaper ideals. Having been denounced as "malefactors of great wealth" by President Theodore Roosevelt, they didn't feel any compunction to play Santa Claus on this occasion. Besides, the whole trend in America at that time was toward making big corporations out of little corporations without falling into the net of the Sherman Anti-Trust Act.

Individual newspapers could not buck such a tide. The day of James Gordon Bennett, Marse Henry Watterson, Joseph Pulitzer, and Henry Garrison Villard was fast coming to a close. William Randolph Hearst, Edward Wyllis Scripps, and a few others solved the problem by setting up newspaper chains. Others like Col. Robert McCormick in Chicago and Harry Chandler in Los Angeles staved off defeat by getting their fingers in other pies and making their newspapers house organs for their various enterprises. But the *Sun* held on, paid its reporters the best space rate in town, and acted as if all were going fine.

If there had been such a thing, I might have been described as the aquatic editor, with particular emphasis on long-distance swimmers. Up to that time, the English channel had been crossed by one swimmer, Capt. Webb, who later had a leg bitten off by a shark. But the swim from Sandy Hook to the Battery had not been accomplished. Several had tried it, one in three tides, attempting to hide behind Ellis Island treading water for eight hours till the tide began flowing toward the Battery again. I covered these events. They were dull, produced a lot of seasickness, and no winners.

On one attempt a Capt. Al Brown found the going rather rough in the lower bay. A launch with newspapermen and photographers followed him. A few miles off Sandy Hook the water became terribly choppy and a hard wind began blowing. It turned over a sailing vessel with seven on board. We came upon them. They were straddling the ship, the white caps pitching them around badly.

I had fears like other persons, but water was not one of them. In my time I had rescued several persons from drowning, and once was rewarded with a saddle by the grateful survivor. Since I didn't have a horse I couldn't do much with it. But it was a nice thought. Altogether I have participated in ten rescues, several of them single-handed.

On the occasion of the upset in New York Bay, I got out on the bow of the official launch, lashed myself to a post, and proceeded to rescue those on the dunked sailing vessel. Our launch would come close, and then back off before a wave could crash us against the upturned fishing smack. I would hold out an oar and the next wave would wash a victim on to our deck. Sometimes a succeeding wave would wash him right off again, but I would yell for him to hold on to the oar and by this method we landed six of them.

Before I could make the first rescue a news photographer from Underwood and Underwood named Jackson pushed me aside to get a picture. He kept shooting pictures as I rescued the drowning men. I thought he was an incredibly hard-boiled character at the time, but one of his pictures was bought by Aetna Insurance and used in their advertising for years. So he knew his business, even if I didn't.

The captain would not grab my oar. He shouted he was going down with his ship. As his ship was not going down, it soon became evident that the idiot was not only romantic but drunk. As we backed away to avoid getting caught in his sails, our launch, now loaded beyond safety, began listing. I had no fear of drowning if we capsized too, figuring I could swim the long mile to shore. But the others were in a panic.

Fortunately a catboat came along. It had a crew of two. One handled the rudder while the other leaned over the side. As they sped past the capsized sailing vessel, one grabbed the skipper by the neck as if he were a brass ring on a merry-go-round and yanked him aboard the catboat. That took care of all the derelicts and we started for the shore of Sheepshead Bay to unload our water-logged human cargo.

The reporters and photographers scrammed ashore before the

derelicts could be carried ashore. Then we remembered that our long-distance swimmer was out there treading away all by himself. In chorus all the reporters said I could have Capt. Al Brown. They were returning to Park Row overland by the good old subway and would meet me later at the *Sun* office.

The officials and I returned to find Brown. We found him.

He was two miles farther from his goal than when we left him. So we picked him up and chugged over the whitecaps to the Battery by motorboat.

In a way it was a good break for Brown. The story made the front page. He got in the opening paragraph and that was about all he got. The rest of the story involved the seven who were saved. The Coast Guard picked up the sailing vessel. It seemed as unsinkable as the famous Mrs. Brown of Denver.

After the college year closed I used to be sent each June to Poughkeepsie to cover the annual intercollegiate regatta. This was a big news event in those days and the *Sun* assigned men like Edwin C. Hill and Thoreau Cronin to write local color stories to supplement the straight reporting of the sports staff. Other papers sent men like Damon Runyon, W. O. McGeehan, Grantland Rice, Harry Cross, Rube Goldberg, and Dan Daniel.

Rowing at the time was the purest amateur sport in America. Members of the crews trained from the previous fall till the following June, and their reward, if they won, was a twelve-foot oar. It was a hard, grueling form of group discipline, which brought nice coats of tan and boils on one's behind. It had some of the qualities of the life of medieval monks who gave up everything, worked around the monasteries, wore hair shirts, and suffered vicariously for the sins of others.

Crowds of fifty thousand used to journey to see these races. The rich viewed them from yachts. Those not so rich saw them from a long train that moved along with the crews. The peasants saw the races from vantage points along the shores. It was like watching needles float in a bathtub.

Columbia, Syracuse, Cornell, Pennsylvania, Navy, Wisconsin, and usually a West Coast champion like California, Stanford, or Washington, participated. Yale and Harvard did not enter but had their own race a week later on the Thames above New London, Connecticut.

Both these regattas drew great crowds and received generous recognition from the press. I covered the Poughkeepsie regatta and in 1916 was assigned to cover the Yale-Harvard regatta as well. I expected that a star reporter from the cityside would be sent to New London the day of the race. But on this occasion I received a telegram telling me I would have to handle the whole story myself.

This could not have been done as easily at Poughkeepsie where the races were all rowed in one afternoon. But at New London, the freshman and junior-varsity races were rowed in the morning and the varsity race at sundown. This gave reporters a chance to clear up the less important features in the early afternoon instead of having to do all their writing between 6 and 10 P.M.

But there were many side features that had to be covered too. It required two men, or one with seven-league boots—not one with only one good leg. Fortunately I met a New London reporter who gladly helped me out. He was Frank Mallen, later a colonel in the Marines and city editor of Bernarr Macfadden's *Graphic* (a tabloid with the restraint of a stallion) which introduced Walter Winchell, Ed Sullivan, and Louis Sobol to New York journalism.

With the notes Mallen collected about yachts and celebrities to add to my own observations, I was able to weave a tapestry that ran to five thousand words. It took hard fast writing to do this between sunset and 10 P.M. The Postal Telegraph as-

signed me a typewriter next to some dynamos which were
humming along while I wrote. Despite this outside pressure
against the inside pressure of a brain working at top speed, I
managed to complete the task well inside the deadline. But
when I got up and went out for some fresh air I had to hold on
to the side of the building lest I collapse.

I didn't return to New York till two days after the regatta.
When I reached the *Sun* office I was praised on all sides for a
magnificent performance. I was heading straight for the select
circle of star reporters.

Within two weeks, however, I was out of a job. In that
interim Munsey had bought the *Sun* and merged it with his
lowly *Press*. Then he proceeded to cut salaries 30 per cent and
fire the *Sun* reporters right and left.

He tried to do the same with the "black gang," but Big Six,
the printers union, told him, in effect, to get lost. They had a
contract with the *Sun* and as long as he kept the name of the
Sun on his masthead he would have to pay for two crews till
their contract expired.

Being a rugged and ruthless individualist, Munsey didn't
cotton up to this arrangement. But it was made clear to him
that if he violated the union contract he would be publishing
no newspaper at all—in New York or anywhere else.

This really opened my eyes. Reporters, college men in the
main, reared in a tradition of anonymity which was supposed
to guard them from self-consciousness, trained in loyalty, and
taught to join no "ism" that would complicate that loyalty,
could be fired *en masse* overnight. But those who handled the mechanical end of the paper had a dignity as human
beings, thanks to their union, which could not be trampled on
at will.

Pope Leo XIII had written that capital cannot do without
labor, nor labor without capital, and that for either to sur-

vive, the organization of each into their respective unions, with equal rights for collective bargaining, was the first step toward peace in an industrial civilization. Later Pope Pius XII called the labor question "the nerve center of the social body" and took employers to task for failure to bring justice, equity, or charity to it. "Unless your justice exceeds that of the Scribes and Pharisees," he added, "you shall not enter the kingdom of heaven."

But in 1916 employers were not interested in social justice, severance pay for long-time employees suddenly thrown out of their jobs, unemployment insurance, or anything of the sort—least of all employers like Munsey, whose last will and testament read, in H. L. Mencken's well-remembered phrase, "like the braying of a disappointed jackass."

The staff of the *Sun* had worse things than that to say about him. They wrote ribald and insulting pieces which they passed around to each other. But it was obvious we soon would have to hunt for jobs in a market where jobs were scarce.

Jack Knox, sports editor of the *Evening Telegram* and a nephew of James Gordon Bennett, had offered me a job writing big league baseball some time before the *Sun* went down, but I couldn't see leaving the *Sun* under any conditions and he gave the job to Hy Daab, who later cut quite a swath as advertising and publicity director of RKO Radio pictures.

Several of our staff were invited up to Grantland Rice's apartment on Riverside Drive and 116th Street for a wake. He took us all out to dinner and in appraising the situation said he thought our *Sun* staff was the best in town at the time, with the *Tribune's*, featuring Heywood Broun and W. O. McGeehan (he didn't mention himself), running a close second. Ever a kindly, gracious, and exceedingly talented man, Granny would have hired us all if he had owned a paper. But he too was only a hired hand who could not solve the problem of unemployment.

I ultimately got a job as managing editor of *The Spur*. This was a glossy, fashionable monthly, the first of the fifty-cent magazines. Its object was to say nothing, but beautifully. It catered to the Munsey sort of millionaires who collected works of art and mixed horse shows, charity balls, and the Met into a richly perfumed manure.

Editing *The Spur* was a dull, easy job. It involved a five-day week bankers' hours, and two hours for lunch. The idea was to make it beautiful but dumb. Our office was on Fifth Avenue. Howard Dietz was writing advertising copy for Philip Goodman in an office on Broadway not far away. He had won five hundred dollars in a college competition. The layout showed two students at a dance, one saying to the other: "Bored? Have a Fatima." *C'est tout!*

Goodman's office was the hangout of George Jean Nathan, John Held, Jr., and many of the Broadway crowd. One of his accounts was Sam Goldwyn. Dietz later became director of publicity and advertising of Goldwyn pictures. When Goldwyn sold out to Metro, Dietz landed aboard the Metro-Goldwyn craft, still head man of his department. Later when the firm became Metro-Goldwyn Mayer he again landed on top. Morrie Ryskind worked for him for a while. Si Seadler—who broke down with t.b., ignored my advice to go west, returned from Asheville, N.C., and made a miraculous recovery in New York— became his advertising manager. Between them they revolutionized the business of exploiting motion pictures. A lad of tremendous drive, talent, and ambition, Dietz, with Arthur Schwartz, wrote musical comedies in his off hours. After a night of this sort of creative writing, Dietz made the rounds of night clubs, scheduling all of his office appointments for between three and four in the afternoon. Then he blew for the day. Once on being chided by a superior for leaving early, he remarked, "But I came in late, you must remember that."

While he was in Goodman's office and I was on *The Spur*, we rented a bungalow at Babylon on Great South Bay and commuted to town daily like big-time executives. We read our morning papers on the train and took the 5:15 from Penn Station back to Babylon each evening. I was constantly surprised by the extra reading he did. No student at college, he raced along unconventional paths after he went to work. He introduced me to many new authors, Chesterton among them. This surprised me, for I saw even then that Chesterton was going my way, not Dietz' or even Shaw's, and I was glad to hitchhike on his amazing paradoxes.

We had so much leisure we even volunteered to write Edwin Justus Mayer's column for two weeks to give him a vacation. He was writing light stuff for the *New York Call*, a Socialist daily miles to the right of the latter-day *Daily Worker*. Mayer, poorly paid for all his obvious talent, borrowed freely from friends, and when later he had a smash Broadway hit, *The Firebrand*, his list of creditors ran into columns. He began paying off. Dietz wrote me in Switzerland: "Eddie's show has been running a year and he hasn't got down to paying off the *D*'s yet, so I doubt if he will ever get to the *S*'s."

Mayer himself pointed out that since he owed both Dietz and me and we were such good friends, maybe it would be easier to straighten out the tangled economic situation between ourselves. The small debt remained a bond of friendship between us for all time. He never paid it, but even in a theater he would climb over people to chat with a guy to whom he owed money. A charming rogue, God bless him.

Dietz contributed frequently to F.P.A.'s column, *The Conning Tower*, under the nom de plume of "Freckles." Once he wrote a lilting piece about the single life he led in that bungalow in Babylon on Great South Bay. Some days later I answered it in the same *Conning Tower*, pointing out that while Dietz led a single life, my work was *doubled*. We never commented on each other's contribution. The game was for the other party to read the reply as we both opened our morning papers on the train from Babylon to Penn Station on our way to work.

We bought a canoe and paddled across the bay to Fire Island for ocean swimming. We caught crabs and clams and staged our own clambakes. We fought water fights inside the bungalow, I, as always, being the champion water sprite, a title I acquired at Columbia and have not lost to this day. Why people get so angry at being doused with nice, clean water still eludes me.

We took the lease for the bungalow from Ralph Barton, a diminutive cartoonist who built up his ego by wooing beautiful women and then throwing them out of his life. As he felt the hot breath of the draft breathing down his neck, he remembered a wife and child he had in Chicago and hurried there to claim them as exemptions, tossing the lease on the bungalow to us.

Among the women he heaved out of his life was an actress who then married the greatest dramatist of the day. That one of his discards should reach such eminence so enraged Barton that he got a job as a dramatic critic. Every time one of the dramatist's plays appeared on Broadway he pounded it to pieces. In the end these self-made potions poisoned him. He died of their effects.

The dramatist went on to win everything from the Pulitzer to the Nobel prize. The moral was obvious: the wages of negative thinking is death.

The wages of underwork has its penalties too. At least it had in my case.

My health broke down completely.

8

Chasing the Cure

•

THE medical suspicion was that I was absorbing toxins from bad tonsils as well as from osteomyelitis. On examination the tonsils proved to be exceptionally large. The diagnosis indicated they ought to come out. I didn't want to lose them. I believed God put them there much as a strainer in a sink. Merely because they were large seemed to me no more reason for taking them out than it would be to cut off one's feet because they were too large. But I felt terrible, especially after luncheon when chills and fever followed by malaise made bed a welcome sight. So I went to St. Luke's for the tonsillectomy.

In the rush of things the staff overlooked the routine check-up of lungs, heart, and other vital organs. As I was being wheeled to the operating room a nurse leaned over my shoulder like a guardian angel and asked if they were using a local or general anesthetic. I didn't know. "Ask for a local," she warned.

In the operating room I advanced this request, but the surgeons were visibly disappointed. The staff had arranged everything for a general anesthetic and, like children who are denied what their hearts are set on, they all but pouted. So against my better judgment and the whispers of my guardian angel I acquiesced to the staff's wishes.

It was one of the biggest mistakes I ever made. At that time, unknown to them and to me, my lungs were holding a conven-

72

tion of tubercle bacilli. A stethoscopic checkup would have revealed this. What the ether did to this smouldering flame was to set my whole being on fire. It was ten days before I got out of the hospital after this minor surgery. I didn't snap back at all. Instead I felt worse than ever.

I was home only one night when I began gushing blood. It was thought that the tonsillectomy had not healed properly, so I was sent back to the hospital. Examination there didn't support this suspicion. I kept having hemorrhages—twenty-eight of them in three weeks—and lost thirty pounds. My sputum was tested and came back positive. I was not only another victim of the then dreaded white plague but in a few short weeks had advanced to what was described as the third stage. All five lobes of the two lungs were involved.

Every subterfuge was used to break this dreadful news to me in a roundabout way. But I had peeked at the chart before the staff could tell me and knew the worst. The prognosis was not good.

Not *good?* It was terrible! I had already lost three sisters with this disease and now at twenty-five it looked as if my number were up too.

The hospital shipped me home in an ambulance because it had no facilities for t.b. patients and was certainly not looking for terminal cases to add to its statistical reports. I was so weak I couldn't read a prayerbook or a paper without trembling. (Today, over sixty, no one has a steadier hand; I can thread a needle without glasses in decent time.)

My pulse raced around 130 day and night. I ran a fever between 100 and 103. At that rate it was obvious I was not long for this world. It looked like galloping consumption and then a short ride over the hill to what we as kids used to call "Cavalry" Cemetery.

But while my body was weakening, my mind was working

hard to get out of this death trap. I went back and reconstructed our family mistakes. I was sure that my beautiful sister Marguerite was the first weak link in the chain. If she had stayed in the Adirondacks I was certain she would have got well. But she was homesick. She came home, infected the rest of us, and died.

One cold night in November, an hour before dawn, my mother was holding my hand and trying to comfort me after I had suffered a new hemorrhage—always a terrifying experience that sets one's heart pumping faster from fright. But I found I could control the bleeding by not moving a finger and could slow the heartbeats somewhat by mental resolve. After an hour I was able to relax a little and think things out. I determined to succeed where my sister had failed. I asked my mother if we could scrape up enough money for me to get to Saranac Lake. She was sure we could. Though a widow now, with no visible means of support, her other son having married, she was sure it could be managed somehow.

"And always remember," she added, "that if the loneliness gets too great the same trains that take you away can always bring you back."

But I resolved to myself either to come back well, or never. God was everywhere. Dying in one place or another was all the same to Him. But it was our job to exercise the free will He gave us and not cower with fright when faced with making a decision.

Drugged with codeine to cut down my coughing and reduce the hazards of a hemorrhage on the train, I finally got to Saranac Lake about ten days before Christmas. It was cold enough to freeze the lungs of a brass Buddha. It was 30 degrees below zero and ultimately went down to 50. I found a boarding house that had a spare room. Bundled in a horse-drawn sleigh I was depressed to find that it was the last house at the

end of the lake. The people were Canadians. They had lost a
daughter and had stayed on to board other patients for a livelihood. I had hoped to get into Trudeau Sanatorium, but my
condition was so far advanced the chances seemed slim. In any
event it would take several weeks, as the waiting list was long.

Meanwhile I settled down to chase the cure. Each morning
after breakfast I bundled myself in a cure-chair and lounged on
a porch while the snow whirled about me. I put in eight hours
a day this way and then went inside, had supper, and climbed
into bed. I had no companion in misery. I thought I would
crack in two from homesickness.

For comfort, I read the life of Edward Livingston Trudeau, a
frail doctor who lived forty-two years after he first broke down
with t.b. He never really got well, but he became so famous he
was elected president of the American Medical Association. He
had founded Trudeau Sanatorium and it had become one of
the most famous institutions of its kind in the world. He introduced the cottage-type of treatment, suspecting that isolation
was one way to check the spread of the disease. He believed
that rest, good food, and fresh air would prolong life and in
many cases bring about a cure. The town of Saranac was a
monument to his beliefs. More than five thousand ex-patients
did all the things a town has to do to survive. Practically every
doctor was a former patient.

When Dr. Trudeau opened his first cottage, Little Red, in
1884, the death rate from tuberculosis was 158 per 100,000.
The disease was the Number One killer of the nation. By
1954, when the Sanatorium closed its doors, the rate had been
reduced to 12 per 100,000, thanks to the introduction of miracle drugs like streptomycin and isoniazid. But in 1919 the
rate was still well over 100 per 100,000.

Except for artificial pneumothorax, which was a type of

minor surgery designed to collapse one lung and let it rest for a year or two while the more healthy lung did all the work, the Trudeau treatment was designed to teach patients to rest out-doors and to learn to take care of themselves. It was really a six-month course in training patients to get to bed by 9 each night, take two-hour rest periods in the afternoon, and follow rules which would protect themselves and others from further infection.

The first command was to control one's cough. A patient who coughed all day did as much work, the staff insisted, as if he had climbed a mountain. Exercise meant walking and noth-ing else. Even that was controlled and graduated according to one's improvement.

After six months, patients were discharged whether they showed improvement or not. If well enough to return to work, they were ordered to go to bed Friday night and not get up until Monday morning and to otherwise follow the regime of the San as closely as possible.

The word "cure" was rarely if ever used. At best the staff referred to "arrested cases" and warned that the microbe could keep alive, even if walled in by nature's calcification, for as long as seven years. Those who showed no great improvement were transferred to neighboring rest homes. But their progress or retrogression was kept track of for the rest of their lives.

After a month on the waiting list I was admitted to Trudeau's famous San. By then he was dead, but his Sanatorium was as lively as a freshwater college. Indeed, it seemed just like one. There were a few large buildings, but most of the patients were scattered over a hillside in what could have been fraternity and sorority houses. No two had the same architecture. Some were new; others were old and not too attractive. But the charges were the same for all—at that time—around fifteen dollars a week.

Dr. Edgar Mayer, later a foremost specialist in the field, admitted me. He had come up from Dr. Minor's "san" in North Carolina to Trudeau where he had once been a patient. Dr. George Wilson, who subsequently took over the medical direction of the Will Rogers Sanatorium for show people in Saranac, was a Trudeau staff member at the time I was a patient.

The nurses were all ex-patients. They were trained at Trudeau, with special courses at Bellevue Hospital, New York. Each spring a group of them received diplomas as R.N.'s. Some patients were ambulant, others confined to bed. Each Saturday the ambulant patients had checkups, and if they showed more improvement, they got more exercise. If they slipped back, they had some of their walking time taken away from them.

In the main they were gay tuberculoafers and proved that good cheer as well as tubercle bacilli is contagious. From a dying lone wolf, I changed to one of a cheerful pack. All of us had our ups and downs but the spirit of most was excellent. I was a bed patient for practically the whole time I was at Trudeau, which was unusual. The doctors normally put all patients to bed for six weeks on entering the San and then put them on carefully graduated exercise. I never got to the second stage—at least not at Trudeau.

We slept outdoors in what were called Klondike beds and wore more coats in the daytime than an onion. We wore woolen helmets at night and I often wished someone would invent a miner's lamp that would hang over my nose to keep it from freezing.

In our cottage were four patients. Two were medical students. One I knew as a member of a championship varsity crew at Columbia. His name was Vince Sanborn. He was so shocked to discover he had t.b. that he said, "Boy, if I get well and a

patient ever comes to my office and says, 'Doc, I feel tired,' I'll
tell him, 'Get to bed and don't get out of it for six months. You
have râles all through your chest. You're dying.' "

In those days few doctors knew anything about the disease
until they broke down from it themselves.

The other medical student was a brilliant Johns Hopkins
man. He was destined to become one of the great men of his
time, except for one weakness. He couldn't leave women alone.
Women were never a problem to me. I could take them or leave
them by simply turning on or off a reservoir of charm—an Irish
asset or curse, depending on how you viewed it. It became
clear to me very soon in chasing the cure that chasing women
could not be part of it. This lesson in personal restraint was
hard to learn because the protein and starch diet was designed
to make patients yeasty. But I soon saw that responding to such
temptations was often the road to death.

Once in a discussion I asked my Hopkins medic if he would
make a deal with God to give up his sex life to become the
greatest scientist in the world. He asked me if I would be willing to make such a bargain to write the Great American Novel.
I said I would.

"I'd be damned if I would," he insisted.

He made a quick recovery, thanks to artificial pneumothorax.
He returned to Baltimore and was soon on his way to great
things in medicine. But the lack of restraint he showed at
Trudeau exacted its toll. He was dead in two years, and it
wasn't from tuberculosis of the lungs, but from a social disease
that also gives a patient râles in his chest.

Other sanatoriums turned out cures too. One of the most
miraculous was Si Seadler's. He had returned to New York
from the famous San of Dr. Minor in North Carolina and one
day in coming from a theatre had a terrible hemorrhage in the
lobby of a Broadway theater. He was rushed to Mt. Sinai

hospital where Dr. Tashman administered artificial pneumothorax. This stopped the bleeding.

He was kept on this treatment for nearly two years, and
when his collapsed lung was allowed to expand again, tests
indicated all signs of the disease had disappeared. He took no
particular care of himself afterward and even so never had a
relapse. Since that was more than forty years ago it may be
presumed even by Trudeau's cautious standards that Si is an
arrested case.

When I broke down, Si wrote to me and suggested that
since I had urged him to go West to get well, perhaps he could
now advise me to return to New York and get a sure cure.

But I belonged to the Robert Louis Stevenson school of
cure-chasers. He too had spent some time at Saranac before
going West and ultimately to Samoa, where he died. There was
a tradition that if one went West to chase the cure he could
not safely return to an eastern climate again for five years after
recovery, without running the risk of a relapse.

In those days climate was supposed to play an all-important
part in recovery. Actually it played a minor part. Food and rest
accounted for 90 per cent of one's recovery. Nina Wilcox Putnam completed a cure on a roof above 42nd Street and Fifth
Avenue. But some cases, and mine seemed to be among them,
needed that climatic 10 per cent.

I had been given artificial pneumothorax as Si Seadler had.
In fact my pleural cavity took as much as 1300 c.c. of the nitrogen gas and even so I did not have a completely collapsed right
lung, proving I had a big chest and must have had adhesions
which prevented a complete collapse and hence complete rest of
that lung. Besides, my left lung had an active t.b. condition,
and it goes without saying that both lungs couldn't be collapsed
or I'd be a dead patient.

Like Eugene O'Neill's hero in *Beyond the Horizon*, I still

felt that if I got over the hill I'd have a better chance. Colorado,
New Mexico, Arizona, and California were the favored places
for cure-chasers in America; Switzerland, in Europe. I returned
to New York to say good-by and then prepared to make the trek
west. I had decided it was forever.

Friends helped finance the trip and I picked a place in Phoenix, Arizona, called St. Luke's Home. I arrived there around
Christmas, 1920, in the worst rain the Salt River Valley had
had in years. It rained almost without a break for two months.
I gritted my teeth and hung on. From bed I edited a paper
called *The Branding Iron*, "the only burning shame on the
desert." Nothing happened much, except for the worse. We
had a visit from General Pershing and another from Governor
Tom Campbell, a tall, eagle-beaked, and handsome man addicted to ten-gallon hats. The Episcopal Bishop of Phoenix
used to take visitors on a tour of the home. We felt like in-
mates in a zoo.

Though St. Luke's Home had a religious foundation and the
superintendent was an ordained minister, the place seemed
singularly lacking in spiritual nourishment. There was a recreation hall and on one occasion a faith-healer from England
came and lectured to us about the laying on of hands. He was a
serious man and laid hands on all of us, but no miracle cures
resulted. In fact two of our group took a turn for the worse
and died shortly after his visit.

The superintendent himself was a small, cocky, cigar-
smoking martinet who rode herd on the patients as if his sanatorium were a corral. Now and then he would wear a Roman
collar, but just as often he would not. He spent the afternoon of
Good Friday playing pool in the recreation hall. A petition
was started to have him fired, but nothing came of it. I may
have started it. It would be just like me, for I never felt that
because I was down I was out.

He realized early that I was a maverick and would just as
soon heave a bedpan at anyone who thought I was helpless because I was bedridden. He was forever ordering patients to
throw out their "junk." That meant practically everything except their pajamas. "Junk?" they would repeat in a helpless,
bewildered way. "Yes, junk!" he would shout.

I was surrounded by a rickety bedside table, an old heavy
Underwood typewriter, portable files, books, and some honest-
to-goodness junk. I gave him a look that would have withered
a giant cactus when he looked in my direction. My junk stayed.
My junk was me.

One winter morning I was reading Michael Williams' *The
High Romance*. The founder of *The Commonweal*, Williams,
had been a San Francisco newspaper editor during the earthquake and fire and previously had been a Socialist of sorts,
sharing in the Helicon Hall cooperative living experiment in
New Jersey when Upton Sinclair was commissar and Sinclair
Lewis was janitor.

Later when life was giving Williams pretty rough treatment,
he sought help from the Carmelite Nuns. I remember that
while I was reading his autobiography I smelled the fragrance
of roses. I looked around to see where it was coming from. We
didn't have a rosebush on the desert and since all of us were
thousands of miles from home, no daily visitors were bringing us any flowers, least of all American beauties.

I returned to reading and a few pages later Williams reported
that when he approached the Carmelite monastery he smelled
the unmistakable fragrance of roses, looked around him and
found none. It gave me an eerie feeling to come on this coincidence.

He learned later—a fact which I didn't know till he revealed
it—that St. Thérèse of the Little Flower of Jesus was of the
Carmelite Order. She lived only twenty-four years and died of

t.b. at Lisieux, France, about the time I was born. A few years after I was reading this reference to her in Williams' book, she was beatified and subsequently canonized as a saint.

This legend of the fragrance of roses she prophesied would be identified with her, and all statues of her now show her holding a crucifix and a bouquet of roses in her arms.

The Carmelites are a cloistered order—except for the one or two who have contact with the outside world. At the time I was reading *The High Romance* I didn't know anything about them at all. Williams confessed that their prayers solved his problem for him. He later became a Catholic convert, one of the earliest of the reformed Reds to learn that man cannot live by bread alone.

When summer came, the Salt River Valley turned into a furnace. This was before the days of air-conditioning. Several patients died of heat prostration before the t.b. bacilli could accomplish this melancholy end. It was decided to ship the rest of us to Prescott, Arizona, a mile-high mining town, famous as the home of Bucky O'Neill and Tom Mix, two of Teddy Roosevelt's Rough Riders. It had also gained a measure of notoriety for the wild life of its Whiskey Row and especially for one dive called the Bucket of Blood. The town seemingly had never accepted Prohibition. Now and then the sheriff would raid a still, pour the contents down a sink, and have it caught and rebottled in the basement where it was sold again at cut rates.

One bootlegger, an ex-soldier, not taking kindly to this type of law enforcement, told a sheriff's posse to get off his premises or he'd let them have it. They didn't get off fast enough and he shot and killed a deputy who had come up from Phoenix for the annual rodeo and had gone along with the posse for the ride.

Because the bootlegger was a veteran and suffering from tuberculosis the jury didn't have the heart to hang him. So they voted him a life sentence at the Florence penitentiary, a place which was hotter in summer, if possible, than Phoenix or Yuma. In fact there was a standard story of a coyote chasing a rabbit through Florence and both of them were walking. I visited this particular murderer in Florence before he died and decided that worse than being sick was to be sick and in jail, and worst of all was being sick and slowly boiled alive in the Florence state prison.

In the Prescott San, which was five miles from town (in itself no metropolis), we lived in crude cabins heated by woodstoves and serviced by slop jars. There were even fewer spiritual comforts. Now and then a Father Paul, a Franciscan, would ride out to see us on a motorcycle and give us the Sacraments. He came from Phoenix—a hundred miles away. He was a gay adventurer on the missionary front and more than once got spilled racing his motorcycle over our mountain passes. But he insisted that the Blessed Sacrament in his pocket always saved him.

Another of our visitors was the cashier of the Prescott bank. He seemed lonely. He told me that he had been superintendent of a Sunday School, a millionaire as well, and that he had lost both his faith and his fortune in a crash. After that he wandered from state to state and job to job seeking some sort of a firm foundation on which to build again. He had joined and left several religious groups and now wanted to become a Catholic. His family, which he loved dearly, was getting a little bewildered and tired of his gropings. He didn't want them to join him until he could convince them that this was the last change he was going to make in this life. He thought I could help him.

He brought them out one Sunday and they were really a beautiful family, inside and out. I answered many of their questions, but I thought he answered all our questions best—at

least for a banker. "If it would destroy the happiness we now
have," he said, "I would not want back a dollar of all I lost."

In time his whole family was received with him into the
Church and he thanked me for what I had done to help, which
when analyzed was merely to act as a sounding board for his
own convictions at a time when I was trapped in a mountain
sanatorium and couldn't get away if I wanted to.

I did a great deal more, I believe, for my cabin-mate. He was
a tall, dark, handsome Irish kid from Chicago named Jack
Keevan. His faith was sort of tilted over one eye and ready to
fall off. He whooped it up like a man coughing up T.N.T.
Doctors agreed that no one could continue to live who presumably had as much t.b. as his lungs indicated. Tests eventually
revealed that most of his trouble came from an unhealed pneumonia condition. Vaccines were just coming in at the time.
They were tried on Keevan. At first the shots made him sick
as a dog, but gradually he showed improvement and after a
month had nothing more than a bronchial cough and shortness
of breath. These did not leave him, but his lungs were pronounced clear and all signs of t.b. gone.

He was a brilliant kid, with a gay humor and an amazing
genius at mimicry. He had only a primary school education. I
learned that he had been in the National Guard and had been
dispatched to St. Louis to shoot down Negroes in a race riot. He
had had to sleep on the wet sidewalks and as a result had developed a lung condition. He was given a medical discharge.

On this slender proof of military valor we pitched for veteran's compensation for him and by pulling a wire here and
there got it. I then decided that he should go after an engineering degree. The doctors at the San allowed him to go to Prescott
High School in the morning. There he took courses in math,
chemistry, and physics. In the afternoon after our rest periods
I tutored him in English, history, and economics.

By the end of the year we sent him in to take the college entrance examinations. He passed them and was accepted with certain conditions in the Arizona School of Mines, one of the best in the country.

While he was at Prescott High he covered sports events and brought the information out to the San to me. I then wrote the stories for the local morning paper. If the event were out of town, he would give me the data and highlights on the telephone. Out of this arrangement we managed to make about ten dollars a week.

The doctors allowed me out of bed to go to town to help get out an "extra" on the Dempsey-Carpentier fight. We laid out the whole front page on the prognosis that Dempsey was going to win. We had a big cut of him and a DEMPSEY WINS IN   TH ROUND headline across the front page.

When the flash came that he had knocked out the orchidaceous Carpentier in the fourth round, I dashed off a lead without waiting for the details to come in. We were in type and on the presses before the details arrived. It turned out I had reconstructed what had actually happened almost blow-for-blow. We were on the street a half hour before the early rounds came in by Western Union. In fact, we were all sold out before our rivals reached the streets with their "extra."

Oddly, I suffered no relapse from this folly. Also while a patient there, I started a book review column and was cited by the *Freeman* for this particular bravery in what had previously been two-gun territory.

From Prescott, Keevan, Al Kieson, and I moved for the college year to Tucson, taking a house near the University of Arizona. Kieson, a tall, tender, well-bred kid from Winnetka, Illinois, had been with us in sans in Phoenix and Prescott. He had broken down in the Navy. Somehow he always had money, but he and his money were easily parted, and Keevan was al-

ways quick to move in for a part of it. In Keevan's book, Kieson
was a sweet chump and just what we needed to survive at all.
All of us were Catholics of sorts.

Keevan made all the arrangements for the house and could
not have done worse if he had been a greenhorn from Latvia.
In fact Kieson could have made a better deal. In a month we
were out of money and had to take in a solvent convalescent to
meet expenses. We had to give him and the housekeeper the
best accommodations and take what was left ourselves. We slept
on back porches and front porches on old second-hand beds that
jailbirds would have rejected. The place had only one bath and
we ran it like radio commercials, except of course for the "paying guest." He could take as long as he wanted. He was supposed to be "totally and permanently disabled." He had a new
car and ran around at all sorts of hours. His philosophy could
be summed up with: "You can get any of them if you have a
car." He got the girls but the bugs got him. He died shortly
after our lease expired.

We were blessed with a wonderful cook. We brought her
down from Prescott where we had boarded with her for a while.
We had had the best room in her house. She slept on a back
porch. Now the shoe was on the other foot. We had to board
her and give her the best room in our house. In addition we
guaranteed her eighty dollars a month.

Though Irish with a lyrical brogue, she bore a Swedish name
when we first met her. She had a son, who was quite a hero in
the Marines, and a daughter, who was secretary to Prescott's
leading law firm. She gladly deserted them to go with us.

This was not the first time she had deserted them. Keevan,
who had the instinct of a private eye, found out that she had
been married to an Irish Catholic miner in Butte, Montana, and
one day had run off with a handsome Swede to Arizona, leaving behind two small children.

Without bothering to divorce her husband, she went through a civil marriage with her Swede and thus lived in a state of bigamy for several years. In time her conscience began to bother her and she left the Swede. Her children, now grown, forgave her and joined her in Prescott. They were good Catholics and she went through the motions of being one.

But Keevan, now knowing her past, needled her about "doing her Easter duty" and such matters, never once letting her know what he knew. He would talk pig-Latin to me and this would drive her crazy, for she suspected, and quite rightly, that she was being discussed. But Keevan, the tall, dark, and handsome Lochinvar, could do no wrong in her eyes.

One morning she came to see me. I was typing, stretched out on a canvas couch with a portable typewriter across my knees. She held a telegram in her hands. It reported that her Swedish husband had died the night before on a ranch near Ash Fork. She was shaking all over. She then told me the hell she had been living through for years. She thanked God for sparing her. "You know it could have been me instead of him," she said. She wondered if it would be all right if she left the house in my care while she hurried downtown to see a priest.

She came home in a couple of hours. She was beaming. Her whole mental attitude changed. She never missed Mass and went to communion now more than anybody else in the house. Keevan was mystified by her change until I explained to him that the Swede's death had released her from a bigamous life and moreover had again restored her in the eyes of the Church to a state of grace. He let her alone after that.

In Tucson I was still a bed patient but improving. I made some money "fictionizing," as it was called, motion picture scripts for fan magazines—a most welcome bone from Howard Dietz. I also wrote short stories for International Features. Agatha Brown (who later married the sculptor, Karl Illava) was the editor. My chief competitor was Sam Hellman. We got five dollars a story. Agatha and I had had a short and flaming romance when she and Ethel Johnston once visited me in Saranac Lake. But we both realized that it had to be a case of ships that passed in the night and that a warm and enduring friendship was not a bad sublimation for a blighted love affair.

After a year in Tucson I was able to move around a little, but I still had to watch carefully my leg as well as my lungs. I sold myself to the publisher of the *Tucson Daily Star* as a sports editor and hired Harry Bryant, a college athlete, to be my legs and lungs. I got thirty dollars a week and paid Bryant half. In addition to the regular sports news, I wrote a daily column of verse and comment. It was called *The Cheering Section*, a title subsequently "lifted" and still used by King Features in one of the magazine sections of the Hearst press.

Sick or well, I seemed to make friends easily. Among those I made in Tucson were Harold Bell Wright, the worst novelist with the greatest success in America; Francis Perry Elliott, who wrote *The Haunted Pajamas, Pals First,* and *Lend Me Your Name;* Larry Evans, an actor who wrote *Once to Every Man;* Rosemary Drachman Taylor, who wrote *Chicken Every Sunday;* Floyd Heck Martin, the youngest university president in America at that time; Governor George Wylie Paul Hunt; Shorty McKale, director of athletics at the University; Charley Barrett, Cornell's All-American quarterback; and Albert W. Atwood, *Saturday Evening Post's* financial authority. Atwood had taught at the Columbia School of Journalism when I was there, but I had not taken any course under him. Merryle Rukeyser was his prize pupil.

Wright, Elliott, Evans, and Barrett had all gone to Tucson as t.b. patients. Elliott, who had once been a Harper's editor and friend of Mark Twain, was closest to me. Though old enough to be my father, he was like a brother. I was allergic to

Wright, but he had been financially generous to Elliott and
that forced me to overlook the fact that in my limited opinion
Wright couldn't write for nuts.

One of Wright's novels was called *The Mine with the Iron
Door*. Appleton published it and I was hired by Franklin Spier
to help in its exploitation. We conceived of the idea of three
cardboard millionaires reading the book in, say, the Union
League Club, New York, and being so convinced of its authenticity that they incorporated for a million dollars and planned
to set out for Arizona to find the mine. As it cost only twenty-
five dollars to incorporate, with no questions asked if you didn't
try to sell any stock, this part of the publicity plan went
through without a setback. I then hired three mining students
under the leadership of Jack Keevan to set up a preliminary
camp in the Canada del Oro.

The newspapers leaped into the quixotic expedition and the
resulting publicity for Wright's book was tremendous. But
about three weeks after the news had died down, a humorless
Indian who called himself Lo came to see me about the matter.

He wanted to know if I were the one who had sent "them
minin' expert engineers" to the Canada del Oro. I said I was.

"The mine's not there," he said. "It's not forty miles from
there."

"How do you know?" I was foolish enough to ask.

He looked me in the eye, pressed hard on my poor right knee,
and said very slowly, "I know because I got the mine."

After an hour of revelations, he convinced Keevan, Kieson,
and me he did have the fabulous mine. All he needed was a
thousand dollars to buy dynamite to blast open a sealed mine
mouth and, *voilà*, there we would find the iron door and behind
it all the gold that the Apache Indians had hidden from the
oncoming Spaniards, far away and long ago.

He talked so convincingly that three of us who knew it was

all a hoax that morning had invested in the mythical mine by that afternoon. This is known as gypnotism in circles where confidence games operate. We were, in brief, victims of our own ruse.

For the next three months we went through hair-raising experiences—I vicariously, but Keevan and the others got mixed up in gun-play, horse-stealing, and all the other ingredients of an old-time western. The mythical mine was far up in the mountains back of Oracle, Arizona. To get to it, you had to pass through a bottleneck, a trading post owned by people who knew the Indian and had seen some of his valuable ore specimens.

He talked the Dean of Archeology into going up to view the ruins. He pried a cap off a rock, brushed it with lamp-black, took a white cloth, and got an imprint. He claimed it was a map of a lost city, maybe one of the Seven Cities of Cibola. He pointed out the outline of wide roads, long concealed. He took specimens of ore and asked the Dean of the Arizona School of Mines if iron were ever found mixed with gold. The Dean told him gold was never found in hematite formation. He showed the Dean specimens and asked, "Is that iron? Is that gold?" The Dean had to admit that through the Indian's alchemy the two somehow had effected an alliance.

But the Indian had so much trouble shooting his way in and out of the diggings that my partners got scared stiff and began going on the eighty-mile rides with him less and less. In the end they left it all to him. Thus we didn't see him for months. But we still had our shares in the Lost Soldier Mine.

The next year when Sol Lesser came into Arizona to make a picture version of *The Mine with the Iron Door* I got myself hired as the company's press agent on location. When he heard of the Indian, Lesser too became interested.

Then one day Wright came to visit me. He had a long telegram from Lesser wanting to know if we could still locate that Indian. He thought Lo could help in the exploitation of the picture. What ideas did I have?

Well, I knew the Indian's claims were on land Geronimo once owned. In fact the Apache chief had once said if the federal government would let him go back there, he would dig up enough gold to pay for all the damage he had done to white settlers. As this amounted to more than five million dollars, it seemed like quite an offer. But the Army, after agreeing to his proposal if he surrendered, double-crossed the Apache chief and shipped him to Florida instead.

I talked to Lo and asked him if he would be willing to go to Washington to see the Big White Father. Then if he promised that there would be no further double-crossing, would he open the mine? He said he would. So I sent him off for Washington with a cactus cane for President Coolidge and a Papago Indian basket of cactus candy for the First Lady of the Land. He went in his blue jeans and battered ten-gallon hat, being the only man I ever saw who didn't know what an inferiority complex meant. I never met anyone who could make me feel ill at ease, and in that respect Lo was my blood-brother.

He got his interview with the President, the papers got their story, Lesser got his publicity for *The Mine with the Iron Door,* and I got my fee.

But Lo never came back to Tucson. In fact I never heard of or saw him again, but I totaled up what I had put into his mythical mine against what Lesser had paid me for my publicity services and it looked as if I had come out just about even.

That, however, was not the end of our experiences in fast shuffles. Keevan had run into some sharpshooters who had an asbestos mine near Globe. He had talked me into going halves with him. One night, however, we were invited to dinner at the Chicken-Every-Sunday Drachmans. We began telling Mose of our good fortune. He had always been a sucker for such enterprises, most of which funneled the family money down the drain. But he was a bank director and Chairman of the Board of Regents of the University of Arizona. When the state was first organized in 1912 he was sent by some saloonkeepers to get the state capitol for Tucson and, failing that, either the state penitentiary or the State insane asylum. When he reached Prescott, however, there was nothing left but the state university. So he had to be satisfied with that. The saloonkeepers all but beat his brains out. A sissy college was not their idea of a fair return on their investment. In time, of course, it proved he had got the cream of the crop.

He went along with our story until he heard the names of the promoters. He took that big. They were, he informed us, the biggest crooks in a blue-sky business. How, he wanted to know, had we paid them? We told him by a certified cashier's check. That looked like the end to him. I looked at Al Kieson, one of our family group, who somehow had not been inveigled into this deal.

"Oh no," said Kieson. "You don't hook me on this one!"

"Listen," I said, "listen, Mr. Drachman, from what you've told us, these are men of great avarice. Now, if we should go to them and tell them we think their deal is so good that Kieson wants to buy in, too, and then offer them a bigger personal check, do you think they would bite on the juicier bait and give us back the smaller check?"

He grinned and said they might.

So we talked Kieson into writing a personal check for *twice* the amount of our original investment and, because he looked like the sort of chump who could never think up a fast switch, we then talked him into driving out with Keevan that night to where the thieves were holed up.

They came back in an hour leaping with delight. The deal

had worked. They had recovered our certified cashier's check, and the crooks had Kieson's personal check.

"Now the job is," said Mose, "to find the bank cashier so you can stop payment on Kieson's check before they have a chance to cash it. I'll phone him to let you in a few minutes before the bank opens in the morning."

So the three of us got up at dawn and sat on the cold curb until employees of the bank began arriving. We got admitted a few minutes before nine and stopped payment. The crooks came in at ten and found Kieson's check was not cashable. We hid out of town for a few days till we learned they had gone on to Phoenix and bigger game.

All this was not designed to improve my health, though it seemed to advance Keevan's career. In time he graduated, became the youngest superintendent in the Guggenheim mining chain, was shipped to boss things in Manila, was commissioned a major, got caught in the Bataan Death March, and died, as hundreds of others did, in that Japanese cruelty now glossed over as something Communists do but nobody else. I had put a lot of myself into Keevan and I shall not forget his loss in this life.

But while we lived together in Tucson we had fun. I finally got the thrill of my life. After eight years, a sputum test came back negative. That didn't mean I was cured by any means, but it meant I had at last made the first step toward some sort of recovery.

I began to see features for national magazines in the area, and one had an incredible twist. I met an old piano salesman who had broken down with t.b. and had discovered a peach tree growing in a dry wash in the desert north and east of Tucson. He found water too. So he cultivated some acres and began growing peaches where they said only cactus would grow.

Fascinated by his experiment, I asked him how he did it.

"Oh, I just love to grow things," he said. "Just love them, and I guess they return the love."

I wrote a feature for N.E.A., the Scripps-Howard syndicate, and when he offered to pay me for some added publicity on a subdivision he planned, I demurred, for I knew he had no money.

"I tell you what I'll do," I said. "I'll write a piece for a national magazine. You name the magazine nearest your heart. If I land the article there, you owe me an acre of land. If not, if it lands somewhere else, you owe me nothing."

He picked *Success,* a magazine now dead but then quite popular. It was published by Orson Swett Marden. I sent it there. It landed. My peach-growing realtor paid off with a deed for an acre. It probably wasn't worth ten dollars at the time. But I held on to it for twenty years and ultimately sold it for two thousand dollars to help one of our children through college.

By now I had learned to resist a certain measure of temptation and to be sure opportunity knocked twice before I got up from my cure-chair to go to the door. I took two hours' rest in the afternoon and became a nine-o'clock fellow in a ten-o'clock town.

Sometimes the temptation to throw all caution to the winds became almost irresistible. One year I had touted the University of Arizona polo team into a national championship. They were to play Yale, but Princeton beat Yale in the play-off; so the matches were arranged between Arizona and Princeton at Hamilton Field, Brooklyn. I got the town of Tucson to put up the money to transport the cowponies to New York and the team slept in the boxcars with their mounts.

Princeton was loaned thoroughbred polo ponies for the event. In Arizona we divided the cowponies into two groups and the teams switched mounts between the halves. This seemed to us to make the game a contest between riders, not horses. We tried to get Princeton to do this, but it was no dice.

I saw our team off from Tucson, for again this was one of those occasions when my health would not permit me to enjoy the fruits of my labors. I had got used to such disappointments. (I was unhappier over Arizona losing the series than over being unable to go.) To have ridden down Fifth Avenue with the team, calling on the Mayor, seeing my friends, and being otherwise fêted would have been great fun. But this was not for me. God had willed it otherwise and I had learned to accept His will.

In homeopathic doses, however, I saw the whole state of Arizona from Nogales to Grand Canyon. My host was Governor Hunt. Wherever I happened to be taking the cure he would stop by and take me for safe rides, put me up at a good hotel, make his speeches, and then return me to my combination sunporch, bedroom, and study. Having been elected seven times, he was practically Arizona's perpetual governor. Today his views would be too radical to pass even a border patrol, though it wouldn't have bothered him, for he was an F.F.V.

His sense of humor was such that after feuding with mine owners he sent all of them copies of Upton Sinclair's *King Coal* for Christmas. When he retired, he warned all hands to run the state right or he would be back and run it again. President Wilson sent him off as Minister to Siam and when he came back, he was appalled at the way the state had slipped. So he got out his Model T, toured the state, and won his old job back.

He looked no more like the typical Western governor than a rhino. He was built like a water barrel, with a weeping walrus mustache, white hair, and a cap. His opponents were tall, lean, you-all characters and wore ten-gallon Stetsons. But their drawing power was practically limited to their own breaths when George Wobbly Paul Hunt threw his cap in the ring. Among other things, he was the father of prison reform.

One time he took me from Prescott to the Grand Canyon on a road inspection tour. Along the way he would talk to working stiffs to find out how the job was getting on. On this occasion he recognized a worker who had once been a boxer and had played bit parts in Hollywood westerns. He had got in some sort of jam in Arizona. (I think it was check-kiting) and when he had served his time, he asked the Governor for a job. Hunt got him one with the highway department.

After talking a while, the Governor asked the reformed palooka if he would like to go with us to the Grand Canyon. He said he would. His Excellency got out a sheet of embossed stationery and had it tied to the shovel, explaining that this particular road-runner was AWOL, meaning, in this case, "absent *with* official leave."

At the Grand Canyon we stopped at the El Tovar, a deluxe dudery of the Santa Fe and lousy with protocol. As we entered the dining room, a line of defensive halfbacks boxed off our extra guest and insisted on putting a coat on him. It was sizes too big for him. He felt like a clown without make-up. The Governor treated the whole episode as a joke.

But the next morning as we gathered for breakfast, our ex-pug was still seething like Old Faithful. The headwaiter and his six Jap bellhops were there with the coat. "Get away, get away," the highway hand growled. They kept coming at him, coat ready for the capture. He gripped his fists. They edged within striking distance. He let them have it. Two of them went out like lights. The rest backed away.

We entered the dining room as a team, our hero still in his shirtsleeves, his dignity as a human being restored. The Governor smiled at him. "Did you ever read *Cashel Byron's Profession?*" he asked. The fighter said no, he hadn't. "I'll send it to you. You'd be wonderful in the part," added the Governor.

I continued to have my downs as well as ups and the Christmas season almost invariably found me down. On one occasion Jim McKale, Arizona's athletic director, brought Knute Rockne for a visit. Rockne had brought his Notre Dame team to Tucson and was keeping the players there till the night before a Rose Bowl game, when he planned to entrain for Pasadena, an overnight sleeper jump.

I asked him why he didn't take the players to California and get them used to the climate.

"They're better here," he explained. "In California they would be entertained and distracted and be all pooped out by game time. We play games to win."

"Like mountaineers who swoop down from the hills and ravage the lowlands," I said.

He smiled and said, "Something like that."

Years later when Columbia was coming West to play Stanford in the Rose Bowl I told this to Coach Lou Little and urged him to do as Rock had done. He did it, and Columbia beat Stanford 7 to 0.

Shortly after Rockne's visit, two sisters from St. Mary's Hospital came with some Christmas presents. One of them was Sister Victoria, the mother superior. A stately, gracious nun, she was distressed to find the conditions under which I was being cared for, called up the hospital, ordered an ambulance, and packed me off to the best room the hospital had.

They were good to me. In fact they were generally good to writers. Francis Perry Elliott spent his last days with them. Though he had been a prosperous author around 1910, he was broke by 1920. He was a gentleman to his Southern finger tips. He had been president of Belmont College in the South before joining Harper's where his chief job was to keep Mark Twain happy.

He never believed an editor could write, but after his wife died he was going through her trunk and found a package neatly tied with red ribbon. "Frank's Plots," it said.

Out of these came *The Haunted Pajamas,* one of the funniest stories of the era. The plot revolved around the fact that anybody who wore them might take on the actions and appearances of someone who had worn them previously.

Though he was an impoverished and broken man by 1923, the way the Sisters of St. Joseph treated him you would have thought he was as rich and as important as Cardinal O'Connell.

We talked of final things, for his end obviously was fast approaching. One day he asked if I would request the hospital chaplain to give him instructions. He felt his strength waning and wanted to lean against the Vatican wall for warmth and comfort.

When the time came for his taking of the Sacraments, the nuns, nurses, and patients acted as if it were the greatest honor that had befallen the old institution. Bishop Gercke came out to the hospital and did the honors. It was a sad and touching scene. The sun played on his head of white hair like a halo.

After this I moved from St. Mary's to Oracle for a few weeks to earn some money handling the publicity of a motion picture company on location. One morning I got a call from one of the nuns urging me to come back to town.

"He is going fast," she said. "He just said to me, 'Don't let me sleep today, Sister. This is my last day on earth and I have lots to do. Get Frank for me!' "

I hurriedly dressed to catch the stage coach to Tucson. It was a forty-mile trip.

Just as I was ready to leave, I was fetched with a pain in

the back as if shot. Gasping, I crawled back to my room and called for help. I began vomiting and nothing could allay the pain.

The nearest doctor was in Tucson. He was there in two hours, prepared to operate. His diagnosis, however, was kidney colic.

"It's the worst pain this side of childbirth," he explained, "and there is nothing to do but give enemas and then try to knock him out."

This he proceeded to do. So while my friend was dying and wondering what was delaying me, I was unconscious forty miles away in a tumble-down shack of a hotel run by a Cherokee Indian and a Negro who had been one of Buffalo Bill's scouts.

By the time I came to the next morning, my friend was dead. I felt I had failed him. It was not for him to have a speedy recovery but he did have a holy, if not a happy, death.

The next day my kidney colic was gone as if it had all been a nightmare. I was, however, ordered back to the hospital where it was discovered t.b. had infected my kidneys. One by one my friends were dying off—and whose number was up next? Mine?

I didn't think so. Though now back on a hospital status, I began to pick up amazingly. Within a short while no trace of those microbes could be found in my kidneys and they were fast losing ground in my lungs.

Not long afterward the hospital had a fire. It was over the ward where Southern Pacific employees were hospitalized. Here the nuns had their sleeping quarters. Apparently through the years they had set aside every dollar to improve their hospital and an adjoining sanatorium. They badly needed accommodations for themselves in keeping with the high standard of the rest of the health center.

I asked that a telephone be installed in my room, and from there I began a campaign to make the town aware of the necessity of repairing this oversight. Everybody responded with such warmth that in a matter of weeks we had raised fifty thousand dollars—a lot of money for a town of twenty thousand.

St. Mary's had a circular two-story brick building, with porches on the inside and the outside. A tree grew high in the patio. The outside porches were not used much. I prevailed upon Sister Victoria to break the wall below each window and put in a Dutch door so that beds could be rolled out to one porch in the morning and to the other in the afternoon, thus providing sunbaths at any time of the day.

Heliotherapy was just coming into vogue and here was a building which had anticipated its popularity by twenty-five years. The building was exclusively for all forms of t.b., and heliotherapy had been found especially effective in bone infections.

Dr. Rollier, whose clinics at Leysin, Switzerland, originated this form of therapy, had written a medical textbook on the subject. It was published by the Oxford University Press. I took every word of it as gospel.

One section dealt with osteomyelitis. A Dr. Amstad related the various methods used to attack this disease and then explained that at Leysin they followed a different procedure. They left the wound wide open so the sun could penetrate right to the marrow of the bone and kill the bugs at their source. They held the wound open with a retractor. "The results are always surprising," he wrote. "Large defects, such as at the head of the tibia, heal in ten to twelve weeks."

I wolfed this down as if it were Peruna. Amstad didn't say the results were *sometimes* surprising. He said they were *always* surprising. Now I wanted to walk more than ever. Here at last was announced a sure cure. I had to get to Switzerland, that's all there was to it.

Tucson had been good to me. It was the nearest thing to a

home I had known since leaving New York. My lungs were improving at last, but my leg was still the old trouble-maker. Climate had proved the deciding factor in my case, but it was not helping me walk without crutches, and I wanted so much to walk like others.

If cured I would come back to Tucson, for I had left my heart there. I knew I could always make a living in Arizona, for I had been doing increasingly better each year.

The nuns were saddened to see me go. They did everything to make my trip comfortable and assured me there would always be a place for me at St. Mary's. When it came time to settle up, they smiled and shook their heads.

"There'll never be a bill for you," said Sister Victoria.

I left with their blessings, and in tears.

9

Sick and in Paris

•

ONE of the most heartwarming things about friends of my college days was that they always gave help but never advice. None of them questioned that a trip from Arizona to Switzerland in search of a sun-cure bordered on madness. Instead, Howard Dietz, who had visited me at St. Mary's Hospital not long before, wangled passage from the French Line for a first-class trip on one of their deluxe transatlantic liners from New York to Cherbourg. Si Seadler, by now a 'cure' and advertising manager of Dietz's department, wired that everything was taken care of and that the trip wouldn't cost me a sou. In New York they'd be waiting for me with open arms.

I had, however, developed a phobia against going back to New York, even to passing through it. The town had broken me down and a pattern, which was half good sense and half primitive taboos, began to govern my life. It was a variation of "he who fights and runs away lives to fight another day." I looked for a way to encircle New York's deadly end. I asked if they could trade in their deluxe passage from New York for something not quite so glamorous going from, say, a Texas port. Used to the caprices of movie stars, they found this switch no problem and fixed me up on a slow scow of thirteen thousand tons which took thirteen days to cross the Atlantic from Galveston to Le Havre.

The ship was subsequently sunk in World War II. I was

surprised it remained afloat that long, for on our voyage it chugged along in a way that reminded me of the derelict ship in Conrad's *Lord Jim.*

Aboard, I met a French priest who was bound for Lisieux, the birthplace of St. Thérèse of the Little Flower of Jesus. The old priest had known her in childhood. It was strange to think of a saint as a contemporary. Usually hundreds of years pass between the death of one who has led an exemplary life and his or her beatification.

St. Thérèse had been born around 1870 and had died in 1894. Thus she had lived only twenty-four years and in that short time had inflamed the religious devotions of millions by her own fervor.

In her own words, she spent her Heaven doing good on earth. No Bride of Christ ever loved Him more. When she died, more consumed by her love of Christ than the devil's t.b. bacilli, she told those of the Carmelite Order left behind that they would know she was continuing her work in behalf of those still on earth when in response to their petitions for help they smelled the fragrance of roses.

I have related how this fragrance came upon me while I was a patient on the desert near Phoenix, Arizona, and how I later read of its happening to Michael Williams in *The High Romance.* It happened to me again on the high seas. I smelled those roses. Later the old priest told me it was on that day that Thérèse was being canonized in Rome and, looking at his watch added: "In fact by now she is recognized as a saint."

When that evening the ship's surgeon got around to changing the dressing on my leg, we discovered the wound had healed! Anyway, it was not draining and the surface was closed over. The ship's surgeon was plainly puzzled, because the day before there had been no indication that the suppuration was slowing down.

For myself, I didn't know what to think. Miracles didn't happen to the likes of me. I still believed more in surgeons' interference and sun treatments than in the intervention of saints. I was conditioned by the material world in which I lived, and it was never more material than in the 20's of the twentieth century. Man, in those days, did not live by bread alone. He insisted additionally on layer-cakes and French pastries. His soul was in the pit of his stomach, and though the rest of me wasn't worth much, my stomach was perfect.

So the possibility of a miraculous cure, on the high seas, of a chronic disease that had been a part of me for fifteen years sent frightening sensations up and down my spine. I hadn't asked St. Thérèse to intercede in my behalf. I thought she was a wonderful inspiration for those who lacked personal courage to fight through their difficulties, but I couldn't see how that included me.

Moreover, at the time, my shrine was the sun god and my destination was Leysin, Switzerland, the Mecca of a growing cult of sun-worshippers. I had no intention of changing my course in transit, of going instead to Lisieux, or Lourdes, or even Rome. I tried to ignore a coincidence that was repeating itself—the fragrance of roses—first on the desert near Phoenix and now on the high seas. What an idiot I must have been to have ignored these offers from one who had said she would spend her Heaven doing good on earth.

The ship's surgeon was sure that the healing was superficial and that below the surface the cavity and infection remained. He insisted on opening the wound and placing a quill in it so the sinus could not heal over again. The quill—as odd a surgical device as I ever saw—slipped out and in a few days the surface healed over again. This baffled him, but since I was going to Leysin for a thorough and basic surgical cleaning out of the infection, he shrugged his shoulders and let it go.

Neither he nor I believed in miracles at the time; so instead of joining the old priest and paying my *devoir* to St. Thérèse at Lisieux, I continued on to Paris. Apparently St. Thérèse washed me off her hands after this obvious lack of faith, for she could see I was determined to have those Swiss surgeons hack away at me. Though I didn't realize it at the time, I had missed the chance to bear witness to Thérèse's first miracle as a saint.

That wound was never to get another chance to heal.

Many writers have extolled Paris in the spring, but most of them were young, healthy pagans, whereas I was a cheerful tuberculoafer with a hole in his leg. The drizzle and mist that began at Le Havre became chronic by the time the train reached Paris. There I was met by Thomas Earl Black, one of our classmates. He had lived for years in Paris. In fact he had been the hundred-metre champion of France before going to Columbia. He found the going in the School of Journalism too hard, flunked out, and crossed the campus to a graduate school where he got a master's degree in French before his Class of '17 J reached its junior year.

He was offered a commission in Hoover's army which carried bread instead of bullets into occupied Belgium, and he sought to include Sok and me in the enterprise. French was a basic requirement. Black bargained with Hoover's high command, saying that his going depended on their accepting us as well. Sok bluffed them into believing he knew enough French, but they were still doubtful about me. We were to have twenty-five dollars a week as an expense account and a Ford delivery truck for transportation. I was the only one who could drive.

Black assured them he could teach me enough French on a slow boat across the Atlantic to meet their demands. I argued that you didn't have to know a language to give food to starving people. I added that I knew German and that the Germans at the time were occupying Belgium. But Hoover had set up his own dictatorship on Belgian Relief and insisted on French as a basic requirement. So Tom Black, a man they wanted badly, walked out because they wouldn't take Sok and me as well.

Till our reunion in Paris, I had not seen him in nearly ten years. He was the same smiling red-headed Hoosier, a cheerful sight in the drizzling, misty rain that kept spraying *La Ville Lumière*. He knew the good and cheap places to eat and to sleep. I spent most of the time in bed resting up from the trip. Consequently, I saw practically nothing of the Paris every tourist knows. Tom lived at Fresnes, across from the prison, and rode in daily to see that I was all right.

It took a week before I felt well enough to go on to Switzerland, and in that time I never saw Nôtre Dame, Sacré Coeur, The Louvre, or The Pantheon, which had once been the shrine of St. Marguerite, the patron of Paris whose prayers had turned Atilla and the Huns away from Paris. Montmartre, the Dome, the Champs Élysées, and Montparnasse were all names to me and nothing more. All I saw was the little garden from my room in a hotel near the Luxembourg Galleries. The hotel had once been a convent and had retained the peaceful atmosphere of its holier days.

When you're sick, I suppose any new city is just another microbe convention which you're anxious to escape. Anyway, Paris in the spring meant no more to me than it does to a French street cleaner. I felt more at home after the train passed the French frontier and entered Switzerland. The mountain air was cleaner and so was everything else. The Swiss even used our sort of electric light bulbs. Their houses were immaculate. But their mountains, to one fresh from Arizona where mountains can be seen for one hundred miles as clearly as if they were a block away, were so close you felt like pushing them off your shoulders.

We passed by way of Lausanne to Aigle. From Aigle we

took a funicular railway up the mountains to Leysin. It was raining as if a new deluge had been visited upon the land. The streets were so hilly there were no motor cars or trolleys. Only horse-drawn vehicles were used in summer and skis in winter. Though a freedom-loving republic for eight hundred years, it seemed to me that the lives of the Swiss were depressingly regimented. Most of them spent the first half of their lives building châlets on inaccessible hills to escape their neighbors, and the second half in building funicular railways to bring their neighbors close to them again.

I was assigned to a *clinique* called *Les Hirondelles* (The Swallows), and it certainly was for the birds. We had one nurse for twelve patients. We slept two patients in a room at night and all of us were rolled out on a long porch at dawn. Of the twelve patients only two beside myself spoke English, one a doctor from Canada and the other an Irishman (of sorts) from Belfast. Among the nine others no two had the same mother tongue. Only one was a Swiss. Like all Swiss, he spoke French, German, and Italian.

After a week of orientation I was wheeled over to the main clinic for my operation. It was done under local anesthetic. The operation proceeded more like a brutal third-degree to obtain a confession than modern surgery. An assistant held me down while Dr. Amstad, the chief surgeon, slashed, chopped, and chiseled in an area that seemed impervious to his particular anesthetic. I screamed as if I were being throttled by devils. His assistant wore no cap and his long curly hair kept shaking dandruff in my face. After an hour Dr. Amstad uttered some guttural German and pronounced the operation over. He placed an *écarteur*, a retractor, in the wound to keep it from closing and shipped me back to *Les Hirondelles* in an open barouche on which a sort of door had been placed so I could lie down. I believe a blanket was thrown over me. I wasn't strapped to the board. If I had rolled off I would not have minded because by then I was too near dead to care.

I went through months of agonizing treatments. That promised twelve weeks to a miraculous recovery gave way to a summer of pain. Summer surrendered to fall and fall to winter. I was less near a cure by then than when I entered. Coles Phillips, a cover designer for American magazines, was a patient at a nearby clinic. He was hopelessly ill from a t.b. kidney infection. He had brought his wife and four children to Leysin with him. On Christmas day, his wife, Theresa Hyde Phillips, learning I was alone in that cold land, brought me a beautiful flowering plant. They were as much disappointed in the claims of Rollier's sun-cures as I was.

My roommate was a Scot who had tuberculosis of the spine. He had to lie flat on his back night and day and could view things only in reflections of a little mirror.

When we were rolled outdoors each morning, a table with "conveniences" was rolled out with us. One day he kept calling for a nurse. None came. I knew what he wanted and it couldn't wait. So I reached into my table, took out a washbasin, and sailed it into the room. It crashed against the door. It sounded like an explosion. Staff members came running from all floors.

"That guy wants a bedpan," I said simply.

He didn't need it much longer. In a week he was dead.

I felt it was time for me to get out of the place before I too was carried out. Coles Phillips felt the same way. We decided to head for the Italian Riviera. I left on crutches, sour at a place that promised to kill or cure and ended by doing neither. I urged Coles Phillips to buy a pair of cheap crutches to make his trip across frontiers easier. He could walk without them, but he was sicker than I was and needed to be spared the ordeals inflicted on all travelers by customs officials.

He refused to stoop to such a subterfuge and got the works, whereas I didn't have to stir from my compartment and my baggage was hardly looked at. My crutches were like diplomatic passports to people who assumed that anyone who used them was a war hero and that all heroes were shot in the leg.

On recapitulation of this misadventure I tabulated that in Leysin we had nine sunny days a month. If Tucson had that few sunny days a month, the Sunshine Climate Club would have been lynched. I grimaced and shook my head to think how I had been chumped by a medicine-show and thanked God I had got out of the folly alive.

The Italian Riviera was full of convalescent homes and I tried many of them—all the way from Ventimiglia, where Dr. Voronoff was grafting monkey glands on men to reestablish their virility, to Rapallo, where Max Beerbohm and Ezra Pound spent their winters. The place I liked best was Santa Marguerita, south of Genoa. There I licked my wounds and tried to think my way out of a mess of my own making. Between treatments I wrote poems, as a sort of convalescent therapy. Like this, for instance:

RATES OF EXCHANGE

I lie and watch the leaves go brown,
The leaves along the boulevard.
I lie and watch my knee go down,
So swelled in pain—so stiff, so hard.

My callers tell me all the news:
"The Riviera at its best!"
"You never saw such pretty views!"
"Exquisite!" "Sad" and all the rest.

I watch the autumn turn to frost
And count the weeks I've lost in bed.
My health will come, but at a cost,
The leaves by then will all be dead.

I could have returned home with Coles Phillips and his family. The temptation was almost irresistible. But I felt I was sure to lose if I admitted defeat that openly.

In a year Coles was dead.

By then I was getting used to beautiful friendships growing like desert flowers and dying shortly afterward. But I was determined to be like Stevenson, Shelley, or Keats in this respect, if no other. I would not go home to die.

10

Picture-Making in Utopia

•

Though on the Italian Riviera I was only a few hours from Rome, I never went to the Eternal City, the fountainhead of my faith. I still was trying to make progress the hard way. There was one great orthopedic surgeon left on the continent and I hadn't tried him. His name was Dr. Vittorio da Putti. His hospital was in Bologna. He also was director of a sanatorium for bone cases in the Dolomites.

I wrote to him, explaining my case, and got an answer inviting me to his clinic in Bologna to see what he could do. Enclosed with the letter was a note in English from his secretary, privately urging me to come, as she felt sure he could help.

He turned out to be a big, handsome, cheerful man. When I said I wondered if it wouldn't be better to cut the damned leg off, he registered horror.

"Why, you can live ninety-nine years with that leg!" he exclaimed. "I make the best artificial legs in the world and I can't make one that can give you as much service as the poor one you have!"

We talked of Sir Robert Jones of London and of Dr. Rollier of Leysin. Dr. da Putti wondered what kind of scientist the Swiss was. He had offered to exchange information with him, he said, and had never got the slightest cooperation. I dismissed Rollier as a man who did quite well as long as he kept his hands off his patients and made them lie around in the sun until they either got well or died.

Da Putti offered to operate for nothing, but assured me in advance that further curettage would simply mean a bigger cavity in my leg and one chance in a thousand of coming out of it any better off than I was at the moment. He rather feared the whole femur had been infected by then, but added it was a low-grade infection and not likely to spread if kept clean.

It is a great man who admits his limitations. I thanked him and asked him to thank his secretary, too, for urging me to come to see him.

"My secretary wrote you?"

I told him about the note in English. He laughed. "She's not my secretary!" He told me who she was. She was an American girl who had married an Italian nobleman. When her marriage went on the rocks she offered to help him with his English correspondence on occasion. I found out who she was and where she lived. I wrote and thanked her. It wasn't long before I found myself in a triangle and the great orthopedist became Signor Geloso to us, for he was madly in love with her. And with reason, for she was a beautiful woman.

He urged me to take the baths at Salso Maggiori and she sent her nurse along to take care of me. The treatments did wonders and within two months I was able to pick up where I had left off in Tucson and do a little writing again.

Howard Dietz came to visit me in Italy and wondered if I couldn't write some features for him on *The Garden of Allah,* which Rex Ingram was making for Metro-Goldwyn in Nice on the French Riviera. I was happy to get out of "Mussolitaly," as I called it, to the freer air of France, though I was leaving the best of friends behind.

Out of these articles developed the first substantial job I had held in years. Rex Ingram asked me if I would take over the task of directing his advertising and publicity. Howard Strickling had left France to return to Culver City. Left behind were Leo Mishkin, now entertainment editor of the New York *Morning Telegraph*, and Michael Powell, who later directed *Red Shoes, Tales of Hoffmann*, and other great pictures. They were young and needed a boss.

I explained to Ingram that I had not worked in an office in ten years and couldn't do it now, but if he wanted me to try, I would run the department from a villa on a hill about a mile from the studio. This seemed satisfactory to him and to Harry Lachman, the general manager. Lachman had been one of America's best painters in Paris. He had deserted his art for motion pictures and was at that time proving himself a great general manager of both Ingram productions and the studio as well.

He had cut production costs from one million dollars down to $375,000 without taking out any of the production values for which Ingram's pictures were noted.

Alice Terry, Antonio Moreno, and Ramon Novarro were Ingram's stars at the time. He was still living on the phenomenal success of *The Four Horsemen of the Apocalypse, Scaramouche, Mare Nostrum*, and *Where the Pavement Ends*.

He had just made a picture version of Somerset Maugham's *The Magician*, but this one had missed more than a few tricks. He was bored by pictures, preferring to lie around the *plage* and tan his body beautiful. He indulged in some sculpturing on the side. He also had taken Mohammed as his prophet.

His real name was Reginald Hitchcock. His father was a clergyman in the Established Church of Ireland. Rex had gone to Yale where he was a classmate of Frank Tuttle, who also became a great motion picture director.

Ingram was more handsome than any leading man he hired and of course was treated like a king. He signed office memos

"R.I." which could be construed as Rex Imperator as well as Rex Ingram.

The studio was built around a villa that once belonged to General Massena, one of Napoleon's generals, and Ingram used it as an atelier for his sculpture, as well as his private quarters for his amours.

Thanks to his making *The Four Horsemen* and *Mare Nostrum,* both written by Ibáñez (who himself was an exile from Spain and lived in Menton), Ingram's name was mud in Germany. His pictures were barred from exhibition there.

When I first met him he had already begun production on *The Garden of Allah.* This novel by Robert Hitchens had been made into a picture before. In remaking it, Ingram started a trend which hasn't come to an end yet. Except for John Ford's remake of *The Informer,* few of these tired duplications have been successful in the picture business, but producers keep on trying.

I wrote in a villa which had a lovely balcony and was supplied with transportation and a secretary. Saturday I would go to the studio, have luncheon, talk with the various persons concerned with production, and go home with enough material to last me another week. While at the studio I would dole out instructions to members of my staff, and the arrangement seemed to work amazingly well.

The Riviera at that time was at its best, and everybody who was anybody (and who isn't?) visited the Ingram studio. Thus I met not only authors like Ibáñez, Maugham, Hitchens, Oppenheim, Fitzgerald, Hamilton, Gibbs, Wells, and Kipling, but people like Henri Matisse, Mary Garden, Mary Nash, Norma Talmadge, Douglas Fairbanks, Harold Lloyd, and scores of picture stars from Hollywood, all of whom envied Ingram his splendid isolation and wanted to see just how he did it.

Though my job paid only seventy-five dollars a week, living

conditions on the Riviera at this time were such as to make this comparable with 275 dollars a week elsewhere. Then too, as often happens when a free-lance writer joins a staff, he finds that the normal expenses which he had got in the habit of absorbing himself are automatically absorbed by the company. I found I was saving fifty dollars a week as a matter of course.

I had an assistant who lived at Villa Grand Vue with me. His name was Lucien A. Sauvage. He was a French-Canadian, and since he could drive a car and knew French and English, I thought he'd make a good assistant.

It wasn't long before I noticed he was uncomfortable while typing. I then learned that he had had a t.b. spine. The infected bone was curetted and a sliver of his shin inserted between two of the vertebrae. He made a good convalescence. He felt all right when standing or walking, but sitting made him terribly uncomfortable. So I got him a high-backed chair such as kings used, strapped supports under his armpits, and hung them from the top of the high chair. This took the weight off his spine and gave him such relief that he could type for hours without discomfort.

We worked together for two years. Then Sauvage returned to Montreal for a visit with his family, planning later to practice law in San Diego where he had previously lived and where he had had the operation on his spine which had saved his life. This plan never matured, but we did meet again in Hollywood in 1934. By then, Sauvage was an attorney, having studied law in the public library. He passed the bar examinations, the fourth highest man that year. Since then he has been our family lawyer.

We discovered in Nice that we had a lot in common. We were Catholics with a liberal political point of view and a fondness for good wine and French peasant food. The peasants' philosophy and spiritual serenity fetched us too. We compared it with the ulcerating madness of the movie business and marveled that such basically vulgar-minded people as Hollywood spawned could turn out so many nice clean pictures, often extolling the best side of mankind.

We discussed how easy it would have been to make *The Garden of Allah* a good picture. Robert Hitchens, the author, had covered most sides of the question, but it seemed to us that Ingram had carefully selected the worst sides. Then one day I learned that his chief reason for wanting to make the picture was to show a monk with a bastard child.

With such a motive, he obviously could never completely conceal his malice toward his subject. One day in the projection room with his father and a few others, Rex called to me and said, "Scully, if you want a story, you can say I had so much religion in my father's house I haven't been in a church since."

His psychophantic fringe gave him the quota of laughter he expected for this gratuitous attack. His father said nothing. Brought up to honor fathers and mothers, and certainly honoring and loving my own, I was shocked into a realization that my own beliefs had been dozing in that unbelieving atmosphere.

The nearer the picture came to completion, the more cynical everybody became about it. Ingram had started a devil's fire he couldn't put out. I found that he grabbed small ideas I tossed off at luncheon as a drowning man grabs at straws. His malice in wonderland was heading him toward a sure-fire fiasco, and he felt it. His big scene was a sandstorm with a renegade Trappist monk and his bride caught in it. Their lives spared, the monk decided to repent and go back to the monastery. The cynical view of Ingram's crew was: "Who wouldn't want to go back to a nice, cool monastery after that?"

Tempers were getting frayed on all sides. My aides at the studio, anxious to help, had volunteered for combat duty. One,

Lee Mishkin, son of the Metropolitan Opera official photographer, joined the camera crew. So did Mickey Powell. Mishkin got the job of sticking the scene board in front of the camera before each "take." In placing it between the camera and a close-up of Alice Terry, the thirty-thousand-dollar star and wife of Ingram, he banged her on her beautiful nose, scraping off the makeup. She backed away and stumbled into a bucket Powell had put down behind her.

Powell was bawled out and Mishkin was fired.

Hours later Mishkin climbed the hill to Villa Grande Vue to tell me the bad news. Only nineteen at the time, he was on the verge of tears.

I must have sensed that things had been going badly because he had hardly finished his sad tale when I handed him a letter. "The Chicago Tribune has started a Riviera edition," I said. "Take this letter to the managing editor." It was a glowing letter of recommendation.

In a few hours Lee reported back, elated. The letter had got him the job. When the Riviera edition was discontinued at the end of the season, his bosses were so happy with his work that they transferred him to the Paris staff. From there he had no trouble breaking into New York journalism. By the time he was a well-grounded newspaperman, he switched back to his early love and became a critic on The Morning Telegraph. We have been like brothers ever since that dismal day in Nice. Years later, on a trip to Hollywood, he found out that Ingram was living the life of a recluse in North Hollywood. He was the last man to interview the director before Ingram died.

But in 1927 Ingram was still Rex Imperator of the Côte d'Azur. One Saturday when I drove to the studio he hailed me with: "Here comes Canon Scully!"

Before the laughter of his yes-men had died down, he noticed that I was taking his sally deadpan. He switched his approach

and invited me to lunch with him privately, saying he wanted
to talk things over.

"I don't know what to think about this picture," he began.
"Alice doesn't like the way it's going. Lachman shares her view,
and obviously you don't like it either. Why don't you move into
the studio and work on it with me?"

He was getting $100,000 dollars for directing the picture; I
was getting seventy-five dollars a week, remember.

I told him it was too late to do much without a lot of reshoot-
ing. In fact if I had been a Thalberg I would have ordered the
whole mess scrapped. But I wasn't and didn't want to be. He
thought it could be saved by re-editing and cutting. I didn't.

"Nick Schenk in New York and the bunch on the Coast,"
Ingram continued, "don't like the rough cut they've seen. The
picture might be saved with special exploitation. Goldbeck suggests some one from Hollywood go to New York. But I'd rather
have you. Do you feel well enough to make the trip and handle
my part at the opening? We could budget 250 dollars a week
for six weeks and take care of all expenses. We could even send
an assistant along with you."

I didn't want to go to New York. That was the place that had
broken me down and an instinct for survival told me to by-pass
any place that had treated my body unkindly. Besides, the
tempo of New York was too fast. For me, as well as Ingram,
the French Riviera was just right. It was just slow enough for
my t.b. tread.

I suggested he get somebody from the West Coast—Howard
Strickling, for instance. But Strickling, he pointed out, was
working under Louis B. Mayer. That name had a number-one
priority on Ingram's S.O.B. list. He insisted his pictures be released as produced by Metro-Goldwyn, *not* Metro-Goldwyn-
Mayer.

"We'll set you up in a suite in one of the best hotels in New York and give you a round-trip ticket if you'll go."

"I'll give you an answer in two days," I said.

It was a terrific temptation. I thought of my mother back in New York and what fun it would be to return home after ten years of chasing the cure, with money in my purse and all the earmarks of opulence. What a laugh we would have together.

But God gave me an answer the next morning, possibly on the intercession of St. Thérèse. While clearing my throat, I felt a warm, salty, substance irritating it. I coughed and blood began to come from my lungs. From long experience I had learned how to control my nerves so that my heart would not start pounding. I quietly returned to bed and didn't move a muscle for an hour. I knew that if nature were given half a chance, it would coagulate that blood and make some small repair at the point of lesion. Then I called a doctor.

Doctors normally treat such a condition by giving a shot of morphine to the patient to quiet him. I had always had a singular control over my nerves in a crisis. All I asked for was a nurse so that I wouldn't have to move a finger for at least forty-eight hours. Any activity, I knew, was like trying to heal a cut on a finger by constantly wiggling it.

Without letting him know what had happened to me, I sent word to Ingram that on thinking it over I had decided not to go to New York. Within ten days I was up and around again.

And then came a cable that removed all desire to return to New York. My mother, tired of waiting, had died.

11

Isadora Duncan "Adopts" Me

•

MORE and more I seemed to be meeting celebrities whose glamorous careers were behind them. One of these was Isadora Duncan. I found she was stopping at the Negresco, the most fashionable hotel in Nice. I didn't know it was her habit to seek refuge in the best hotels when she was broke. They never turned her away. To them she was a great artist, not an American tourist who had run out of money.

It was not long after her Russian husband, a young poet and madder than most, had died by his own hand. Paris Singer, father of her two children who were accidentally drowned in the Seine, had turned over to her a high-powered car, and she was driving it recklessly around the winding Riviera roads, hoping one day to take a wrong turn and end it all.

This suicidal melancholia was heightened when she discovered that another young Russian, a pianist, with whom she was infatuated, had cast his eyes too lovingly on an American girl they both knew. She decided she could take this sort of thing no longer. She walked on the waves, or at least she tried to, and went down. The pianist and a British officer rescued her easily enough, but when the British officer went back to salvage her fur coat from the waves he nearly drowned.

The press was on her trail about this escapade when I called her, and she was so relieved to learn that I merely wanted her to pose for some pictures with an Oulaid Nail dancer we had in the picture that she gladly consented.

She kept dragging the young Russian pianist into the photographs, but I didn't mind, figuring the photographer could always cut him out when he enlarged the prints. He was in his twenties, fairly tall, definitely dark, and astonishingly handsome. Quiet, esthetic-looking, he was potentially a Russian genius—if the easy life of the Riviera didn't wash him up as a gigolo. And as yet, though he was paired with the maddest of Americans, he showed none of the vices of foreigners simulating La Vie Bohème. I could see that all Isadora adored in her vanished beauty she saw in him.

Afterward I took her and her young pianist to luncheon, only to learn that she had not had breakfast. She ordered five shots of Irish whiskey, which was her idea of a substantial way to start the day.

(She was fat and fifty at the time, but sweet, motherly, and fun when she could forget the past for a moment. She confided in me things I would have difficulty telling my father confessor.)

The members of the press kept trying to find her. The next morning she arrived at our villa, hoping to elude them. She asked me to drive with her to Antibes to see a friend.

We stopped at a tobacco shop while the pianist went in to buy some cigarettes. She leaned over to me and whispered, "He's a genius. I only associate with geniuses."

As she was associating with me every day by then, I was mighty flattered.

She was sure we would be invited to a sumptuous luncheon at Antibes. However, the rich friend was not home, so I had to settle by treating Isadora to five more slugs of Irish whiskey at a nearby bistro. This sort of thing went on for days. Then one day she told me she was writing her life story. I thought of a friend who might want to publish it. I cabled them I could get an option on it for them for a few thousand dollars.

While awaiting word from America, we visited a little studio she had in Nice. It was cold, dark, draughty, drab. An old housekeeper was taking care of it. When we walked out into the sunlight, Isadora remarked that we would have to do something for her. "She's lonely. She needs a home and people to care for. We'll have to get her a house."

Though agents, the midwives of the arts, were considered prosperous parasites by producers and publishers, I seemed to have played their rôle several times. But I always did it as a friend and would have considered myself lower than a prostitute if any one had suggested I should pocket the traditional 10 per cent for the service.

My friend turned down my suggestion, but another publisher grabbed it and sent a thousand-dollar check as an advance. Isadora had difficulty cashing it. Not long before her mad Russian poet hanged himself, while the two of them were flying over Germany, he had snatched all the papers in her purse, torn them up, and tossed them out of the plane. Her passport was among the trivia thus disposed of.

As soon as I could help her convert the check into francs, she said she was going to buy a villa. "I'm going to give Scully a room with a balcony overlooking the sea and nurse him back to health. I'm going to give Patterson three bottles of whiskey a day."

Patterson was the British officer who had rescued her from drowning.

"Why Patterson three bottles of whiskey a day?" asked the Russian pianist.

"Because I feel sorry for him."

Patterson had lost a leg. I thought he had lost it for king and

George W. P. Hunt, Arizona's perpetual governor, and the author in front of ruins of Tumaccacori Mission near Nogales, Ariz.

...lly as editor of *The Branding* ..., Phoenix, Ariz. (1920).

Scully and Al Kieson at Prescott Arizona (1921).

...e horizontal col-...nist of the *Arizona* ...ly *Star*, Tucson, ...z. (1923).

Sime Silverman, *Variety* editor, author of the famous quote: "Need any money?"

"Nurse" Evie Currey—who took the night shift.

With "Nurse" Alice Pihl in Nice before she became Mrs. Scully.

Relief "Nurse" Adele Clifton of "No, No Nanette."

country, but it seemed he had crashed through a skylight while on a bender and had practically severed a leg in the escapade. The pianist didn't think Patterson should go through life grousing about his misfortune.

"I don't care what you say," she repeated, "Patterson gets his three bottles of whiskey a day."

"But that's silly," the pianist insisted. "It's like me. I can be a Russian refugee for one year, or two years, but I can't make a career of it. Patterson—"

"Gets three bottles of whiskey a day," Isadora concluded.

He didn't, however. Before Isadora could get around to a house, she was talked into buying a car.

By now the old one was a wreck. One of those flowing veils which she habitually wore around her neck caught in one of the wheels of the new car, yanked her from the seat, and choked the life out of her.

Most Americans who had known the dancer in her prime thought it was all for the best, though the French—to a man, woman, and child—mourned the loss as if it were a national tragedy. I shared the view. She was sweet to me.

Her book became a best seller, but she was no longer among us to share in this belated good fortune.

By then Ingram's picture had been completed, had been shown in New York, and had died too. Metro-Goldwyn, with or without Mayer, decided to say good-by to its lotus-eating director. Lachman said good-by to him too. He formed his own company with Nina Wilcox Putnam as his writer and partner and Mickey Powell as their star. They elected me president of the company.

Lachman had more canvases in the Luxembourg than any other American, living or dead, Whistler included. But he thought painting was a dead art and that the spirit of the age was best exemplified by speed and mechanics. He felt that if a painter were worth his salt, he would place his talent in the frame of its time. Painters in centuries past were a vital asset in great men's lives. If they wanted to have some visual proof of how beautiful their castles were in Spain, they sent a painter down there to paint them. If they wanted to impress their descendants with their importance as ancestors, they had their portraits painted. But with the invention of the camera—and this was even truer with the invention of the color camera— that sort of painting had outlived its usefulness and was therefore living on borrowed time.

For this reason Lachman wanted to be a motion picture director. For an artist, he had singular skill as a business man, and though he started on the Ingram lot as a still photographer (about the lowest thing on a motion picture lot), in six months he had climbed to general manager of the studios and had cut production costs 60 per cent. But still he wanted to direct, and Ingram still wanted to keep him in the front office. They parted company on that issue.

Lachman, no Adonis, held an unusual fascination for women, particularly singers. Mary Garden, Marguerite Namara, and Jue Quon Tai were among them. But he never married until Jue Quon Tai came into his life. She, the daughter of a Chinese ambassador under the old regime, had come to the South of France to study for opera under Bartelemy. He had been the coach of Enrico Caruso, Mary Garden, and Grace Moore among others.

Tai had made a success in vaudeville and musical comedies, but she wanted to be the first opera singer of her race. She met Harry Lachman, through Rex Ingram, I suspect, and from then on the conversation around the table, though it might begin on the subject of music, invariably turned to movies.

Tai had a rare voice, a contralto of great range, warmth, and beauty—Mary Garden said she had never heard a voice to match it—but after she married Lachman, Tai found her talents gradually pushed more and more out of the picture.

Tai once overheard the remark that while it might be all right for her to be married to a "white man" on the Riviera, she would never be accepted socially in Hollywood. This really burned her. As a result, when Lachman was later called from Paris to Hollywood to direct for Fox Films, she determined to knock this social bias into the Pacific.

She put on parties worthy of the late Mrs. Cornelius Vanderbilt. As many as two hundred dined at her home at one time, and they were the *crème de la fromage* of Hollywood. When she exhausted the list and had got every holdout to her table, she closed the doors and became practically a recluse. She had vindicated her social position and that was all she wanted to do.

One day at our house Mary Ford, the wife of John Ford, about the most famous of Hollywood directors, and Olive Carey, the wife of Harry Carey, on noticing the length of Tai's finger nails, asked her what she would do if she saw some lint on the floor.

"How would you pick it up?" Mary wanted to know.

"I'd call a maid," said Tai imperiously.

On the Riviera, Lachman saw in me the sort of person he wanted to replace himself so he could direct pictures. He knew that I had no ambition to direct and couldn't do the physical side of it if I wanted to. But I could organize and get people to do things—which is what an executive needs most.

With beautiful backgrounds wherever we turned and fascinating, though often primitive, industries to be discovered in the dying hill towns, we decided to see if we could make visual education amusing and painless. Our slogan was: "Like study-

ing geography under Charlie Chaplin." I suggested that we take
the wine industry. "Let's take a Frenchman and an American
sitting on the terrace of the Negresco hotel," I said. "They pick
up the wine card. The American says to the Frenchman, 'Why
is it that in this country wine is always cheaper than water?'
'Why?' echoes the Frenchman, 'I'll tell you why.' And with
that we lap-dissolve into the whole industry of growing grapes
and making wine. At one point we'll have the peasants take off
their dirty shoes, climb into the vat, and explain that the weight
of their feet was just enough to bruise the grape and free it of
its juices without crushing or destroying its bouquet. Next we
will cut to two beautifully dressed people on this same Negresco hotel terrace, show a waiter opening a bottle of wine and
the diners breathing its exquisite bouquet, then cut back to the
peasants' dirty feet squashing the grapes. At the end we'll have
the Frenchman saying to the American, 'Now is it clear why
wine is cheaper than water in France?' And the American saying, 'Nothing could be clearer, not even Einstein.'"

It was a quaint idea. We made a dozen pictures like this.
But we ran into a snag. By then Hollywood had been wired
for sound and our silent gems heading toward New York were
met in mid-Atlantic by prints of *The Jazz Singer* heading toward Europe. We were sunk without a trace.

Our only chance to recoup our costs was to move eastward
ahead of Hollywood pictures equipped with sound tracks. We
did fairly well in England and on the Continent and then retreated to the Far East. There our little gems met a thundering
herd heading west from Hollywood and were heard of no more.

The net result, however, was that we got offers to join a Brit-
ish company in Elstree. But just as I would not buck the New
York climate, neither would I go to England. So Lachman and
Powell left for London and I said good-by to them in Nice.

We made plans for my joining them for the summer, perhaps

in London, but I really did not bank on the prospect. I had got used to choosing between a climate and a career.

I had to take time out for another operation anyway. That leg was kicking up. The new flareup forced me into the Queen Victoria Memorial Hospital. It was another one of those agonizing things with a local anesthetic, but I was ready to leave the hospital and return to my French *pension* in two weeks. By this time I had more or less lost count of operations.

I had an ironing board strapped to my leg and I hung it out of a Ford roadster as Sauvage and I drove from the Quai des États Unis to the Promenade des Anglais and up the hill to Villa Paulette. I now had a second-floor room with a balcony so that I could lie in the sun. To get up there I sat on the steps and backed up the stairway while Sauvage held my leg in its splint in the air.

Convalescing from operations was always a busy time for me. On this occasion I had to wind up the affairs of the company. Among our assets was what I suspect was the first deluxe trailer ever made. It had belonged to King Albert of the Belgians. He had used it as a field headquarters in World War I. It was hauled by a Renault truck. About thirty feet long, it had sleeping accommodations for four, a kitchen, and toilet facilities. I had hoped to make a tour of France in it, but the company's obligations became so pressing that I had to sell it. It brought about 2500 dollars.

Unasked, I wrote a column on the motion picture situation in Europe and sent it to *Variety*. Sime Silverman accepted it, paid me twice his regular rates, and asked me to write for him as often as I felt up to it. Thus began an association with the bible of show business that passed its twenty-fifth anniversary in 1954.

It did not appear I was faring badly because I refused to go to London. My career by now was pockmarked with renunciations of this sort, but in refusing to go to London I was soon to learn that a divinity was shaping my destiny in a beautiful and enduring way.

The sick eagle, however, was getting sick of looking at the sky. He had always felt he shouldn't weigh down another with his woes, but his resolution in this respect was getting weaker. Too long had he agreed with those who argued that misfits like himself should not marry and multiply, that he was destined for the scrap-heap, and that eugenics had all the answers.

Women had never been a problem—except to get rid of them. It had been easy through the years to convince most of them that I had no future and would prove a burden once the honeymoon was over. Besides, I had a deep religious conviction about marriage. For my kind it was once to every man and only once. The cold breath of middle age was beginning to breathe down my neck, but I was still playing the role of the perennially convalescent bachelor.

I had plenty of mature friends. Henri Cain who wrote the books and librettos for Massenet's operas was a next-door neighbor. Maeterlinck was a visitor. Queen Marie of Roumania and Talbot Taylor, who first put U. S. Steel and Anaconda Copper on the market, were nearby neighbors, and when I was well enough I got invitations to dine at their places.

Villa Paulette had its quota of beautiful and attractive women too. Mme. Andrée Aulois, who owned Villa Paulette, was not the least charming of these. She originally was from Burgundy, spoke exquisite French, and played Chopin beautifully. Her brother had been one of the finest painters of military subjects in France. His paintings of horses and uniforms of a long dead era were magnificent. In his time this was a highly regarded talent, though since then, France has got her fill of military subjects. He was killed in the First World War.

Mme. Aulois herself was a war widow with one son who divided his time between mountain-climbing, skiing, and commercial art. He subsequently became an art director of French pictures. His mother and he treated everybody as a star boarder and did not exclude me from their gracious and heartwarming hospitality.

One day they sent a mother and two daughters, who had lived for some years in America, to visit me in the hope that a few hands of bridge might relieve the monotony of convalescence. They were Norwegians. The mother, Fru Sophie Pihl, was a severe and regal-looking woman. Her oldest daughter Astrid was a luscious blonde of perhaps twenty-three. With them was a small *pike* (pronounced peeka) who was said to be eighteen and looked all of twelve. Her name was Alice Mellbye Pihl. She had the trusting and limpid eyes of a gazelle and moved around like a tomboy who would rather run than walk like a lady.

They came to play bridge, and did my morale a world of good. I remember I foolishly bid five hearts and made it. I didn't know the little *pike's* heart was among them. I have never since had time to play bridge with them or anybody else. That card game was the beginning of the end of the Convalescent Bachelor.

12
Princes and Peasants

•

THE French Riviera was populated with eminent exiles in the 20's and 30's. As in Arizona, many of them either came for their health or were waiting for the sheriff to die back home. People as diverse in their views as Grand Duke Alexander and Alexander Berkman from Russia, Frank Harris and W. Somerset Maugham from England, Isadora Duncan and Nina Wilcox Putnam from America, and Blasco Ibáñez and the Bourbon dynasty from Spain lived near each other and in peace.

Former kings like Carol of Roumania and Manuel of Portugal, various surviving members of the Hohenzollern and Hapsburg royal families, and fugitives from fleabitten monarchies in the Balkans and the Near East, as well as Sir Basil Zaharoff, the "Death King" who had sold munitions to all of them, contributed their quota to "royalty at liberty." So did Mohammedan lands whose shahs, sultans, cherifs, and beys found it better to skip than stay.

The exception was the Aga Khan. He was there by choice. The religious leader of a large Mohammedan sect, he specialized in breeding and racing horses. Seemingly this could not unhorse him. He spent most of his time wining and dining almost everybody except his flock. He was said to be richer than Otto Kahn, who visited the Riviera now and then to see how the opera talent he was subsidizing was getting on. Some people confused

130

them, but it was our job as newspaper correspondents not to.

Fugitives from Teapot Dome scandals were neighbors to actors, playwrights, and authors like Chauncey Olcott, George Broadhurst, E. Phillips Oppenheim, Mary Garden, Emma Carus, Maurice Maeterlinck, Maxwell Bodenheim, Maxine Elliott, Ignace Paderewski, Leopold Godowsky, George Antheil, Elliot Paul, F. Scott Fitzgerald, Bob Brown, Johnny Weaver, Robert W. Service, Rudyard Kipling, Kay Boyle, D. H. Lawrence, James Joyce, and Ernest Hemingway. I knew most of them. Except for the White Russians, they seemed to have no financial troubles, and many of them were inexplicably well off. The royal exiles, like all the rest, were gracious, democratic, and hospitable, as most sick people are. And exiles, whether willingly or unwillingly, were all sick in one way or another.

The English claimed to have "discovered" the Riviera. Considering the monuments, aqueducts, arenas, and ruins left behind by the Romans and the still-standing hill towns built by Saracens, not to stress the contributions of the French themselves, this Anglican claim seemed a bit far-fetched.

Actually the English discovered it as a winter resort, which was its worst side. They came after Christmas and left before Easter. This was the rainy season. Its winters were frequently cold and now and then it snowed. But of course at its worst it was better than England in wintertime. The houses were not built for this sort of weather, but the English, used to underheating, didn't seem to mind.

From April to December, however, the climate was ideal. In summer a sirocco would blow gently across the Mediterranean from Africa and maintain an even 80 degrees day and night. We dressed in polo shirts, slacks, and *espadrilles*—a costume acceptable even in the most fashionable places in summertime. It practically never rained from May to November.

Now and then a distinguished Frenchman managed to own

a villa on his own Riviera. Henri Matisse and Henri Cain were two of these I knew. Jean Renoir also had a place which he had inherited from his father, the painter.

The whole area was reminiscent of the medieval free cities. Nobody minded paying the few dollars demanded for a *carte d'identité*. Many did not have even passports, but if they paid their bills and did not disturb the peace, they could even plot counter-revolutions and not be bothered by the Sûreté Générale.

One coup d'état against the small monarchy of Monaco, which was surrounded by French soil, almost looked as if it would succeed. But it was called off because it rained. So Monte Carlo was spared, which was a relief to Zaharoff, who had bought the Hotel de Paris and the Casino to have a place where his Spanish duchess would not be socially slighted.

I found I convalesced faster on the Riviera than elsewhere. Instead of taking months to get over an operation, I got up and around in weeks—till the next attack.

Sometimes I had to send inexperienced ambassadors on most delicate missions. Once, needing material for a feature article, I sent Mishkin and Sauvage to interview H. G. Wells. He was living at Villa Pidou, near Grasse, a perfumed hill town back of Cannes and about twenty miles from our Niçois pension.

They arrived at Villa Pidou, rang to be admitted, and waited. No one responded. They tried again. Again no one answered. They walked around the walled estate to the rear. Trained by me in the art of gate-crashing, they hopped over the wall and all but landed in the eminent author's lap.

He was having tea alone in his garden. He ordered them off the premises. They explained they couldn't leave because they had been sent for an interview.

"Who sent you?" he demanded.

"Frank Scully."

The name meant nothing to him. Bewildered, he looked from one to the other and caught Sauvage trying to take a picture of him.

"Here, here!" he cried. "None of that. Get on with you now!"

But they insisted they could not leave without an interview. "Scully will be furious."

"What do I care how furious Scully will be?"

"Oh," they told him, "that's because you don't know *Scully*. You don't know how furious he can *get!*"

The thing began to get ridiculous to him. "Very well," he said, "I'll let you take three pictures. You can entitle them: 'Friends of Scully and an Unknown!'"

They took the pictures and Wells began to get more fetched by their Yankee brass. In the end he granted them an interview. . . . When I met Wells later, he told me they were a lot of fun and he enjoyed reading their interview.

Now they were leaving, Mishkin to work on *The Chicago Tribune* in Paris, Sauvage to return to Montreal to see his family and then to lay the ground for our invasion of San Diego. It was up to me to hunt for other assistance.

Because my convalescent quarters had become an office, bedroom, clinic, and workshop, I had long ago found out that a male assistant worked out best for all concerned. Half the time I had to work in bed, the bedspread strewn with papers and books and a portable typewriter over my lap. In Switzerland I had learned to type lying on my stomach while I was taking a sunbath.

After Sauvage left, I tried to carry on alone till I could find a young man to replace him. What I found instead was a profile Sauvage had apparently been working on. Among the things my Boswell thought of me were:

Scully is a great hand for doctors. He warns them to look out when they use a stethoscope on his chest because, though he looks the picture of health, what they will find there may shock them to death. They never listen. Several have died that way.

He sometimes quits smoking for as long as three years and lays off at least six weeks every year. That's during Lent. He never misses Mass.

He says he hates to travel, and to prove it he went from New York to Arizona and from Arizona to Paris and from there to Switzerland and from there to Italy, and from Italy to France. He met Mussolini in Locarno, but he didn't like him even before then.

He always carries a writing board and some sheets of paper. Instead of reading magazines in doctors' offices, he scribbles notes.

He says he never pays any doctors who send their bills through collection agencies. The remaining few get paid in time.

He was once compared to Mark Twain, but the only thing they had in common is that they both liked to write in bed.

Whenever he is invited out to dinner he warns his hostess he does not like garlic, onions, or spiced food. He says he wouldn't take a house on Cap D'Ail (Garlic Point) if they gave it to him.

He rarely closes a door. Not even to bathrooms.

He dresses in tweeds and is very fussy about the color of his tie. He hates those with designs. He owns no umbrella.

He never kisses and tells. He laughs at authors who tabulate their amours, saying if he had that few he'd be ashamed to list them in print.

He is especially careful about his teeth. He should be. They with his hair are about the only things that he doesn't have something wrong with.

He's a great one for ignoring all the red tape and credentials foreigners need. He drove a car around France for years without a license for either him or the car.

He never gambles, claiming he gets more gamble in his daily life than Nick the Greek.

He likes most Russian refugees, but says they do not wake up until midnight and by then his own mind is practically asleep.

He looks like a cross between St. Francis and George Washington, but claims when he was young he danced better.

He says anybody who hates his guts is wasting his time, because that's the strongest part of him.

He's a character.

Sauvage's departure for America left me shorthanded, but since I was short of funds I faced the loss of hands philosophically. Besides, at the time I didn't so much need a secretary as one who could run errands, drive the car, and sterilize surgical instruments. The little Norwegian *pike* might do. When she ran errands, she really *ran*. The real test, however, would be whether she could drive the car through the narrow gate of Villa Paulette without scraping off the fenders. She had a little six-horsepower Renault of her own, and I noticed she passed through the high iron gates beautifully. Everybody else backed and scraped, or gave up and parked on the narrow road.

She was a tiny thing, around five feet tall, and weighed perhaps ninety-five pounds. She wore a blue beret and a boy's

brown leather jacket, lisle stockings and saddle shoes. Her hair
was bobbed, much like the boyish Italian haircut that became
the rage around 1953. She used no makeup or lipstick. She had
beautiful features. Her cheek bones were high, her nose straight,
her mouth well-shaped and small. Her skin was clear, smooth,
and clean, with a touch of pink in her cheeks. She was neat as a
pin. She looked nothing like a *femme fatale* or an habituée of a
Bar Américain. In fact, she looked the nearest thing to a perfect
"errand boy" one could find.

One morning shortly after Sauvage departed she entered my
particular wonderland with her mother and sister. They were
going to town and asked if I needed anything. As we talked, I
noticed that Little Alice said nothing.

"Do you speak English too?" I asked.

She looked at me and smiled, those gazelle-like eyes shining.

"Yes," her older sister assured me.

Whether the little *pike* didn't answer out of shyness or because she didn't know English remains in dispute. Her contention is that she didn't understand the sort of English I used,
and my French (hers was flawless, the French all agreed) was
even harder for her to understand.

I learned later that she and her sister knew what they
wanted. Her sister wanted to marry an American and little Alice
wanted to marry (when she grew up) a Norwegian. So her sister
married a Norwegian and Alice in time married an American—
me, in fact. Both marriages turned out to be supremely happy.
At the time I speak of, however, my little *pike* didn't seem
mature enough to be even a child-bride in India.

After a few days of her small services I wondered if she
couldn't do them regularly. I figured I could pay her fifty francs
a month (two dollars). When I learned she was actually eighteen, not twelve, and had been graduated from high school, I
wondered if she couldn't learn speedwriting.

As she and her mother and sister were going to the mountains for a few weeks, I suggested she take a typewriter along and practice. I gave her a letter to copy. I told her to type it until she had twenty perfect copies.

She brought them back in two weeks. They were flawlessly typed. I was thrilled. I had stumbled on the perfect girl Friday. She didn't tell me until ten years later that she had to waste a ream of paper (500 sheets) to make those twenty perfect copies. She was a great one for keeping her own counsel. So I hired her.

I have it on the authority of her mother that one day she came running into the garden of Villa Paulette exclaiming, "Mother, he will have me!"

Her mother professed to be baffled.

"Mr. Scully wants me as his secretary!"

Her mother protested that her little Alice didn't know English, or whatever else was required of secretaries, and though she personally liked the *malade Américain* she wasn't so sure she wanted her daughter completely absorbed in the life of "that charming convalescent." To her he was a sort of male version of *La Vie Bohème*.

"He thinks I can do it," Alice insisted. "But I must learn stenography and typing and drive him around and answer the telephone."

Her mother reflected and decided perhaps it would be good training for her daughter—as long as she could keep an eye on her. The child could use some of this to good purpose if and when the family returned to Norway. There was a young medical student there who had had his eye on Alice for some time. She was still too young for this sort of thing, though, her mother reasoned. Still, she already had had a proposal of marriage from a young Indo-Chinese boy who was even smaller than she was. He kiddingly offered to give up his rights to three hundred wives if she would marry him. To prove his serious intent he actually showed Alice the proper way to cook rice. All this was laughable to Mrs. Pihl.

It would have been laughable to me, too, had I known about it. I thought she was a cute kid, but just a kid. She was smart and learned fast. She knew little English, at least little of *my* kind of English. In teaching her, instead of going all the way back to Chaucer, I "cut to the chase" and tutored her from copies of *Variety*. It was a strange English, even to most Americans, but it was a language understood by millions in show business, the fourth largest industry in America, and I reasoned it would serve her better if she ever went to America.

I learned with astonishment that she actually had been born in America. It seems her father had been a construction engineer who had built railroad bridges in the West for the Union Pacific. His home and office, however, were in Pittsburgh, where Alice was born.

When she was six years old her father died suddenly and the widowed mother took herself and her two little girls back to Norway. It was during wartime, and one of her earliest memories is of a German naval patrol boarding the ship off the Orkneys and taking the father of a motherless little girl off the ship. They cruelly left the little girl behind.

Alice's family in Norway was distinguished. Her mother's brother Johan Mellbye was a member of the King's cabinet. He was the owner of Grefsheim, a huge farm and one of the show places of Norway. Her great-grandfather was Norway's foremost historian. The first statue on the University of Norway campus was erected in his honor.

She was so innocent she thought grandfather clocks were called that because they actually were built by the grandfathers of the families that owned them. This had been true of her family. Why not others? One invented by her grandfather told the day, month, year and season as well as the time.

Coming from America, a child of six, she had nowhere to turn for conversation except toward the mother of her father. She, an Ipswich-born lady, had lived in Norway for fifty years. All that time she insisted her grandchildren, and indeed everybody else, talk English in her presence, if possible. This practice continued until she died when more than ninety years old.

Alice, however, was made of softer stuff. Not being able to talk Norwegian, she dummied up and wouldn't talk at all. This went on for two months. She felt she was a foreigner, though with her platinum blonde hair, she could have passed as a native-born. But she feared her tongue would give her away. Instead of talking she listened. She listened to conversation on all sides. Then one day when she thought she had mastered the native tongue, she burst into prose. It was perfect Norwegian, with a slight English accent.

At first the family lived in Oslo in a huge house, surrounded by acres of fruit-trees, with Grandmother Mellbye. Then the widowed mother bought a place in Lillehammer, a health resort in the mountains. Sigrid Undset was their next-door neighbor.

Alice was a good student as well as a good sport. Like all Norwegian girls of the best families she was taught all the elements of good housekeeping. Many of these apprentice as maids in other families for a year to learn how to run homes of their own properly later. They learn knitting, sewing, cooking, hostess manners and *politesse* generally as well as domestic science.

When Alice finished high school, Mrs. Pihl decided to take the girls to France to complete their education. They boarded a cargo boat for Bordeaux. From there they traveled south to St. Jean de Luz. In France little Alice felt homesick and lost.

Again she felt like a foreigner. Again she dummied up until she could learn the language. She went to French movies and copied down every word she didn't know. When in time she broke out in French it was practically perfect in accent, syntax and grammar. In fact France became the only country where people didn't think she had come from some place else. She spent some time in the Pyrénées, particularly in Tarbes, the home of Marshall Foch. She and Mrs. Foch became great friends.

She studied dressmaking and got a diploma as a designer and cutter. Her mother took her to Nice for a little vacation and picked a house that Alice didn't like. For once the mouse-like little *pike* voiced her objections. She didn't like the house her mother found, because being the youngest she got the last choice in beds. One side was so flattened she would roll out of bed several times at night.

"Very well," said her mother, "you go find a better place."

Alice found a *pension de famille*. It was called Villa Paulette. And there's where I came in.

I was the M'sieur Scooly, the talk of the *pension*, the *Américain malad*, who lived upstairs and pounded his typewriter on the balcony in the sun.

And I was looking for someone to run errands.

13

Alice in Wonderland

•

Noт long after Alice began to work for me, M. Lincoln Schuster, the boy publisher, now long outgrown the short pants he wore on entering Columbia University, visited Nice and began singing a new song. From a Beethoven-lover to a Mozart-lover, it seemed decidedly off pitch. He said it was by Larry Hart and Dick Rodgers, and it began: "I took one look at you, that's all I meant to do, and then my heart stood still."

I used to sing it: ". . . and Larry Hart stood still," for it was his best song, and not many years later his heart actually did stand still, never to beat again—a great loss of a great talent. At the time Larry wrote these lyrics, Hart, Schuster, and I were about the last bachelors of our bunch. They might have imagined that love was like that, since apparently it had not come their way as yet. But it didn't happen that way to me. As far as I was concerned, things were standing still too long. I was half-way to seventy and hadn't done a thing to brag about, except not die.

One day John Maxwell, president of British International Pictures, which I used to refer to in print as British Inter*urban* Pictures, and A. E. Dupont, the German director of *Variety*, Emil Jannings' first great picture, came for a visit.

While they were sitting on the balcony of Villa Paulette, I suggested that they try to live up to the pretentions of their incorporated name. When asked how, I pointed out that England had the greatest name in show business and ought to use this as a shield to advance in the field of truly international pictures. When pressed for specific subjects which British producers could develop to get into this world category, I grabbed the name of Shakespeare. *The Loves of Shakespeare* would lend itself to this sort of appeal, I suggested.

Knowing how quick all such characters were (and are) to pick the brains of those around them, I said there was a play by Frank Harris called *The Loves of Shakespeare* and suggested that they buy this and go on from there.

Actually the name of the play was *Shakespeare and His Love*. It was a modest thing. At least it was modest for Harris whose ego bowed to none. Except for Shakespeare, Wild Bill Hickok, and Cervantes, he admitted few equals and no superiors. My idea was to show Shakespeare as a youth who had been terribly handicapped, forced to give up one girl and marry another in a medieval equivalent of what today would be called a shotgun wedding, and yet had climbed to a great love and a great success.

Dupont and Maxwell wondered how they could get hold of the Harris play, and, ever the obliging chump, I said I'd take care of it for them.

This involved heaving overboard certain prejudices. I believed what most people had to say about Harris—that he was a lecherous old roué with no moral or economic scruples and a highly overrated talent. Harris had been trying to meet me for a year, and now it looked as if to make good on this offer to the British producers I would have to meet him, whether I wanted to or not.

I had Alice drive me to Cimiez, where Harris then lived. It was like moving into an antique shop. Works of art were crowding every corner of the apartment. His wife Nellie Harris and her sister Aggie O'Hara lived with him. Nellie (of what the French call *un âge incertain*) was still a beautiful woman. She had a refined and helpless air, beautiful skin, red hair and blue eyes, and always carried a chiffon-and-lace handkerchief which she delicately touched to her nostrils now and then in the tradition of great ladies. Her sister Aggie was plain, thin, and, to be brutal about it, pathetically homely. They had a Pekinese dog and this about constituted the Harris menage.

Harris was in his seventies and amazingly full of bounce. Short, stocky, with a voice that you might have expected from one twice his size, he had a head full of his own hair and wore a black mustache which was probably dyed.

At this period of his career he was in practically everybody's doghouse. He had published four volumes of his *Life and Loves,* and they had been suppressed everywhere but in France. Aside from a collection of love affairs that were about as exciting as gynecologists' clinical reports, there was a great deal of contemporary history in the volumes which was well worth salvaging. Most people leafed through the love affairs and, finding them mediocre, never bothered to read the rest of the material in the volumes. They sold for about forty dollars and were almost the only source of income Harris had at the time.

He told me the first volume had given him such a black eye in America that the royalties from his *Contemporary Portraits* and his original researches on Shakespeare and Oscar Wilde had dropped from about six thousand dollars a year down to practically nothing. He seemed to keep going by writing dunning letters. These must have had great sales-appeal because old friends kept sending him sums now and then.

This type of endowment ran back many years. When he lived around Washington Square before World War I, he set up a Frank Harris Brotherhood, the objective of which seemed mainly to keep Harris solvent. He had run through *Pearson's*

Magazine (which he owned), and his hate of the British had made most people jump to the conclusion that he was pro-German. This wasn't true, but it might just as well have been because he got into a fight with the Wilson administration, and A. S. Burleson, the Postmaster General, suppressed his publications. After that, he invariably addressed him as "A. S. S. Burleson." This on the envelopes addressed to the Postmaster General may have produced some laughs, but it certainly was no way to get himself off the Postmaster General's blacklist.

He had to tell all this to me before I could tell him the reason I came was to see if his *Shakespeare and His Love* might be used as a vehicle for a motion picture. Harris' eyes lighted immediately; you could almost see a million dollars dancing in each eye. I didn't think that British International Pictures would pay much more than one thousand dollars for such a springboard, but even a thousand dollars was a lot of money to Harris in those days.

He began walking Alice and me around his art gallery. She was timid, well-mannered, and dressed as usual in her French beret and leather jacket. After we had viewed the art gallery and had made an appointment for another day, we returned to Villa Paulette.

In a day or two I asked her to take a manuscript back to Harris, but she quietly and politely begged to be excused from doing so. This puzzled me. I asked her why. She wouldn't tell. I didn't find out till years later. . . . While we were viewing a painting of The Virgin and Harris was extolling it as a work of art, he had pinched Alice's bottom.

This was so in character with Harris that it doubtless meant no more to him than pinching the cheek of a baby. He probably pinched every girl. He must have learned it from Italians along the Galleria in Milan. Any girl who ever shopped there and didn't get pinched had reason to feel insulted.

British producers, on learning my contacts with their own island-born authors who had homes on the Riviera, would sometimes ask me to soften the way for them. One asked me if I would sound out Somerset Maugham for anything he had which was priced within reason. On one occasion while at the Villa Moresque, where I lunched with Maugham, he walked me around to see what remained unsold on his book shelves.

He confessed he couldn't quite understand how minds of picture producers worked. Often he suggested a story which he thought might make a good picture and offered to sell it for as little as five thousand dollars. They refused, he would work the story into a play, and then they would think nothing of paying thirty thousand dollars.

He picked out one story from *The Trembling of a Leaf* and said, "I think this would make a good picture." It met the same fate as the others. All of the stories in *Quartet* and *Trio,* which became such outstanding successes in 1950, were in this category at the time.

In the summer of 1928 two eminent persons of the theatre came to the Riviera—George Bernard Shaw and Alexander Woollcott. Shaw rented a few rooms in a modest hotel at Cap d'Antibes and Woollcott leased a large villa nearby. I wrote to both of them, asking if they would mind if I dropped in as part of my *Variety* chores.

By this time I was able to drive a Model T Ford by making a hinge of two boards and attaching one end to the brake and the other to the floor where it met the seat. By pushing on this hinge with my right hand I spared myself much of the braking, which was hard on that weak right leg.

From Woollcott I received a warm and gracious telegram asking me not only to drop in but to stay for lunch. From Shaw I received a postcard telling me to leave him alone and adding, "You forget that I am a journalist too, and crows shouldn't feed on crows." I went over to Woollcott's and had a grand time. Harpo Marx and Ruth Gordon were also there.

When they learned that I knew Harris, they asked if I could arrange a meeting for them. I said of course. So I arranged a luncheon at Harris'. Harpo Marx couldn't come, but at luncheon Woollcott said he would like a set of Harris' *Life of Oscar Wilde* for Harpo. Harpo was not like the people who have their walls lined with beautifully bound books they have never read. He said he had read every book he owned. At the time he owned three.

I don't think Woollcott meant to pay for them. He was used to being inundated with books for free from publishers. But I knew he was in the money, and Harris was broke, so I said: "Eight dollars." Woollcott paid it. Later he wrote in *The New Yorker* about Harris. He said Harris was dressed like a racetrack tout and peddled his books along the Riviera. Actually this was not so. Harris loaded down practically every visitor with books at this time, and his memory was so far gone that he frequently gave them to old enemies as well as new friends.

About a week after the Shavian rebuff, I was invited to the Harris' to a tea to meet the master. Emma Goldman was coming too, Nellie Harris added. I said, "Nuts to the master. I offered to travel twenty miles to pay him a courtesy call and don't wish to meet him on a social level now."

This was probably the start of some of the worst slugging the master had to take in print from a Nobody. It went on for years.

I got the gist of the repartee from Emma Goldman and the Harrises the next day. It was the first meeting between Shaw and Harris in fourteen years. Mrs. Shaw had not come with the master. She had burned Harris's *Life and Loves* and Shaw, the old gossip, had passed this literary tidbit on to Harris. It had left the old buccaneer burning with a low blue flame ever since he heard of it.

From the first word even their compliments were conditioned. Shaw asked Harris what kept him looking so young. He was seventy-two at the time—six months older than Shaw.

"Good meat, good whiskey, good wine, and plenty of women," said Harris. "And look at you on your diet of *legumes* —white, nearly bald, and thin as a rail."

"My complexion is the admiration of Europe," Shaw replied. "I have not a bald spot on my dome, and my thinness is a quality—not a fault, and yet you enviously go around telling people I'm undersexed!"

"I never said it!" cried Harris.

"Yes, you did—in a lecture in Berlin last winter."

"Well, if I did, I'd forgotten it. But it's true."

"It's not true. If anything I'm oversexed!"

Harris looked at him in astonishment. "You oversexed?" Harris repeated. "Why you told me you came to London at nineteen and that your first overt act took place when you were twenty-nine. That's ten years. If that had been Shakespeare or any normal person, it would have been ten days."

"Ah," said Shaw, "but that's because you and Shakespeare and other normal persons had not been brought up on Handel and Mozart and Michelangelo and Raphael as I was. If your sense of beauty had been properly nursed you couldn't have touched anything so prosaic as a real woman at that age."

Remember, these were two old men. Their interest in the subject could not have been more than academic, but it is a fair comment on them and their times that in their tiff over chastity neither of them quoted St. Paul, the Commandments, or the Founder of Christianity they professed to admire.

Shaw went back to entertaining motion picture stars at Cap

d'Antibes with exhibitions of how he made a short showing Mussolini (whom he admired) how to act, and taking nude sunbaths for the entertainment of those with field glasses.

Between those two old goats I favored Harris by the smallest of margins. Somewhere within him was the seed of salvation. He simply made the mistake of telling his life and loves to the wrong people. He should have told them to a father confessor. As a matter of fact, when he felt the end was near, he tried.

But at the time I first knew him he was still struggling to keep his head above water in a physical, not a spiritual, sense. He importuned me to help him. Helping older people had become a pattern in my life and I accepted it much as one accepts a drab wallpaper pattern in a hotel room. He showed me a fragment of a manuscript that had been lying around for years and wondered if we couldn't build it into a book and split the royalties.

I learned that he had been a cowboy in the 70's and had been on the trail with Wild Bill Hickok. By borrowing from the less pornographic parts of his autobiography, which few—even critics—had bothered to read, I saw I could build a beginning, middle, and end around his fragment and give the book a moral ending, for many of the cattle he stole in Mexico ended, after being driven across the plains to the stockyards, in the Chicago fire. I titled it *My Reminiscences as a Cowboy* by Frank Harris. It sold thirty thousand copies and got nice notices in both New York and London editions. It was clean from beginning to end.

Alice typed this manuscript. It was her first and she did amazingly neat work. She had grown in many ways in a year, and though she still retained her shyness and quiet modesty, these were highly commendable and even noticeable virtues in a world peopled mainly by exhibitionists. She met notables like Paderewski, Godowsky and Tadlewski, Shaw, Olcott, and Durant—most of them two and three times as old as she was. What she thought of them she kept to herself. This was a virtue that grew in importance as the years went by and strangely attracted the attention of many geniuses who were beginning to tire of the sound of their own voices. It was a virtue that seemingly had raised Calvin Coolidge to the Presidency and was even rarer in women than it was in men.

Her behavior reminded me of the story of the man who went around without a shadow, which caused a sensation when the loss was discovered.

14

Vamping Till Ready

•

AMONG those nearer my age, if not Alice's, for even I was nearly twice her age at the time, was Albert Tadlewski, who became the adopted son of Paderewski. How this came about is a warming illustration of the easy, breezy character of friendships on the Riviera between wars.

Paderewski was playing benefit concerts around France for war orphans. At one of these Tadlewski, who was a fellow Pole and had been badly mauled in the First World War (he was killed in the Second), went back stage to pay his respects to Paderewski. This was at the Palais de la Méditerranée, which Frank Gould had built on the Promenade des Anglais in Nice.

They walked out together and kept walking until they reached Tadlewski's modest little home. Tadlewski invited the master in. Paderewski asked Tadlewski to play. He tried a piece of no great length. Paderewski asked for an encore. In fact he kept urging him on until Tadlewski had played for two hours!

"Good." said Paderewski. "Now I will do something for you. In return for your playing for me, I will play for your pupils."

Tadlewski could hardly get his breath, he was so choked with gratitude.

"But I do it under one condition," warned Paderewski.

"Yes, Master, anything."

"I do it on condition that you double your prices afterward!"

Tadlewski told the story to me and I, the sentimental pragmatist, said, "Listen, Alberto, this is too good to waste."

"But we mustn't say anything about this," warned Tadlewski.

"We must say *everything* about it," I insisted. "How else are you going to obey his orders and double those prices if you don't give his *beau geste* all kinds of publicity?"

"But how?" asked Tadlewski. "Mr. Paderewski might get annoyed."

"Leave that to me," I said.

Left to me, it began to build. I got the story spread all over the Continent and it even showed up in *The New Yorker*.

Paderewski's concert for Tadlewski's pupils attracted all sorts of celebrities and was such a huge success that the Palais de la Méditerranée invited Tadlewski to hold his own pupils' concert there and two thousand paying guests attended.

Out of this little thing Paderewski adopted Tadlewski as his son, the Chauncey Olcotts adopted Janet Clerico, a fourteen-year-old prodigy from Monaco, and Tad and I became practically blood brothers. Paderewski thanked me no end for helping his fellow Pole.

A year later when I was fighting for my life, Tadlewski, who had studied medicine in Vienna before taking up music, offered to close his school and take me to the best surgeons, and Paderewski said if closing the school were impractical he would keep it open till we returned to Nice.

Tadlewski had won the *Prix de Rome* and had the war not all but destroyed him, he surely would have been another Paderewski. Shrapnel, gas, and wounds, and a period as a prisoner of war, had permanently impaired his eyesight and his intestines. He was a well setup young man, six feet tall, weighing about 175 pounds, full of charm and warmth and an appreciation of

American humor. He spoke excellent English and of course French, German, Polish, and Italian.

But as a result of his war wounds he could no longer stand the rigors of concert tours and so had to settle for a modest little villa where he could teach a limited number of poor little rich girls. That Paderewski could recognize in an hour's playing a talent he would have been proud to father was eloquent proof that among artists, at least, blood is thicker than bullets.

Tadlewski, for all his gaiety and talent, was destroyed by those enemies of mankind who look on all below them as material to be crushed by their steam rollers to make smoother military roadbeds. He was swooped up after Mussolini attacked Nice in what Franklin D. Roosevelt called "a stab in the back." Being an internal wreck to begin with, a second period in a war prison camp was a death sentence. It wasn't long before he was a dead genius.

We also had a visit from Leopold Godowsky. His was a scattered family by this time, but Papa Godowsky, Mutz, and Dagmar were spending a holiday on the Riviera. Dagmar had known Tadlewski in Vienna. Alice and I took Godowsky to see him while he was still in Nice. On this trip Godowsky wanted to see everything. A small, stocky man, he had been court musician to the old Emperor Franz Josef, and though he had none of the showmanship of men like dePachmann and Paderewski, he was revered by all of them. Once dePachmann at a concert saw Godowsky sitting in the audience. When the applause of the audience was at its height, dePachmann ignored everybody and turned and bowed to Godowsky before sitting down to play.

After the performance, Godowsky went backstage to congratulate him. The audience was still clapping and shouting. DePachmann grabbed little Godowsky and tried to drag him on stage, but Godowsky would not hear to any such nonsense, and when dePachmann wrestled with him, he slipped out of his coat. DePachmann walked on stage holding the coat and said to the audience: "I couldn't get the master to come out, but here's his coat." It was dePachmann who said: "When it comes to playing, Godowsky makes the rest of us look like blacksmiths."

After Dagmar married Frank Mayo, the actor, Godowsky talked Carl Laemmle into signing him to a fat contract at Universal. Dagmar became a *femme fatale* there, herself. She and Natacha Rambova, the daughter of Richard Hudnut, became close friends in Hollywood. In fact she was with Rambova when the Hudnut heiress eloped with Rudolph Valentino.

Dagmar herself was between marriages on this Riviera trip. She had been divorced three or four times and carried her credentials in her purse as proof she was free to do what she liked. Her father was most tolerant of her follies, though he could be severe on occasion. In fact his hostility toward one son's marriage to a dancer drove the youth to suicide. But Alice and I found him a warm and simple man. He worked hard to keep his family well provided for.

Yascha Paii told me how Godowsky was asking his way to a concert stage one morning, when he ran into a workman. Godowsky asked the man what he did around the place.

"I move pianos. Hard work. What do you do?"

"I move audiences," said Godowsky. "That's even harder."

On the Riviera he was the one who was moved. He was like a schoolboy on vacation. Everything delighted him. We took all of them to the Harris' for luncheon, and when Godowsky heard about the dying hill towns he wanted to see them all. We settled for places not so dead—like Vence, St. Paul, and Grasse.

As they were leaving for Paris, Godowsky heard about Cagnes, a medieval hill town a few miles off the Nice-Cannes road. He decided he had to see it—then and now. Dagmar and Mutz decided that they preferred the comfort of the Blue

Train. They got on board at Nice and Alice and I drove Godowsky to Cagnes, planning to let him catch the Blue Train an hour later at Cannes.

There was plenty of time for this, except that Godowsky became so enamored of Cagnes that he kept darting in and out of places like a fox terrier. When he learned this was Renoir's home town, he wanted to see the old *mas Provençal* where Renoir had lived.

As a result of these rapid-fire researches, it looked as if he would miss the train in Cannes. Alice and I practically forced him into her little Renault. We raced down the hill and hurried toward Cannes to pick up the train which Dagmar and her mother had boarded at Nice. Within ten miles of Cannes we had a blowout. As we were changing tires, Godowsky suddenly said, "Oh, my goodness, I have all the tickets!"

We assured him the *Train Bleu* enjoyed a long stop at Cannes. But Godowsky became so worried that I flagged a truck going toward Cannes and asked the driver to take him aboard. We pushed him high in the air and seated him next to the driver of the *camion*. Then we returned to change the tire.

Suddenly down the road we saw Godowsky running toward us. It seems he had forgotten a copy of the *New York Times* which he had bought for Dagmar. It was the Sunday edition. In those days, as now, it weighed a ton. We gave him the paper, the truck backed up, and we heaved him aboard again. Alice proceeded to change the tire and, as predicted, we arrived at the station a half-hour before the train left. Godowsky was aboard, but he looked like a mighty worn-out tripper. We promised to meet again in a few weeks in Paris and then waved them good-by.

Alice and I then went looking for a little restaurant near the port to have dinner. We didn't find what we wanted until we reached a place on the *quai*. It had enough atmosphere to cut

With Max Schuster and Harry Lachman at the Rex Ingram Studios, Nice, France.

With authoress Kay Boyle and new husband, Laurence Vail.

... and Iva Broadhurst, "Skip" and ...ly, at Villa Variety in Nice.

... and Jae Greenberg come to stay at Nice (1931).

Leo Mishkin is assigned by Scully to interview H. G. Wells, at Grasse.

Scully, Dagmar and Leopold
Godowsky at Nice (1929).

Dagmar, Alice Pihl, "Papa" and "Mutz
Godowsky at St. Paul, near Cannes.

Isadora Duncan, with her arms around a Russian "genius" and an Oulaid
Nail dancer. An Arab dwarf is in the tub. This is the last picture taken of
Isadora before her tragic death in 1927.

off chunks with a knife, but the supper didn't turn out to be a meal to remember. Still, we had a lot of laughs discussing the charming naïveté of really great souls like Godowsky. As we talked, the seventeen years that separated Alice and me seemed nearer seventeen seconds. The little *pike* became the flower of all womanhood that night, and I began to feel I'd be a dolt to ever let her go. She wasn't a tomboy any longer. A year had changed her miraculously into a charming and beautiful young woman.

She had developed into an amazingly competent manager of a sick writer's career. She took to all my friends easily. One by one they had visited us and all were pleased by her way of taking care of me. She could do everything, even change a tire, when dressed in her best, without losing any of her dignity. She was growing by leaps and bounds and, what was more to the point, she was growing on me.

We drove home slowly in the moonlight. I remember she said we would have to stop at Juan les Pins and telephone her mother that we would be late. She had time and consideration for everything and everybody.

As we drove along the tideless blue sea, I knew I was falling in love with her. I didn't tell her so because I was still her boss and she was too precious to be told such things unless the words meant everything, and I couldn't see at that time that I was in any position to offer her anything but moonlight and roses. So I kept silent.

When we reached Nice, I said goodnight and thanked her for helping me through a lovely day. The words in themselves meant nothing, but I felt certain I had not fooled her at all. She knew—without a word spoken.

15

The King's Secret

•

Her mother may have begun to suspect the secret, also without a word having been spoken. Anyway, Mrs. Pihl began making plans for taking her daughters back to Norway.

I had already decided to go to London for the summer to take some pre-antibiotic treatments called "ferments" under Henri Spahlinger, the Swiss biochemist. With the ferment going on in my heart, I was determined more than ever that I must get well before taking the next step, which would be to ask Alice to marry me.

The mere thought of such a step kept me awake nights. It meant a complete change for me. I had always been against invalids marrying. I minded it even more when old crocks used beautiful young things to round out their declining years. I simply would have to get well and stand on my own feet financially or this affair was off.

Moreover, there was a religious impediment to our marriage. Alice was a Lutheran; I was a Catholic. Worse, she was a good Lutheran, whereas I was a mediocre Catholic. Even if we got a special dispensation, she would have to promise to raise the children, if any, as Catholics.

Suppose in her quiet way she secretly hated Catholics? The Scandinavians, I had always felt, were as civilized a people as one could find, and these particular Lutherans had not bolted at the sight of Catholic cathedrals, chapels, priests, and nuns in France. In fact they had spent a great deal of time at Lourdes, which was more than I could say for myself.

Next in line of obstacles was the economic factor. I was thirty-seven years old and had no more assured future than a beaver in the Sahara Desert. Somehow, often with friendly grants-in-aid, I had kept solvent, but could I carry on alone? Could I, to go even further, support a family?

Those of my old friends who had met Alice took to her immediately. Some, like Jae Greenberg, Max Schuster and Ed Anthony, may have suspected what was going on before I did. Jae Greenberg was on a deferred honeymoon. So was Ed Anthony. Romance was all around us, and much of it crazier than ours.

Ed Anthony had recently written an amusing book called *How to Get Rid of a Woman*. He got married on the royalties and took his bride, Esther, on a Mediterranean cruise. This was shortly after he had handled the publicity in Herbert Hoover's successful bid for the presidency and years before he became the publisher of *Collier's*.

By now Alice had become pretty indispensable. The "errand boy" had become a "shapely lass" and a highly competent secretary. She enabled me to earn more as a free-lance writer; and her own wage had moved up from fifty francs a month to a thousand. If I had to continue forever to share my earnings, what was wrong with sharing them with a partner—a member of the family?

It was a nice thought and in fact may have occurred to Mrs. Pihl, too. Lest the thought take more irreparable form, she decided the Riviera was getting too hot and she was taking her daughters back to Norway—*instanter*.

I decided to travel with them as far as Paris. This, they thought, was just dandy. Paris is such a lovely place in spring to say *au revoir* but not good-by. It promised a painless solution to the eternal sorrow of separation, and we all entered into it for all the fun we could get out of it.

In Paris, Alice, Godowsky, and I had a joyous reunion. We became three musketeers in search of a good Russian dinner. On one occasion while we were dining in a Russian restaurant Godowsky said, "You know, I'm afraid this civilization will break down trying to keep up with itself. It is inventing so many things so fast that the human mind cannot expand fast enough to absorb its own ingeniousness, and it will crack while trying." A few weeks later while making Columbia records in London Godowsky himself cracked. He suffered a stroke and one side of his body was paralyzed. He would never play again.

Alice's mother continued to worry. We were stopping in hotels quite near each other. One evening we were walking up the Boulevard Montparnasse in a group. I walked with a crutch under my right armpit and put my left arm around Alice's shoulder.

Her mother looked reprovingly, which was laughable, for in the Latin Quarter couples *not* walking arm-in-arm were rare indeed. "I have my arm around Alice's shoulder for support," I said, "but of course if you object I'll put it around yours."

I did, and she didn't object. She was at heart a Bohemian, but she looked like a severe maiden aunt assigned to chaperone a convent-bred niece.

Nevertheless, Alice and I did get a little time to ourselves. Seated close together at a small sidewalk cafe, I managed to say the secret words. Nobody paid any attention to us. We were lovers, as far as our neighbors were concerned, and nobody pays any attention to lovers in Paris.

I didn't have an engagement ring for her. In fact I have not got around to buying one to this day. But I did have a precious token of affection. It was an 18-carat gold pencil, one of the pioneers in automatic pencils. It wasn't perfect, however. It had a dent in it.

I told her it had once belonged to a preacher I had befriended in Arizona. In his youth he had rowed at Amherst. His crew had won the intercollegiate regatta. It was about the only victory in the history of the little New England college and he was quite proud of the feat, for not only was Amherst a small college, but he was a small man—about five feet six and weighed perhaps 145 pounds. But he was a man of iron with the courage of a lion.

After he had been ordained, he had gone to Tombstone, Arizona for his wife's health. There he opened a small church. The town was a wild and lawless place in those days. His chief job seemed to be reading the burial service over dead bandits at Boot Hill.

Once in a holdup of the Tucson stagecoach a wild bullet hit him in the breast. The bullet was deflected by his gold pencil and this good fortune saved his life. He gave the pencil to me, I suspect, not only as a mark of affection but as a talisman.

Though normally I couldn't keep a pen or pencil long enough to identify it if lost and recovered, I somehow had kept this one through all my wanderings. Yet I was sure it would be safer in Alice's keeping than in mine, and besides it was the only thing of value I possessed. So I gave it to her to plight our troth. She has it to this day, and if it's ever mislaid, there's no peace around the house until it's found.

So we parted an engaged couple. We agreed to meet again in London in the fall and then get married. She did not choose to tell her mother how things stood between us. After all, a bullet-dented pencil was not quite the same thing as a diamond engagement ring to most people. Maybe she didn't quite believe it yet, herself.

As her old boss I had written her a letter of recommendation.

It was possibly the finest love letter I had ever written. No prospective employer on reading it could believe she could be that perfect. So all I succeeded in doing was to get her bilked out of jobs. After she stopped showing the letter, her chances improved.

I had asked Sime Silverman, of *Variety*, if he could find a berth for me in his London bureau while I was taking the Spahlinger treatments. He replied he certainly could. "Make your arrangements with Jolo," he wrote (Jolo was Joshua Lowe, manager of the London office.) "If you don't think the arrangements are satisfactory, don't tell Jolo. That's not because I don't want Jolo to know, but because I know Jolo. Accept his proposition and tell me what it is, and if it's not right, I'll make up the difference from New York."

Spahlinger had moved from Geneva to Mayfair, the fashionable part of London. His vaccine to halt bovine t.b. had been purchased by the British government. Into its perfecting had gone the entire Spahlinger fortune of more than half a million dollars. He was about the last of the one-man microbe hunters.

His family estate, a beautiful acreage at Carrouge outside of Geneva, had been converted step-by-step into one huge stinking laboratory. His family had owned some of the best hotels in Geneva.

Before World War I, Spahlinger had worked out a vaccine for the treatment of tuberculosis and had amazing success with it in one British hospital. During the war he was asked to go to Russia to see what he could do to stop a plague of tetanus which was killing more Russian troops than German bullets were. He stopped it.

After the war he returned to his laboratories in Geneva, but he never seemed to have the success he had had before. The suspicion was that he had lost his formula, but he said this wasn't so. The trouble was he didn't have the money to buy the best essentials. Among these were Irish hunters. From these horses he got his serums. After the war he was down to old nags which couldn't even pull ashcarts any longer, and the laboratory results were equally melancholy.

He was now working in another direction and getting fair results. He called his antibiotics "ferments." He thought injections from these new "ferments" might get at the low-grade strep infection which nothing else had been able to knock out of the marrow of my thigh bone, and also might help my chest.

I found him in excellent spirits. In Geneva I remembered how desperately serious he would get. The huge dining table with places for twenty had piles of folders where gold plates once were. One day on the hunt for a special Eberhard Faber eraser he became so temperamental he tossed whole piles of files in the air in search of it. I made note of his *faiblesse,* and every so often sent him some of these five-cent erasers. It was the only pay he would ever accept from me.

Within a week of starting his treatments I began to feel improved enough to go to work.

London itself was in a turmoil. The Labor government had just come into power. The conservative press was certain that a revolution was only a matter of days. The *Herald,* the Labor paper, was practically dancing in its blue jeans.

I couldn't see any cause for despair or elation. It seemed like the same old London to me. A neighbor of France, England had been close to revolution many times and had never been visibly disturbed by these periodic convulsions of mankind. Tradition and ritual had always been stronger than law in England, and this particular side of English character had not been changed merely because one group of established politicians was taking over the offices of another group of established politicians. Had the new group been completely unknown— as unknown to the English as Lenin and Trotsky were to the

Russians—it might have 'been otherwise. But such was not the case.

To me at least all was calm, all was bright as I walked down to St. Martin's Lane in Trafalgar Square to the *Variety* office. It was in an old building four stories high. It had once been the home of a mistress of a long-forgotten king. But now from the office windows the staff looked out on the statue of Edith Cavell, the English nurse who had been executed by the Germans for helping prisoners-of-war to escape. The first word I observed at the foot of the statue was "Sacrifice." It seemed to me an omen, and that the world, the British Empire included, would have to eat the word if imperialism continued to dominate cabinet meetings everywhere in the world.

While I was waiting, Jolo came into the office. He was the most unbelievable *Variety* mugg I had ever seen. He arrived in Harris tweeds and plus fours. He lived at Windsor and motored thirty miles each day to the office. His speech and manner were brusque. He had worked with Sime Silverman in the early days of *Variety* in New York and from there had gone to London where he set up that office. There he remained a fixture till he died.

Since I didn't plan to work in the office, or for that matter didn't know how much work I could do, I asked Jolo for four pounds a week. Jolo stuck up five fingers to show what a big-hearted guy he was. Having solved the problem of room and board and what to use for money, I began talking about things in general, and Hannan Swaffer in particular. He was the dramatic critic of Lord Beaverbrook's London *Express* at the time, and among critics he was considered a George Jean Nathan using one-syllable words. I told Jolo I admired Swaff's writings and thought him very readable. In addition to his *Express* stint, Swaff was writing a column for *Variety* called *London as It Looks.*

While Jolo and I were discussing Swaff, he walked into the office. He lived in a flat above. He was married to a very gracious and retiring wife. But he himself was an exhibitionist of the first order. He was tall and thin and looked like a guy who had tried to play the part of Hamlet and had never made it. He wore a blue serge suit and over it a blue serge overcoat. Both were stained and spotted. His neck was wrapped in a black Ascot production which was known in the lower orders as "a dirty shirt-hider." His hair was gray, streaked with yellow, and hung down his neck. For a hat he wore a black Homburg that hadn't been cleaned or blocked since it was bought, and that must have been a long time before this meeting. His fingers were stained yellow from smoking cigarettes until they all but burned his nails.

We had scarcely exchanged amenities when we got into our first argument. It was perhaps one of the silliest that any two men ever engaged in. Swaff was exulting over the election returns and I, acting the role of the great pacifier, tried to tell everybody, Swaff included, that the election would not materially change things. "I have just flown over from Paris," I said, "and the countryside looked just as I thought it would. Everything was peaceful and orderly, and driving in from Croydon I saw people playing golf, others cutting the golfing greens, and everybody doing his work as of old. In town the traffic moved along in an orderly way too. The bobbies remained unarmed and the drivers obeyed the wave of a hand which in Chicago would have got the cop's hand shot off and in Paris would have got him screamed at by taxi drivers as an imbecile, an idiot, a *cochon!*

This didn't sit well on Swaff at all. He saw great changes just around the corner, and he didn't want anyone to tell him that there would be no changes to speak of. When I went on to say that Ramsay MacDonald was not straight out of a mine but had had years of conditioning in the House of Commons and now wore golf clothes, not dungarees, and that he would change to clothes that befitted his high office, Swaff was even more annoyed.

"He'll step into silk knickers," I said, "and on bended knee swear his loyalty to his King, and from that moment on ritual will mold the social-minded Scot into a servant of the Empire."

"Well, what would you have him do?" demanded Swaff.

"Well, if this is a revolution," I said, "I should think instead of consuming all this time and ending with a long parade led by a carriage hundreds of years old, and horses not much younger, Ramsay would telephone over to Buckingham Palace, tell the King he was sending over a messenger on a motorcycle, and to have ready the keys to the strong box, as he had to get on with his work. The old way blocks traffic for hours and must result in the loss of millions of pounds. But he will do it the old way because men on this island simply are incapable of revolutionary changes."

"Well, I happen to know," shouted Swaff, "that the King's a Socialist!"

"Golly, Swaff, print that!"

"Don't tell me what to print! I was an editor before you were born!"

"Well, if you were a good one, you'd print it," I insisted. "But you won't print it because tradition says to lay off the King, except to comment on the bloom which has returned to his cheeks after he has been laid up a few days with a cold."

"*You* print it!" Swaff ordered.

"Okay," I said, "I'll print it, and I'll say you said it. But it won't make any difference because tradition here is even stronger than print."

Subsequently I did print it in *Variety*, and of course it didn't have the slightest repercussion.

Swaff and I parted the best of friends, which was the way
we started out. I then went hunting for two things—a flat and
a secretary. I found a flat in Bryanston Street near the Marble
Arch, thanks to Michael Powell and a Russian sound engineer
named Leonti Planskoy. Powell and Planskoy had a flat next
door on the ground floor. The one they got for me was one
flight up. This was as high as my general condition of health
and purse would let me go. Once installed, I got myself a
secretary. I paid her two pounds ten shillings a week out of my
five-pound wage. I had long resigned myself to this. If I were
to earn any money at all, I would have to split it with someone
whose legs and lungs were sound.

The weather, for London, was unusually sunny and mild.
Everybody was complaining. So much sunshine was burning up
their lawns. Rain was what made the British countryside so
beautiful, and that summer there was very little rain.

This made it ideal for a visitor like me, a healthseeker whose
work took him out in the evening to the theatres and now and
then to motion picture studios which were as far as thirty miles
from town.

On one of these excursions I visited the studios of British
International Pictures. A week before, I had written a little
piece that Jack Hylton had been bilked out of one hundred
and twenty-five pounds owed to him for a short subject he had
made for them. The top executives called me in and assured me
they had paid Hylton and could show me in their books they
had paid him.

"Which set?" I asked. "You keep three."

They let that insult go by, but went on to say that I had
libeled them all over America. They even demanded a retraction.

"You can call every big producer in the business 'Brother'
by now," I said, "because I've libeled them all."

"No, seriously," they insisted, "you libeled us all over America, and we demand a retraction."

"Well, you'll never get it," I said, "by *belittling* me!"

This left them speechless. "How did we belittle you?"

"By that crack you keep repeating, 'all over America.' When I libel anybody it's *all over the world!*"

They were certain now they were dealing with a madman whose ego was out of this world; so they rang for a tea wagon and served me tea.

Thanks to Spahlinger's injections I felt so improved I decided to brave a trip to Malvern, where the first festival of Shaw's plays was being staged. This was an attempt of Shavians to steal some of the thunder of the Shakespearean festival held annually at Stratford-on-Avon, just over the hill from Malvern.

The Shaw festival was scheduled to open with *The Apple Cart*, a new play starring Sir Cedric Hardwicke and Edith Evans.

The trip took about four hours by train from London and we passed Oxford on the way. Malvern looked like a dowdy Victorian health resort, but it did have a good theatre.

When I came out of the manager's office I happened to look down a flight of stairs leading off the lobby to a basement. A young man came over and asked, "Would you mind not watching Mr. Shaw's rehearsal?"

I said I'd mind very much not watching Mr. Shaw's rehearsal.

The young man turned away, walked a few steps, and then came back again saying, "Mr. Shaw would be furious if he saw you doing this!"

"From what I've seen, that would have more life to it than the rehearsal," I said, and kept right on looking down the stairs at the Master.

It was obvious to the young man by now that I was a

An original by Ivan Opfer. It has never before been published. Shaw gave
it to Harris and Harris gave it to Scully. Shaw liked it because it was not
a caricature but a serious study.

bounder, a boor, and not easily impressed by Shavian protocol.

Before we could continue with our sprightly dialogue, Shaw came trudging up the stairs. He was carrying a lunch basket. I greeted him and we shook hands. This was our first meeting, though we knew of each other's existence.

"I'm up here for *Variety*," I said, "and God help you if you're not good."

He gave me one of his smiles that looked so much like a sneer, asked if I had come all the way from Nice, and how did I leave the Harrises, and with that backed out of the lobby with his lunch basket, waving good-by.

It turned out that God didn't help him much. Maybe because he didn't ask.

The review of *The Apple Cart* is one still prized among *Variety* muggs. "This thing," I wrote, "has ninety laughs, one gag, and a pratfall. If it had sex appeal, it would be a hit. It hasn't. It isn't." It wasn't!

16

From Shaw to Trader Horn

•

Bᴀᴄᴋ in London, I found a lot of mail but nothing from Alice which indicated she was looking forward to the day she could join me in London and we could head south together. Though we wrote each other twice a week, we wrote as if an invisible censor were screening our words, if not our thoughts. I dictated my letters, which more or less guaranteed that they would be kept impersonal. She answered with the reserve of state papers.

We both acted as if we were not quite sure what the other would be forced into doing. If her people would not let her come to me, I was grown-up enough to see that all the logic of nipping this thing in the bud was on their side. They obviously had nothing against me. They even thought me charming. But between charm and marriage was a channel much wider than the North Sea.

I did not, however, have much time to dwell on such thoughts. Between treatments and literary stints I had a full day, every day. Sometimes I joined in fun that for me was sheer folly and could easily have set me back among the bed patients.

On one occasion I received a note from Alfred A. Smith, a wanderer who had had the foresight to change his name to Trader Horn. This saved him from being confused with Alfred E. Smith (they were both celebrities at the time), only to be identified with *another* trader named Horn—the sleazy South Seas character in Maugham's *Sadie Thompson*.

This one was also known as Zambesi Jack on the Ivory Coast "in the Earlies," as he described the 70's and 80's. His lifestory had become a best seller two years before and was being filmed in Africa by Metro-Goldwyn-Mayer in a production starring Harry Carey, Duncan Renaldo, and Edwina Booth. The first of these jungle "westerns," *Trader Horn* started a trend that was still going strong twenty-five years later. It brought bad luck to Harry Carey, destroyed Miss Booth with a lingering and fatal fever, and landed Renaldo on McNeill Island in a federal penitentiary on a falsified passport conviction.

The cause of it all, sunning himself on the beach at Hastings, was coming to see me. He arrived in a big cowboy hat and a salt-and-pepper tweed overcoat to which was attached an Inverness cape. A pipe was half buried in his soft white beard. He had a soft and beautiful voice and was soon off, conversationally, covering continents as easily as I cover the length of a room.

As it was midsummer, I couldn't understand the Inverness cape until I discovered it made a convenient hiding place for a bottle of Scotch. He professed to have picked up a bit of a cold while teaching a young lady in Hastings how to drive a car (he was over seventy at the time) and was using the Scotch as a sort of anti-pneumonia vaccine.

In a few minutes he was heading downstairs.

"Wait a minute," I said, "I'm having lunch sent up for us."

"I saw a pub next door when I got out of the taxi," he explained.

"Oh," I said, "I'll take you to a good restaurant."

"Aye," he said, "but I prefer a good pub."

After luncheon we went off to see some motion pictures in a West End projection room, and while waiting for things to start, the Trader disappeared again. He had gone to say hello at another pub. When he returned, we settled down to watch the film. It was one of those early gangster pictures which no doubt gave rise to one of the Trader's earlier nifties: "The Americans—a moral people, except when it comes to murdering and so on." Of this one he said: "Good sob stuff—and you have to consider that when you're making things for schooner-rigged females."

By dinner time, weary and hardly able to stand, I urged that we go home and rest a bit before eating.

"You must be tired," I said. What I really meant was that I was out on my feet, but since I was playing the host, and was only half his years, I couldn't admit that he was such a fast stepper I was dropping out on the homestretch.

"A rest will buck you up," I urged.

"Oh, I'm an old tiger," he said.

"I know," I countered, "but even tigers get tired."

He patted my shoulder as if he were a Viking father and I were a weakling son who was letting him down. Then he pulled me off to another club. Or pub. . . . By then I couldn't tell which.

"You remind me of a tiger I once had," he said. "As a cub he used to sleep across my feet. But as he grew bigger he grew heavier and one night, unthinking, I pushed him off. Well, do you know that one kick broke that poor tiger's spirit? He was never the same after that. It shows how careful we must be of the other fellow's feelings."

I lost track of the clubs and pubs we visited. We finally got to dinner about 10:30, when the lower order of London pubs were closed by law. We took a new quart of Scotch home with us under the Trader's cape.

I tried to get the old fellow to bed by putting out pajamas for him. In a little while he returned to the living room, stripped

to his long woolen underwear and his Stetson hat. He also had
the bottle of Johnny Walker. Thus arrayed, he sat down by the
fireplace and began telling what a great gag it would be to discover Noah's Ark and put it on Coney Island. He added, with
a confidential wink from his deepset laughing eyes, that there
were big financial possibilities in exhibiting the Ten Commandments too, adding that he knew where they were. "But it will
cost a million to get them out."

As he turned to his bottle again, I asked him why he didn't
carry a flask.

"I don't favor them," he explained. "They make it look as
if you drink all the time."

Sitting there in his long drawers and cowboy hat and his
long, soft, white beard, he looked like Santa Claus of the plains.
He told me of his early days and his schooling at St. Edward's,
a Catholic college, and how he had gone off to the Ivory Coast
in '70 or '71.

His adventures among the Mpanque cannibals where he and
Little Peru, son of a Peruvian president, rescued Nina T——,
the white goddess, from the Joss House, and gypped a priceless ruby in the bargain, were told with laughter in his eyes
that made it hard to tell whether he believed half of them himself.

Many times he had been fairly well-to-do, but in his old age
he had found himself reduced to "the meagre light of philan-
thropy." He lived in a doss house at Johannesburg and sold
kitchen utensils to housewives—gridirons, toast forks, and wire
kitchen goods which he made himself.

Thus matters stood until John Galsworthy, on a visit to
South Africa, was introduced by Mrs. Lewis to the "Old Visitor"
and announced to all the world that here was an authentic literary discovery.

The Trader once met General Grant on a visit to the Ivory

Coast and sold him a gorilla for museum purposes. Specimens
for museums were bottled in alcohol or "spirits," as Trader Horn
called it, and shipped by steamer. One of the difficulties with this
method of transporting specimens was that sailors had a habit
of draining the alcohol from the vat and drinking it. "A strange
animal, *homo stultus,*" the Trader opined. "They even did this
with the body of Lord Nelson—so you couldn't expect them to
be fussy about a gorilla."

He packed the gorilla for President Grant and got it ready
to ship aboard the *Alaska.* He also had a poor fellow, a gold-
smith from Accra, sleeping his last sleep in a vat of spirits and
awaiting a ship to take him home to his own people. "Mind
you, 'twas a burial which—as a temporary measure—would
have suited many. The Duke of Clarence, for instance, never
would have turned up his nose at such a purgatory."

Well, the Trader labeled the one vat *Accra* and the other
Grant—but he got the labels mixed. After the *Alaska* had sailed
he found he had put Joshua of Accra aboard for General Grant.
The spirited gorilla was still on the dock.

"I never heard any complaints," the Trader told me. "I meant
to write the General, but it would have been a long business.
As it was, I was a gorilla to the good and was doing a lot of business with the museums at that time."

The next day I took him to the station. He laid a brawny
fist on my shoulder. "Au revoir," he said, "and stay away from
homo stultus!"

I assured him I would, as I said good-by to the last of the
convivials.

The motion picture production of his book was a tremendous
success. I was with Max Schuster when the first rave review
of the book appeared. It was written by William McFee, author
of *Casuals of the Sea.* Max and I were driving to the Ingram
studio at the time. Ingram was looking for African material.

This was ideal for him. But he missed the bus. He had no more faith in his own judgment, mine, or Simon and Schuster's (publishers of *Trader Horn*) than anyone else in Hollywood had, until it was a hit. When the people made it a success, Hollywood bought it, and since their caution had made millions for them, it was silly to call them stupid for following it.

It took me a week in bed to recover from the Trader's visit.

Spahlinger felt I was improving so much that he wanted me to remain for a year of continuous treatments to prove the worth of his "ferments." He offered to put me up for the winter in his fashionable Mayfair flat. But the idea of a winter in London scared me more than the ghost of Hamlet's father. I felt I had been most lucky to have had the driest summer Londoners could remember and I was anxious to fly south like the birds before the town reverted to its usual beastly weather.

That Alice had not appeared from the north to join me was a source of disappointment, but I tried to convince myself that I was an old hand at love-'em-and-leave-'em and could absorb this rebuff too. I could not blame her people for wanting to break it up and I bore them no ill will. So when the winds and rains and fogs came back to London I climbed aboard an old crate and headed back to Paris.

I had once tried going the old way of trains, customs, long walks down docks, old Channel steamers, seasickness, and all that sort of thing, and had decided that even one such experience was enough to last a lifetime. Plane travel, even in those days, was vastly superior to the older method of crossing the Channel. Customs nuisances were practically nil. Even in freighter planes the trip from London to Paris took only about three hours, whereas by steamer and train it took all day.

It had been a wonderful summer. My health had vastly improved, and I certainly was no worse off for money than I had been before I left Nice for London three months previously.

Abel Green had come over from New York to set up a *Variety* office in Paris, and I had scarcely landed there before he was inviting me out to dinner and a show. It was called *Hallelujah*, a Parisian version of *Hit the Deck*. Borrah Minevitch and his Harmonica Rascals were in it. Minevitch joined us for dinner at Prunier's.

Afterwards we all piled in a cab for the theatre. Minevitch sat next to the taxi driver. He swapped hats with the chauffeur and otherwise acted like a crazy American. While fooling around, he purposely knocked the flag up with his elbow. Near the end of the ride, he knocked it down again.

Then after we got out he asked, "How much do I owe you?"

The cab driver looked at the meter and could scarcely believe his eyes. It registered five francs. It should have been at least twenty-five francs. While waiting for the driver to break the bad news, Borrah handed him a fifty franc note, told him to keep the change, and walked off.

"These crazy Americans," the driver kept mumbling. "Something went wrong with my meter. Alors, so he gives me fifty francs. The meter reads five francs, and he says, 'Keep the change!' *Quelle pourboire!*"

Well, he was crazy, in a lovable way.

That, *malheureusement,* was my last happy memory for a long, long time. As I was preparing to leave Paris for Nice, a new sort of pain developed back of my right knee.

It never went away.

17

"Coupez!"

•

For anybody who lived through it, it may be hard to believe that there was an American alive anywhere in the world who did not know about the egg Wall Street laid in 1929. *Variety* even expressed it in these words in a front page headline.

Dailies like the conservative *New York Times* were recording the worst stock crash in history, the trading of twelve and sixteen million shares in a day, and losses running into fourteen billions of dollars (nearly half the national debt at the time). By November, desolation, misery, unemployment, breadlines, and Hoovervilles were facing the "millionaires" of early summer—the people who bought heavily on margin, putting down 10 per cent of a stock's value, only to be wiped out because they could not find more margin. As the prices tumbled, millions of white-collared people were bankrupts and many had become suicides before the sickening crash finally hit the bottom.

With this plummeting from riches to rags in a material age, it is doubtful if many were putting their hearts into prayers of Thanksgiving that year, or dreaming of a white Christmas either. Men who were now without bread were privileged to read of Admiral Byrd's flying over the South Pole and dropping food supplies in the Arctic wastes to lighten the load of his plane on the trip back to Little America.

The country was sick. It was one huge hospital. Its stock quotations were its fever chart. Those who were still on their feet went about whistling between the hospital and the graveyard. On December 12, the Bank of United States closed its doors.

All these catastrophes meant less to me than the directions for opening a box of cereal. Though I was only a chip on a raging sea, drifting thousands of miles from home, I was a chip in personal agony. Even Our Lord for one second became weak enough to cry out, "My God, why hast Thou forsaken me?" So if I could not feel the financial collapse of America, it was because I could not feel anything but my own agonizing pain.

The sunshine of Nice seemed to have an ache in it too as I hobbled off the train from Paris. I felt that perhaps I had made a great mistake in deserting Spahlinger and that I had not improved matters by ignoring the pain in Paris. I should have gone to the American Hospital at Neuilly. A country club for some who sowed their oats too wildly around Paris, it had, on the other hand, good bone surgeons.

The increasing pain convinced me that a bone abscess was demanding more space. Tadlewski got me a modestly priced suite in the Hotel de Paris. Surgeons were consulted. X-rays were taken. They didn't seem to show what I felt. Nevertheless, the surgeons made an incision down to the bone to give free drainage. Done in the hotel room, it was literally a dirty operation, because within a few days the drainage took on a green tinge. And the pain increased. They obviously had not tapped its source.

Tadlewski decided to move me to an Anglo-American clinic in the hills back of Nice. There I kept slipping like the stock market. The best surgeon in town was called in for a consultation. Mine said he thought nothing short of an amputation could save my life. The consulting surgeon couldn't believe his ears. He let out a stream of French indignation and walked out of the consultation.

The whole affair took place in my presence. They reminded me of Joseph Jekyll's observation:

> See one physician, like a sculler plies,
> The patient lingers and by inches dies.
> But two physicians, like a pair of oars,
> Waft him more swiftly to the Stygian shores.

As I was in continual agony I could hardly be blamed for siding with the surgeon who wanted to take the leg off—this despite the fact that I had been told for years that such a radical procedure would kill me. It could not be done under general anesthetic because my lungs would not permit the use of ether, and under local anesthetic, or even spinal anesthetic, the shock would be terrific.

Tadlewski wanted to walk out with me and the consulting surgeon. He repeated he would close his school and take me to Vienna. Mme. Evie Currey, one of Tadlewski's pupils and the wife of a retired British colonel, said she would accompany us as nurse.

This Vienna solution conformed with the feelings of Alice's family in Norway. Her uncle was one of the best doctors in Oslo and he had trained under the top men in Vienna—the same men Tadlewski had studied under. The senior surgeon was eighty years old and still considered the greatest in Vienna. His son, around forty, was considered by many to be even more skilled than his father.

Among all these good friends it was arranged to take me to Vienna. The operation, they were assured, would cost nothing. But I couldn't go. By this time I was so critically ill that a trip even across town was almost a death warrant. I was moved from the Anglo-American hospital to the Belvedere Clinic, a mile or two away, and in that short ambulance trip contracted pneumonia to add to the agonies of the bone abscess. Once I recovered from this, it was decided to proceed immediately with radical surgery.

I asked Tadlewski to let my confessor know their decision. He was an old abbé, tall, slender, rosy-cheeked, with hands gnarled from years as a wood-chopping missionary in the wilderness of Canada. He looked like the Curé d'Ars. His name was Abbé Van den Daele. He was Flemish and was living out his years in retirement taking care of English-speaking Catholics in Nice at a chapel called Sacré Coeur.

It had been part of what had once been a big church, but most of the edifice was in ruins. Whether ravaged by nature, an earthquake, or frenzied Frenchmen during one of their fights with the faith of their fathers, I didn't know. But the chapel itself was a warm and living fragment of what remained good in an evil world.

The Abbé, who had a smile that showed how little the ravages of an unbelieving world had hurt him, came almost immediately. He heard my confession, gave me communion and extreme unction, and left me at peace. It was not the first time that I faced the future unafraid, and I prayed that if it were not now God's will to call it a day I would try to do better in the future.

Evie Currey had written to Alice and also to some of my friends in New York. She told them all about the same thing. The surgeons were going to operate and very likely would have to amputate the whole right leg. "But don't worry," she added, "he'll be all right."

It was this last touch that had the shock of an earthquake. It was before transfusions, sulfanilamide, penicillin, streptomycin, or other miracle drugs began worrying low-grade bacilli. But it was not before the era of friends. Sime Silverman chided me for not telling him of the bad deal I had made with Jolo in London. He enclosed a check for two hundred dollars.

Howard Dietz sent a thousand dollars which he apparently had hidden behind the Mine with the Iron Door and out of the grasp of margin-calling brokers. The Frank Scully Marching Club, Silas Seadler, Secretary, all maimed by the mayhem of Wall Street, announced a special dividend.

It has been frequently said that even celebrities known to millions really have no more than half a dozen friends. All my life I have felt I had hundreds I could call on in a pinch. I never have, but frequently when they thought things were bad, they came to my aid. This was one of those crises.

That request "not to worry" was the straw that broke the back of my little *pike* in Norway. It seemed to her that if things were going that desperately, the request not to worry was as far south as one could go in understatement. If it were meant for a solace, it scared her stiff. She broke down and wept.

"I had closed my eyes," her mother wrote later, "to the fact that letters came and went between the two. She was invited out to parties and dances. I encouraged that. But it was of no use. She was silent and not in good spirits. The morning the letter came from Evie Currey was the first time I had seen Alice in tears in many years. I thought, this is life or death, both for him and for her. I told her I thought she must go to him. She sprang up a changed girl, threw her arms around me, and that told me everything."

Mrs. Pihl put on her hat and coat and was gone for several hours. When she returned she said, "Alice, there is a boat leaving tomorrow for Antwerp. I will help you get ready. Here is your ticket to Nice, a new hat, and some warm clothes."

What this decision cost her, Mrs. Pihl never said. "I'm letting you go now," she said to Alice, "because Frank needs you, but you must come back here before you make any final decision about your future."

As Alice was clanking along from Paris to Nice on those hard wooden seats, I was taking my jouncing ride to the operating room. Clinique Belvedere was a transformed Riviera hotel. The elevator to the operating room was so small the nurses had to bend either my head or my legs to get me in. The operating room itself could have served for a basketball court. There were three operating tables about thirty feet from each other. Another operation was going on as I was wheeled to my table. The surgeon who had walked out of my consultation was performing it. He waved his scalpel to us as we passed.

It was decided to try a spinal anesthetic. The best friend I had around the table was a tall, slender doctor from Normandy. He had a soft beard and a soft, assuring voice. Moreover, he talked a soft, assuring English, a language completely unknown to the rest of the staff. The nurses must have been trained as milkmaids and not the cleanest of these. Indeed the whole place cried for the hand of Lister or Pasteur.

After chopping and chiseling for nearly two hours, the chief surgeon said with a shrug that he could find no healthy bone left and wondered what they should do next.

By this time the spinal anesthetic was wearing off.

I cried, "Coupez!"

At this, the surgeon who had walked out of our consultation came over to see what his confreres were up to and, observing the mess they had made, agreed there was nothing left to do but amputate.

Preparations were hurried to proceed with an amputation. By this time I was awake to everything. It was decided my condition was so critical that no further anesthetic of any sort could be employed. The operation proceeded under what must have been the equivalent to Civil War surgery on the battlefield.

Whenever I blacked out under the pain, they would slap my

face to bring me back to consciousness. After three hours they sewed me up and rolled me more dead than alive back to my room.

The amputation partially solved the elevator problem, but even so a nurse had to bend my head against my chest to get what remained of me out of the elevator and into my room.

For the next twenty-four hours life was a matter of living from one breath to another. I remember that it really was a fight for life and if I didn't fight for each breath, the next one would not be there. Evie Currey, now dressed in a nurse's uniform, served me sips of water and never left me during those first twenty-four hours.

I learned later that Alice had arrived from Norway shortly after I had been wheeled back to my room. For the sake of those raised on the romantic school of literature, I wish I could say that our eyes met and from that moment on I knew the fight had been won. But the fact is she was not permitted to see me, nor I her, during those critical hours.

Evie Currey gave her errands to run. Though now obviously a grown woman, she was still being treated as an errand boy. She found herself accommodations with a Norwegian friend of her family's and while on her errands never passed a chapel without going in to say some prayers.

After a day and a night had passed, I could breathe again without struggling. Nature, which has been working for fifteen years to supply calcium to a bone which was continually losing it, began tossing this essential salt into other organs of my body. The pain in my leg eased, but I began having excruciating pains in all my joints. I had traded osteomyelitis for arthritis.

It soon became evident that whether I would live or die depended on nursing care. Evie Currey took the night shift and Alice the day shift. Alice then, as always, learned rapidly. She first learned the textbook way and immediately made practical application of her knowledge. Thus within a week under her self-imposed speedup course, she was qualified to become a nurse and in fact was registered as such by the hospital and given her cap.

Her first duty was to hold an open bottle of ether and pour it on the gaping wound while the surgeon removed and cleaned the drainage tubes and washed out the sinuses. She thought she would keel over. She grew pale but she hung on, figuring that if she did pass out she would raise some dust, smash the bottle of ether, and find herself a patient instead of a nurse. She braced herself against the bed until the treatment was completed and then sank into a chair.

In the room where they kept "sterile" equipment the janitor hung his white coat which the surgeon used when the janitor was not using it. On one occasion Alice took an inhalator out of it to give me a treatment. The dust was so thick on it, she took it over to the sink to wash it. One of the nurses came in, threw her hands in the air, and shouted, "Don't do that! That's been sterilized!"

But, as Alice said to me later, "She didn't say when."

Alice asked them to wash the floor of my room, not simply go over it with a dry mop. She was informed the floors were never washed while a patient was in the room. The length of time a patient remained was his tough luck. My room was mopped, however. Evie Currey got down on her hands and knees and did it. So did Alice.

Alice had to wheedle and beg to get one extra clean sheet a week. She held on to the soiled one and began washing the extra sheet in the bathroom next door. Thus I got fresh sheets more often than most.

As an Easter present the year before, I had given Alice a small electric iron. She unscrewed the handle, turned the iron upside down, and used it as a hot plate. As the meals were meagre and often served cold, the improvised hot plate proved to be a great blessing. She would supplement the meals with food she bought at the market in the morning on the way to work at the hospital.

One time I developed what appeared to be a rash. On further examination it was discovered that the mattress was full of little worms. She asked for a new mattress. They claimed they didn't have one. Alice and another nurse moved me onto a high narrow stretcher, thoroughly cleaned the mattress, disinfected it, and put it in the sun to dry. This took four hours. I couldn't move a finger all that time; the stretcher was so narrow that any move and I'd be on the floor.

Evenings when she left I had Alice leave books near me, not so much for reading as for protection. The night nurses were really clodhoppers. One of them discovered that by lifting my good leg and suddenly letting it drop, I would emit a cry of pain that seemed to be music to her bovine ears. She wanted others to enjoy the wounded bull.

The next time she went near the foot of my bed I grabbed a book and heaved it at her. She ducked. Others near the door laughed. I let them have a couple too. They all escaped unharmed. The next morning when Alice returned to duty she had to clean up the scattered library.

As nursing is essentially cleanliness and seeing that things are done on time, Alice turned out to be one of the best nurses since Florence Nightingale. In fact months later the staff doctors pleaded with me to let her stay on. But that wasn't what she came for in the first place and by that time she was concentrating on her main objective.

She began a habit of dropping in to the Chapel of Sacré Coeur to pray for strength and courage to carry on. Often she felt too tired to pray and would just sit there. It gave her aching body comfort and her soul peace. Abbé Van den Daele often found her there. Sometimes he would stop and talk to her a little. Other times he would give her a soft assuring smile and leave her to her thoughts.

For more than two months she would go home in the evening after twelve hours on duty, never knowing if her patient would pull through the night. There was no hint during all that time of future plans, together or separate.

"As I think back now," she confessed years later, "I was going steady all right. So was Frank. But we were not going steady with each other. We were going steady with Death. I prepared myself for the worst every time I left my patient and the relief of finding him no worse when I came back than when I left him was always welcome. Without discussing it, we took each hour as it came, deciding not to worry about the next hour, or day, or week, or month, or year till it came."

One day she came in and remarked cheerfully that the patient next door had got well enough to go home.

"Don't tell me anybody ever gets out of here alive!" was all I could say. It gave her her first laugh in months and got me out of the doldrums too.

After three months the doctors decided that I could leave the hospital and continue treatments at Villa Grande Vue where I had lived a few years before. There I had a large room facing the sea and a wide balcony with French windows. It was five miles from the place where Alice stayed but was near the home of Evie Currey. Alice came by tram each morning.

By the beginning of the summer season I was well enough to go around a little on crutches, though by now I had three draining sinuses in a stump instead of the one I started with. Maybe that represented surgical progress, though I doubted it. From the long, lean, cadaverous thing I had been in the hospital, I began to get back some weight and color and ambition.

Sime Silverman bucked up my morale no end by asking me to

take over the "Hannan Swaffer" column in *Variety*. He didn't seem in the least concerned by the fact that my activities would be confined for some time to what I could see from a hillside villa. He put me on the payroll at forty dollars a week, though this was the spring of 1930 and thousands of Americans were still bemoaning how much they had lost in the stock market crash of the previous October. Because I was bound like Prometheus, I called the column ironically "The European Runaround."

Considering my own personal crash, it is not surprising that I knew less about the billions suckers had lost than a man in Mars. Having owned nothing, I lost nothing, and as a consequence faced dry-eyed all those who were telling how much they had lost when Wall Street laid that egg.

One of my visitors was Talbot Taylor, who lived near me. He had the most prized estate on the Riviera. He knew Wall Street and he knew horticulture. Outside these two fields he was as illiterate as a cow. As I have related he had put U. S. Steel, U. S. Rubber, Anaconda Copper, and other stocks on the market. He was the son-in-law of James R. Keene and had managed Keene's end of a fight with Edward H. Harriman over control of a major railroad. Harriman won by getting James Hazen Hyde to let him borrow from the $100,000,000 assets of Equitable.

I asked him what would have happened if Harriman had failed. He shrugged his shoulders and said the millions of policyholders who had paid their twenty-five cents a week on life insurance policies would have lost the money, not Hyde.

Believing these things always involved a payoff, I asked about this.

"Oh, Hyde didn't want money," he explained. "All he wanted was for Harriman to help him get appointed U. S. Ambassador to France."

This left me more bewildered about high finance than ever.

When Taylor went in for making beautiful gardens in Europe, he retired from Wall Street. "I wouldn't trust a dime of mine, unless I were in the same room, with my best friends," he said.

He came down to ask if I could help him write a book which might prevent recurrent panics by reforming the security laws so that company officers and directors might no longer manipulate stocks in which they had a directing interest.

Two years before this interview, I had sat on Taylor's terrace when Charles Mitchell, president of National City Bank was there. They were drinking Old Hermitage, a whiskey aged before the Civil War. Mitchell was regaling Taylor with some smart operations of their friends.

"You fellows are crazy," I heard Taylor say. "You'll ruin the country."

Mitchell looked at him bewildered. "Tolly," he said, "you're getting to be an old fogy. It's not the same Street you knew."

Taylor heard this so often during the boom days he thought perhaps he was an old fogy. Now he was coming to me to see what we could do between us to save the country.

But I could not get very excited about saving the country from the wolves of Wall Street. I was more concerned with saving my little *pike* from the wolves of Norway. I wrote her mother asking her consent to our getting married in France. I thought it would be easy.

Her mother, no doubt prompted by all the uncles, aunts, and cousins (whom she reckoned by the dozens) to propound the conventional questions, asked me my prospects.

I replied that they were pretty dismal, as far as I could see. I had one lung and one leg. I was making forty dollars a week, but this was on a week-to-week basis and was coming from America where fourteen million persons were unemployed. So how long it would last was anybody's guess.

Still, I knew God did not give any of us more adversity than we could stand and I felt the worst for us was over. Besides, I was in love with a beautiful girl and she, she confessed, had been willing to take me, for better or worse, almost from the first moment she laid eyes on me.

Protocol having been complied with, the most wonderful mother of the girl of anybody's dreams gave her consent.

18

Riviera Honeymoon

●

I<small>N AREAS</small> of the world where young people can get tight one night and say "Let's get married!" and it's done by dawn, it may be hard to understand a place that demanded the fulfillment of all sorts of legal conditions, requiring weeks of research, before two persons, never married before, could meet even the *civil* requirements of a marriage contract. But that was "loose and immoral" France around 1930. Nobody could marry in haste and repent at leisure there, Congreve to the contrary, though he could marry in leisure and repent in haste easily enough. It was the world's hardest place to marry and the easiest to get divorced until Russia, Mexico, and Nevada decided to debase the holy sacrament of marriage to the level of marts dealing in trade-ins.

We could not have a church wedding without going through a civil ceremony first. To meet this first proviso we would have to get affidavits of residence and many other legal papers from our own countries, all of which would take time.

Between times I had been talking with Frank Harris about writing a biography of George Bernard Shaw. A critical appraisal by the man who had practically discovered Shaw would have a cleansing effect, I thought, and should sell well among those who were getting pretty tired of Shaw's deification of Shaw.

But I did not feel well enough to work as hard on such a book as I had on the cowboy reminiscences. I felt if I roughed out the book and let Harris polish it in his own idiom I would be earning my salt.

Harris at first wasn't much interested, believing Shaw of insufficient stature to carry a whole biography, though as a matter of fact several had been written around the master's cloistered life and lack of loves.

Barring possibly Chesterton, no writer of stature had stood up to Shaw and appraised him as an equal, or possibly as a superior. "What did Shaw ever do?" Harris would complain. But he complained even more about the need of money. It seemed that he thought it was my mission in life to provide it in one way or another.

In his second volume of *Contemporary Portraits*, Harris had published a fifteen thousand-word portrait of Shaw, but it had been published in 1918, which was a war year, remember. I felt certain few people had read it and fewer had remembered it.

M. Lincoln Schuster was in Europe. I wrote him about the project. He was going to Vienna but wired he was changing his plans and coming directly to Nice.

He and Harris so fired each other as they sat on a balcony overlooking the mountains above Nice that it was a delight to see. Harris blossomed. Indeed, he ranged the whole field of literature in his time. He even quoted Lord Alfred Douglas, a man he said he detested personally. "But he wrote immortal sonnets," he assured us. All in all, he put on a show that Shaw, quite an actor, could never have equalled.

At one point, however, Harris, who in his youth could quote *Paradise Lost* from beginning to end, stumbled. His memory failed him and he had to go and hunt out a volume to support his contention that Douglas was a great sonneteer.

Schuster asked Harris how long it would take to write the Shaw book, for it already was tacitly agreed by then that if he would write it, Simon & Schuster would feel honored to publish it.

Harris, as cocky as he had ever been in his life, said he had most of it written and the rest would take about a month.

I just about collapsed at the audacity of this fighting cock.

Schuster urged him, however, not to rush things. It was agreed to arrange for simultaneous publication in London and New York in the fall of the following year. The publishers would advance 7500 dollars in installments, 2500 dollars on signing and the rest as the installments of the manuscript were delivered.

Schuster had scarcely gone on his way when my Harrisian tiger-rose began to wilt. I fixed up a memorandum of agreement between him and me following the general lines of the one between us on the cowboy reminiscences. I was to get 30 per cent of the royalties. But when we came to sign, Harris demurred, explaining that he had to pay a lawyer 10 per cent in New York and since I didn't plan to do as much on the Shaw book as I had done on the cowboy book, he felt 20 per cent would be fair. I pointed out to him that in that case I would be paying his lawyer. We argued the thing for a while. I finally agreed to his terms and signed.

When I got home I discovered that *I* was getting the 80 per cent and Harris the 20! I doubt if he ever would have noticed it, and as it turned out, 80 per cent for me would have been a just distribution of the returns. The next morning I called him and laughingly explained what we had signed. I told him I'd draft another contract, which I did.

I thought we would have a nice leisurely summer in Nice, writing, loafing, and convalescing (I still had five draining wounds.)

Within a few days, however, Harris was sure all of us could work better if we went to Vittel in the Vosges mountains. He had a White Russian secretary who had been there some time previously and remembered it as an ideal place where one could take the cure and have no distractions during writing hours.

The next thing we knew we were all on our way to Vittel, the Harrises in a taxi (with the meter running all the way), we by train. Altogether it was about a nine hundred-mile trip. We carried a full trunk of notes, books, and manuscripts.

This switch to Vittel botched our private life because it made any preliminary work we had done on clearing the legal obstacles to our marriage null and void. It meant we had to start all over again in Vittel. A priest told us he could do nothing until all civil obstacles were removed.

We discovered that the hotel Harris' secretary had picked for us was on the wrong side of the tracks. In fact it was hardly off them. Freight cars, mostly carrying fertilizer, backed and pulled all day long, starting at 6 A.M. The hotel also carried the most earsplitting gong for calling its absentminded guests to meals ever heard outside a firehouse.

It rained ceaselessly the first few days, and Harris was cold and thirsty from the moment he arrived. He began ordering cognac and soda to allay his chills. The *femmes de chambres,* not being fast enough in their service, got their *derrières* pinched. They were urged to hurry. Old as they were, they jumped.

For five days Harris shivered, pinched bottoms and drank cognac. Nellie Harris smiled benignly, touched her nostrils delicately with her crepe georgette handkerchief, and took it all quite calmly. Finding brandy and overcoats no protection from the frigid rain, Harris decided to return to Nice.

I had started treatments to clear up those five draining sinuses and was loath to follow my aging collaborator in his wild goose chase for inspiration. I began to suspect the Shaw biography would get on faster if we didn't see Harris for a while.

Our unwillingness to hop back to Nice so distressed Harris that he decided we should all go to a movie. He liked cowboy movies, but was so absent-minded he would buy tickets for the best seats in the back before he realized he was shortsighted and couldn't see back there. Then he would move up to the first row and pound with his cane for action. He even taught the Vittel kids how to organize a racket to speed up the showing of the picture.

That was all Harris contributed to the Shaw biography in Vittel. He and his wife went back to Nice, while we prepared to go to Paris to see if we couldn't get faster action there on our marriage plans as well as possibly better treatment for my aching stump.

Before leaving, we called in a little country doctor for consultation.

On examing the wounds, he sadly assured us that there must be some slivers of bone floating around deep in those sinuses, and to get these out might require another operation. I explained to him that my surgeon in Nice, testing to see how clean the wound really was, didn't change bandages for four days. That appalled him. He shook his head first sideways, then up and down. "Go to Paris," he said. "See Martel. Unfortunately in Vittel we have no facilities which could cope with such a discouraging development."

Just as we were about to leave, a royalty check for twenty-five hundred dollars arrived by cable from New York. I forwarded it to Harris in Nice. According to our contract, I was to be paid 20 per cent of this sum immediately.

I wired them that we needed money to get to Paris. Instead of five hundred dollars, which was my due, a thousand francs, or about thirty-nine dollars, arrived, with the explanation that only two thousand dollars had come through, as the New York lawyer had extracted five hundred dollars for past debts. Harris had forgotten I had forwarded the full sum. Already I was being squeezed from both ends.

My contract with Harris read that I should be paid directly by the publishers, but by now his absent-mindedness had become so contagious that everybody forgot to insert the clause in the contract. Still, thirty-nine dollars helped us get to Paris.

There we ran into J. P. McEvoy, who was gathering material for Dixie Dugan on tour, a novel to follow *Show Girl* and to be called *Society*. He drove with us to the *Variety* office where we picked up the mail. There was a letter from Sime Silverman. We opened it and read it in a taxi. Our eyes fell on a paragraph: "Hear you're getting married. Oh boy!"

Mac looked at me and then at Alice. "Are you?" he asked.

"What an editor! No wonder Winchell hangs around him all the time!" I said.

The Quiet One at our side said nothing. But she must have been baffled nevertheless. How did such news get around? The only American we had talked to was George Canty, U. S. Trade Commissioner. Had he cabled Sime the news that we were shopping for ways out of the marital maze?

We checked Alice into a little hotel in Neuilly. Finding some delay about entering the American Hospital, I checked in at the Hotel Rovarro near the Étoile. McEvoy liked the place and moved over from the Ritz.

He had gone far in a few years. At Notre Dame he said he had held the lowest job on the campus. "I was the waiter to the student waiters." As a sports writer he had known how to create suspense. In his first story for a South Bend daily he had reported everything but the score.

He had been the poet laureate of the greeting card racket. He had made a fortune regimenting sentimental concern over Mother's Day, Father's Day, and Everybody's Birthday. He had written Broadway hits—both plays (*The Potters*) and musicals (*Americana*). He had been one of the earliest to make a fortune with a comic strip (*Dixie Dugan*). He had been the first of popular novelists to pitch for pocket-sized paperbacks (*Denny and the Dumb Cluck*, 1930).

He had novelized such singularly American heroes and heroines as greeting-card salesmen, cartoonists, radio comics, show girls. Long before Runyon, he was. He was Zola with a sense of humor, Dickens with brevity.

He might have won the Nobel Prize had he stuck to writing novels. But a year or two after I met him in Paris he lost one hundred thousand dollars backing one of his own Broadway musicals. He made a fast switch. Like Caesar, he cut his Gaul (and Mac had plenty) in three parts. He sold them to the highest bidders. Hollywood got a piece, the *Post* got a piece, and *Reader's Digest* got the rest.

What had once been the most promising creative talent in the country was quietly embalmed and laid to rest in Forest Lawn. As a fact-finding roving editor of *Reader's Digest*, he had time to rove and become rich again. In time he rejoined the landed aristocrats, with places in Havana, New City, New York, and Bearsville. He hopped around the world with the verve of a cub reporter covering fires in a Cadillac. After his own and adopted children had grown up, he married again and fathered a brand new brood. He knew what he wanted and he certainly got it. He was, in Ben Hecht's phrase, "the only writer I ever knew who wasn't a financial idiot."

The night before he was leaving for New York and I for the hospital, we had dinner at a sidewalk cafe. He wondered how I paid for all my surgical interludes. I explained that the last one was a sliding-scale deal. The surgeon was to get twenty thousand francs if it were a success; five thousand francs if it were a failure.

"It was a flop. So he sent me a bill for twenty thousand francs."

"So?"

"So I'll pay him five thousand francs. He won't dun me. He knows he'll get paid in time."

He wanted to know what a job like mine on *Variety* paid. I bragged and said fifty dollars a week, ten over what it did pay.

"What are your ideas on borrowing and lending?"

"Well," I said, "I give what I wouldn't miss, instead of loaning what I couldn't afford to lose. If a guy needs a dollar and I need a haircut, another few weeks without a haircut would not bother me particularly. If it's big money they want, I at least start them on their way with, say, five dollars. I did that for a fellow only yesterday. He was really in a jam.

"You know, it's sort of flattering in a depressing way to have friends who think you are better off than they are. I mean if someone does not think of me as sick and crippled, he is giving my morale a great boost, and if there is a bite involved—well, so is there a bite involved in morale-builders like plays or musicals, or movies or books. Our Lord could tell those with financial worries to consider the lilies in the field and that if God took care of them so beautifully, why would He neglect those made in His own image? But even the disciples who lived with Christ didn't quite believe in what He preached, so I doubt if in this material age a fifth carbon copy would impress the impoverished of today. There's no worse sickness than being broke, unless it's the inability to help those who believe they are worse off than we are."

Mac told me about a novel he was planning to write next. It concerned the rise and fall of a comic strip artist who got in a bad jam. (It eventually emerged as *Mr. Noodle.*) We talked about this unique American breed—rich illustrators. He told me about Sid Smith, cartoonist of the *Andy Gump* comic strip that was the backbone of the *Chicago Tribune* circulation figures. Gump's real creator was a little Jewish jeweller. After years of rich living off this strip, he and Smith fell out. It wasn't long before Sid Smith died on the vine. The well of his inspiration had dried up.

That night after we parted Mac came back later to my room. I had been asleep. He said he didn't want to disturb me but he was leaving a cable and would like me to send it for him in the morning.

"It's all paid for," he whispered and then said goodnight.

I turned over and went to sleep again. In the morning I opened the envelope. Besides the cable, which could not have cost five dollars, was a check for one thousand dollars!

I was instructed to cash it, pay doctors' bills, get married on it, think of it as a wedding present, or use it for a literary foundation for my own advancement. I dressed and left for the hospital in practically a state of shock. In fact I doubt whether I have ever recovered from that staggering *beau geste.*

The surgeons, however, tried to take the bloom off my rose. They decided a spur had grown out of the amputated femur and was poking into the sciatic nerve and would have to be chopped off and then hit with X-ray treatments to prevent its growing again. That, they assured me, was the cause of those drainage canals refusing to dry up.

"Not any slivers of bone, not any sequestra?" I asked hopefully.

They assured me the mess was much bigger than that.

Well, I had had operations no end. They were no novelty. But getting married, that would be something new for me. Why not try that instead?

I told the surgeons I'd think over the operation for a few days.

Meanwhile Alice had begun the dismal marital negotiations all over again while I worked on the Shaw biography between treatments at the hospital. Once when she got bogged down and couldn't seem to move in any direction without getting into another bottleneck, she called on me for help. I felt like a knight in the Tower of London who had to get out somehow to help his lady in distress. The American Hospital had a roof garden and certain patients were wheeled up there for a few hours when the weather was good. I had got myself on this list. But I didn't want to go up. I wanted to go down, and out.

Sometimes I wheeled myself to the elevator, and on this occasion, with my clothes on underneath my bathrobe, I said to the elevator boy, "Down." He took me all the way to the basement and I wheeled myself out. After he went back up to the main floor, I took off my bathrobe, picked up my crutches, and sneaked out the laundry exit. Alice was waiting and we hailed a taxi just as it was leaving the grounds. We told the driver to take us to the Neuilly City Hall.

We first asked if Alice could move to a better hotel. She couldn't even move in with Dr. and Mrs. Claude Lillingston, head of the Red Cross in Paris, and friends of her family for thirty years. They had offered to be the witnesses at our marriage. In fact they were about the only ones who approved of the marriage without reservation.

They had started out worse than us, they assured us. Shortly after they were married Dr. Lillingston broke down in health and spent the next three years flat on his back in a sanatorium. In time he got well, or at least well enough to take on such duties as he was now performing as head of the Red Cross.

"Love is the only thing that counts," they insisted, and since they had been married twenty-five years and seemed to us the happiest couple we had met in Europe, why listen to the advice of other people? Why, particularly, listen to the advice of failures? It seemed to Alice that whenever she listened to any woman who ever gave her unsolicited advice on marriage she never failed to find either a divorce or some other indication of unhappiness. On the other hand, the Lillingstons were our sort of people and they approved of what we were doing.

To them my poor health, our lack of money, Alice's youth, my years, her Lutheranism, my Catholicism didn't matter as long as we loved each other.

The authorities told us Alice simply could not move without throwing all the negotiations back to scratch. I could move, but at the time it would have been a matter of moving from one hospital to another, and I was quite happy where I was. But I was beginning to become incensed with the lack of gallantry being shown, in a land famous for its *politesse,* toward my lady fair.

Losing all restraint, I shouted loud enough to wake the dead in the Neuilly bureau of births, marriages, and deaths: "I can now understand why so many people live in sin on the Left Bank. They can't afford to cut all this red tape, grease all these palms, and wait this long, because they have only one life to live!"

The *chef* assured me he was not making things difficult for us. "It was," with a shrug of his shoulders, "the law." And what was the law? Well, first, if you're foreigners, you have to collect the signatures of all the concierges where you have lived for the six previous months. These you must take to the various chiefs of police, who will certify that the signatures of the glorified janitors are not forgeries.

"Armed with these, you must get an attorney approved by the U. S. Embassy to draw up a certificate of eligibility." This was needed to prove that characters bent on holy wedlock were not already bigamists in their native land. This must then be taken to an ambassador, who must swear that the attorney was not disbarred in his native land and was indeed an honorable fellow with only one weakness—a love of champagne cocktails before noon.

All this, of course, costs money. *Papier timbre* must be used and official *timbres* pasted on all these documents. Signatures have a varying price structure. American ambassadors are worth a dollar a word; a French Minister of the Interior comes as low as fifteen cents. Special treatment, of course, can run into big money, but in the end not much time will be saved.

"Once you have these basic documents, you can then apply for a marriage license," the *chef du bureau* told us. "But you cannot get married until the banns have been dispatched by mail to your home town, posted on the bulletin board of the City Hall for ten days, and then mailed back to Paris. This is figured to take six weeks. During that time, one of you may not move from one hotel to another without throwing the whole thing back to the beginning."

We argued that banns were not posted in our homeland any longer; so he advised us that we could eliminate this proviso if we could find a cabinet minister in office long enough to read it, waive the requirement, and take his fee.

You can judge by now that anybody insisting on a legal or holy marriage in France must really be serious about it.

It is wiser to send the lady into this red tape alone. She has the only dissolvant—tears. France may be more bogged down with more bureaucrats than Washington, but they are still easily fetched by a woman's tears.

In our hunt for happiness, I sent Alice in to get a "yes" from a cabinet minister while I sat outside in the sun and talked the whole thing over with the taxidriver. He told me of a woman who had spent two years trying to knock over these obstacles to wedlock. "She, too, was a foreigner," he said. "She spent a fortune. She bribed everybody. Finally, her purse empty, she broke down in tears. They fixed the papers within minutes. Everybody kissed the bride-to-be and sent her merrily on her way. Her chief difficulty was that she had seven marriage certificates but could dig up only five divorce decrees. She wept the other two out of the record."

It was a beautiful sunny autumn day. The taxidriver and I watched as Alice approached. She was dabbing her eyes. We asked her if she had got the waiver signed. She nodded her head and burst into tears. The taxidriver was so touched that he too wept quietly at our side. He drove us back to the *chef* of births, marriages, and deaths. The *chef* read the document.

"Imbecile!" he cried. "The Minister of the Interior doesn't answer my questions at all. All he does is write 'yes' for everything. Some of the answers should have been 'no' if he favored giving you permission."

Then he saw some tears staining the document. He looked up and saw the bride-to-be's eyes were still moist. He rubbed the back of his neck, bit his thumb, shrugged, and okayed the document.

"*Voilà!*" he said.

This solved everything? *Au contraire!* It permitted us to marry in ten days instead of having to wait around for six weeks.

Early on the morning of the wedding the Lillingstons came to pick up Alice at her hotel. They gave her our only wedding gift, a beautiful little goldplated alarm clock. They explained that they had been so excited about it that they had unwrapped it in the subway to look at it and had dropped it and broken it.

That misfortune was quickly forgotten when we suddenly realized that in unwinding all the red tape we had forgotten to buy a wedding ring. Dr. Lillingston gallantly suggested that we might borrow his wife's. She gladly consented. But Alice wanted her own. So she and Mrs. Lillingston went off to find a ring. On Place St. Ferdinand, they found a shop on their own. It was about the width of a dusty door and about two doors deep. It looked as if it had not had a client in years.

Alice had her own ideas about a ring—not too wide, not too narrow. But she was now up against the urgency of taking what fitted.

"I want one like this," she said, picking one out of a dusty collection.

It was the only one of its kind. It was just her size. The old lady began fussing around, looking for a piece of chamois to polish the ring. "Is it long before it will be used?" she asked.

"In about one quarter of an hour, if you hurry."

She began speeding up her motions like an early movie, and wishing Alice all kinds of happiness between polishes.

"It's real gold, you see."

She very impressively showed the gold markings. They were on the outside, so that everybody might see it was real gold. That part wore off in two years, but the ring was real gold, and still is. It cost seventy-five francs—$3.

When they got back to the hotel with the ring, Dr. Lillingston and I were outside waiting for them. I was wearing a pale-blue shirt. That was Alice's favorite, though we had decided on a white one.

"Why did you switch to my favorite?" she whispered.

"Because the white one was too tight in the neck," I said. I was a very romantic fellow in those days.

At the *Mairie* we met our old "friend" from the Deceased

Bureau. He was very nice—like vinegar with sugar. We were ushered to red velvet chairs in the room for marriages. Paintings of nude women adorned the walls. The Mayor came in with a wide red band across his chest. He talked and read aloud in rapid French. Neither of us understood much. He asked in the same monotonous voice if I would have Alice as my wife. No answer. He looked up at me. Still no answer. He didn't seem to understand that I didn't know what he was saying. He read the long question over again. Still no answer. Alice gave me a gentle prod. I woke up. "Alice Pihl? Who?" I am alleged to have said. The Mayor accepted that as sufficient answer.

"Sign here, *s'il vous plaît*," requested the clerk.

We signed one document. Another. Another. Nine papers had to be signed and then they gave us a book. It was called a *Livret de Famille*. In the first page was our *certificate de mariage*. Then there were six pages for birth records—places for twelve children. Six more pages told us how to take care of children and prevent diseases. There were instructions about wet nurses and all infant care, even to warning us not to dry diapers in the baby's room.

We went out on the shadeless square in front of the *Mairie*. We asked Dr. and Mrs. Lillingston to lunch with us. They thanked us but wanted us to be alone. So we hailed a cab and asked to be driven to Sacré Coeur and then to La Chaumière, a quiet high class little restaurant behind the palace of the *Président de la République*. There we ran into Philip Eliot, the husband of Nina Wilcox Putnam. He was driving a big new car, a Moon, and was leaving for Nice. Why not drive with him?

We started out with so much baggage we couldn't sit together. I sat up front with Philip. Alice sat in the back with handbags piled all around her. The trunk with manuscript notes had to be roped on the back because there wasn't room inside.

Normally, Philip was the world's maddest driver, but he outdid himself on this occasion. It turned out that he had a very good reason for speed. He had given somebody in Paris a check on a bank in Nice but didn't have sufficient funds to cover it. As kiting checks was a serious crime in France, he had to get to Nice before the check arrived and borrow enough from Nina to cover it.

Though we raced like mad, he insisted we stop every few hours for drinks. We dined at the most expensive restaurant in Fontainebleau, the one that looks out on the palace, and then went in search for a pharmacy for some aspirin to stop a juicy cold Philip was brewing.

Then we leaped into the Moon and started south at racing speed. After dark, Philip's lights began acting badly and in his haste and the rain he got off the main road. He couldn't understand it. He had traveled the right road no end of times.

Alice had volunteered to drive when he felt tired, and on this slippery road he remembered the offer. She did nobly, but he insisted on taking over again. She was driving too carefully, it seemed. At Auxerre he picked the wrong street and got into the market place with hardly open space enough to walk, let alone drive a car. It took an hour to get out of town. Such delays drove him to a hundred kilometers an hour. We sped through Lyon and on south.

Philip was convinced that all peasants delighted in nothing so much as giving false directions to traveling tourists. "Couldn't you see the sneer in his grin?" he would ask. "I tell you, these people delight in misleading you." He would listen to their directions and then veer off on another road. We lost hours and, eventually, the trunk.

It was proving a nuisance anyway and Philip thought we ought to have shipped it by train. As it contained all the notes, reference books, and letters for the Shaw biography, neither of us leaped at the idea.

Then in the black night, with the rain pouring down, on a slippery and untraveled road we met a car. Philip swung out. The car passed us and suddenly reared like a frightened horse. Its motor died and, with its front wheels up in the air, it came to a stop. We stopped too.

After a good deal of shouting back and forth we got out and found our poor trunk kicked half to death and lying beneath the other car. We took its bleeding body from beneath the angry iron horse and bound its wounds.

Philip was all for an immediate burial. But I insisted a best seller was in that mess. Roped again, we tied it on the trunk rack, covered it with a rubber cloth, and drove on through the rain.

Daybreak found us on the last lap to Nice. The road was all winding, twisting, mountain trails. Even so, we rarely did less than ninety kilometers an hour and passed everything—Rolls Royces, Isotta Fraschinis, Bugattis, and even trains.

The last was by far the most exciting. In that section of France they had chains across the grade crossings. We beat a train to one of these and the guard let down the chain after having put it up. Presumably he decided we could pass without getting killed.

This struck Philip as such good fun that he tried another one. The train traveled in a straight line, but the road kept weaving in and out of the mountains, crossing and re-crossing the tracks every mile or so. It was just like a chase in a movie, only a bit more exciting for Alice because she was sitting in the back and all the suitcases kept tumbling down on her.

By the time we reached Digne we were reeling and nauseated. We tried to still our heaving stomachs by eating an apple which Alice found in my pocket. It tasted funny, but everything seemed funny at that moment. A little bottle of a Chinese headache cure, which Jue Quon Tai had given me, had lost its cork and the sedative had poured all over the apple. A few drops of it on one's forehead was a treatment, Tai had assured me. We had swallowed enough of the hashish to kill a horse. But we could not stop for a rest because Philip had wired on to Nina to meet us at the Ruhl Hotel in Nice. He planned to cover the distance between Grenoble and Nice in five hours—an incredible performance. He actually did it.

We arrived at the Ruhl shaken, but all in one piece. Nina greeted us with all her old affection. She looked the prettiest ever in an ensemble of black and white topped by her platinum blonde hair and a black beret.

All that night we reeled and retched from the mad ride and the "headache cure," but Eliot had arrived in time to beat his rubber check from bouncing him into jail. We too received good news. Abbé Van den Daele had got us a special dispensation from the Bishop to marry. It would, of course, be a ceremony involving such old-fashioned words as "love, honor and obey."

Alice went up to the Harrises to invite them to the wedding. They would be very pleased to come, they said. She explained where the little church was.

"In the Quartier Sainte Hélène. On Avenue de Californie. Just down the hill and two blocks further on toward Cannes than Villa Paulette."

After a while Mrs. Harris said: "Oh, Alice, I don't seem to remember where it is. Can't you come and fetch us at 3:30?"

Alice thought of the big mauve car Lady McCarthy had given them. She thought of the little Jap in chauffeur's uniform with a mauve band around his cap. She thought, further, that there is only one Avenue de Californie in Nice and one little Ste. Hélène church there.

She hadn't ever said "no" to a thing Mrs. Harris had asked

her before, not even to sending cables for them with her own few dollars.

But that day? Her day? Why should the bride have to fetch her witnesses? she asked herself.

"I'm sorry," she said, "but I won't have time. I'm getting married today."

At 3:30 Nina Putnam came to fetch us. She had a basket of white flowers and orange blossoms for Alice. She was Alice's witness. Mrs. Harris was mine.

The church was an old, impoverished chapel, named in honor of Sainte Hélène, the mother of Constantine. (She is credited in Church history with having found the true cross near Golgotha in Jerusalem.) I went in to church to make my confession and Alice sat down to say some prayers on this most serious day of a girl's life. The others waited outside. When they came in, Frank Harris sat down beside her. "What's that woman doing over there?" he asked in his booming voice.

"She is praying," Alice whispered.

"Praying? To whom?"

"God."

"What is that statue over there?"

"It's Jesus."

"And that?"

She didn't want to answer. She wanted to pray. She wanted to be alone. He persisted with other questions. She answered some. And then he said, "And all this for one man."

She got up and chose another pew. She was going to be married in a few minutes and she wanted to say some prayers, not be distracted by a bewildered old pagan.

We were called into the vestry. It was a gorgeous, sunny day, that third day of November, 1930. The ceremony was short, about fifteen minutes. We were the first couple our dear Abbé had married in English; so in between the different prayers he had to look up the next part of the ceremony in the index.

We took each other from that day forward for better, for worse, for richer or poorer, in sickness and in health until death did us part. We took each other in Latin, French, and English.

The Curé of Ste. Hélène, a short man with his hands folded on his bulgy stomach and his spectacles far enough down on his nose so he could look over them, stood beside the Abbé. When it was all over he said, "I didn't understand the English, but I'm sure it's all right."

We signed the registry. Alice and I, Nina, with her imposing legal name, "Nina Wilcox Putnam Eliot," and Nellie Harris. Frank Harris elbowed his way in and insisted on signing too.

We were all invited to a champagne party at the Ruhl with Nina. The strict rules of Abbé Van den Daele's order, we were sorry to hear, prevented him from accepting our invitation. Mrs. Currey, who had nursed me, went with the Harrises.

At the Ruhl the champagne flowed freely. Frank Harris was very talkative. He flirted with Nina, forgetting she had known the old goat years ago in Greenwich Village. She didn't let on. It was her party for us, and so she played her hostess role charmingly. When Harris asked her if she were married, she said, "Oh, I have already *had* three husbands."

Years later when the last of them destroyed himself she moved to Cuernavaca and became a Catholic.

We took Mrs. Currey home on our way to Cannes. She begged us not to have children. "I'll give you a little dog or a little cat, but, darlings, don't have any babies."

She had two beautiful daughters herself, both in their twenties. We said good-by to her, leaving her with her shattered dreams and retaining our own illusions as to what gave the most happiness in life.

We drove slowly along the shore road, driving toward the setting sun. First we thought we would stop at Juan les Pins, but then we decided to continue on to Cannes, the place where it all began. We pulled up in front of the Hotel Victoria —perhaps because we felt by then like mid-Victorians, married at last after overcoming the sort of obstacles nineteenth-century novelists put in their romances. We picked a room with a balcony overlooking the sea. Our room was in keeping with the hotel's name. Even the wallpaper was Victorian.

Alice opened her suitcase and began revealing a trousseau that opened my eyes. Had I married an heiress, after all? She had several dainty frocks and one aquamarine ensemble had the lining of a full-length coat of the same delicate material as the frock.

I examined the coat because the lining looked handsewn. Since she had practically no time to call her own after she had left Norway for that long hard trip to Nice ten months before, I wondered how the miracle had been accomplished.

She explained that she designed the dresses, and had a dressmaker come in nights to help with the fittings.

I was fascinated by the workmanship and the way she had kept all this a secret and a surprise. She had a trousseau that the *haute couturières* of Paris didn't get around to until the next spring.

We opened the mail we had picked up in Nice. Several letters had been addressed to "Mr. and Mrs. Frank Scully." One was from Elliott Sanger, head of music station WQXR in New York, the first one of its kind broadcasting classic and semi-classic music. A line was drawn down the middle of the letter. The left side was addressed "Dear Frank" and the right side, "Dear Alice."

Alice was sitting at my right as we read the letter. It welcomed us into the married circle of Columbia '17 J. It warmed her heart and mine. It meant, as the Victorian novels used to say, that we could now come home and all would be forgiven.

Most of my friends were writers, publishers, or publicists, and all of them knew that writers might be great lovers, according to their own unsupported confessions, but as good providers in a bourgeois world they were dubious bargains. If one were sick, in addition to the infirmities shared by all, he would be considered no bargain at all.

But this was the philosophy of pragmatists in an unbelieving world. That was where we got off. We had hope, we had faith, we hoped we had charity. We were sure that, doing the best according to our lights, God would help us.

In addition to the letters was a batch of telegrams—fifty-one in all. Fifty were for Alice and one for me. Well, it was her day, and, after all, who was I to dissuade her, then or any time later, that she had not made an excellent catch?

We had traveled far in a few years and Little Alice had carried the heaviest part of the burden. I felt she had more than earned a breakfast in bed. To me this was no novelty. I had had thousands of meals in bed. But she was not a nurse, for this day at least, and I was not a patient. We were honeymooners and were having breakfast in bed. It came on a huge tray, the silver polished and shining. The sun poured in as the waiter opened the French windows. There, shimmering in the sunlight, was our tideless blue sea.

My little *pike* had grown to a beautiful woman and now was married. I was too. And what was most incredible of all, we were married to each other!

19

Ghosting the Great

•

Wɪᴛʜɪɴ a week of our marriage we were plunged into so much
work that there was precious little time for adjustments, lovers'
quarrels, or even small spats. These may be part of the first
year of marriage. If so, they eluded us. What we produced instead were fifty columns, four books, and a baby.

We had hardly settled in a three-room apartment of Villa
Grande Vue when the first minor miracle occurred. The last
of my stump's draining wounds dried and healed. As one of
my wounds had healed once before (on the occasion of the
canonization of Ste. Thérèse), I wasn't too sure of its finality
this time, but since the wounds have now stayed closed for
twenty-five years, I suppose the osteomyelitis can be called
cured. That the area aches now more than it ever did before
the amputation cannot be charged against surgical interference.
At least now it is a dry ache.

Our first visit to the Harrises after the honeymoon revealed
that my honeymoon with Frank was over. I had sent him
twenty thousand words from Vittel and Paris, but on returning
to Nice and asking him about the material, I learned he had
mislaid it. All he could find was about sixty-five pages of an
old manuscript held together by a brass paper-fastener. The
material had been cribbed from many sources but not credited,
and by then Harris had long forgotten where the notes had

come from. Each time he read the stuff, it was all news to him.

Several times he pushed the material onto me, asking me to tell him what I thought of it. I told him I had read it before and that it was only notes, the sources of which his secretary would have to credit if she knew them. Once he insisted I take the morsel home to read. I did.

To my horror I learned one day that he had sent off the sixty-five pages to the publishers—all in appalling disorder and not one new line written in the four months since the contract was signed. This he labeled his first installment, for which he demanded, and received, an additional thousand dollars. Then he informed them he couldn't write any more and would they be kind enough to send him what was still due and let it go at that.

Though he owed me 750 dollars, I had never received more than the 39 dollars sent to me in Vittel, and had it not been for my weekly *Variety* stipend and the largesse of J. P. McEvoy, I would have had a difficult time supporting the literary life of Frank Harris, the brigand of letters who, in Shaw's opinion "sailed the Spanish Main with the blackest of flags, the reddest of sashes, the hugest of cutlasses, and the thinnest of skins."

The editorial report on that first installment of Harris' was devastating. Clifton Fadiman, the editor, made no bones about how badly the publishers were being *roulé*. He presented a ten-point indictment of the fragment. The pages, in his opinion, lacked organic planning, and the piece was neither criticism nor biography. "There is not a single new fact or insight in these sixty-five pages, except those provided by Shaw's two letters, one dealing with his sex life, the other with his early career," Fadiman pointed out.

It became clear as Riviera sunshine that all Harris had collected would have to be thrown away and the job started all over again from scratch, or the whole thing called off.

I dug out the carbons of notes I had sent Harris and decided to try my hand at a new opening—all in Harris' name. I had believed there was a great book on Shaw in Harris, but it had completely slipped through his hands. We were all paying a pretty stiff fee for the memory test.

As the publishers were friends of mine from college days, I felt particularly distressed over the fiasco. If I now gave it the old college try and a report came back that the second effort was no better than the first, I would have to confess that the jig was up and bow out.

Meanwhile Dick Simon, the publisher, got sick and in the hospital found himself without a house organ to read. When he got well, he vowed to do something about it. As the guinea pig that had made good, a graduate of twenty-five hospitals in several countries, I had been trying to do something about solving Dick's problem for years. But the best way to get a book accepted is to have the publisher discover the need for it himself. I was asked what help I could give the project and ended by taking it over completely. When I supplied the title *Fun in Bed* for Simon and Schuster's convalescent handbook, our success was assured.

From almost my first operation I saw the need of such a book as *Fun in Bed*. Many writers had milked their personal woes for laughs, such as Irvin S. Cobb and his *Speaking of Operations* and Will Rogers and his *Ether and Me*. But after I had made about a dozen trips to hospitals, the idea of being as funny as a crutch on a crutch struck me as something less than sidesplitting.

I felt more like a middleman. I had arrived in a good spot to do some brisk trading between the place where the surgeon stepped in and the mortician took over. In that middle ground there was plenty of room for a glorified trade paper, and if it would be played for laughs, fine.

Radio and television were not widely disseminated around hospitals in those days. Those specializing in occupational therapy had not even got around to projecting moving pictures on the ceilings. So the idea of dividing a book into acts like a musical comedy and having all-star casts "perform" for those temporarily confined to linen prisons was sufficiently new to spill over onto the best-seller lists of the general book trade. Or maybe the title alone did it.

I insisted the book's format be large enough for writing letters. For love-interest we added a Venus pencil.

After that it was just a matter of counting up the editions. They ran on for years—until everybody got tired of counting. Thirty printings at least. Every notable who got into some sort of domestic trouble had to listen to the joke about the old lady who asked a bookseller for *Fun in Bed*, believing it was the title of the red-faced celebrity's autobiography. In the span of a generation the joke was hung on everybody from Jimmy Walker to Jimmy Roosevelt.

In addition to Harris' life of Shaw and *Fun in Bed*, I had two wraith-writing jobs in the hopper at the time. One concerned an old lady of seventy-five who took a seven thousand-mile trek through the African jungle because her doctor at Capetown ordered a change of climate! She was born on the Cape in 1856, the daughter of a commander of a squadron of the English fleet assigned to break up illegal slave traffic.

She herself married a naval officer who was a boon companion of King Edward VII and, as near as I could make out, one of their responsibilities was the rearing of one of His Majesty's children, presumably by Lily Langtry. I had met the girl in London and had found her quite charming and talented. The running account of their trip from Capetown to Cairo by car and eventually to London was quite exciting. At least they thought it was. But as a book it didn't do very well.

I also was juggling with the literary confessions of another problem child. He, too, was in his seventies. That was Tolly Taylor, the retired Wall Street tycoon. He loved to come in at tea time. We had six people working in three rooms. One of them was an English secretary; another was Alexander Berkman, the eminent anarchist who, being Russian-born, also liked a cup of tea. Taylor was hoping that in all this activity we could squeeze in a book of his reminiscences. I gave the animadversions the title of *Between Panics*.

To give us some vacation from the grind of the Shaw biography, Taylor would invite us up to his palatial estate on Sunday afternoon for tea. We were too polite to say we'd rather rest on the Sabbath than listen to his belated beefs against an economic system which had enriched him handsomely. His teas were elaborate productions compared to ours, involving sitting gingerly on the edge of *petit-point*-covered chairs and watching our manners while being served by two uniformed maids who opened double-doors and carried in a ready-set table. Immaculate linen, highly polished antique silver, and the finest of China featured the repast. The tea was good, too.

This contrasted with the sort of tea party we gave. Actually Tolly Taylor much preferred Ovaltine, but it didn't seem to fit in with the formality of tea at his own home. At our place he could ask for it and get it. He would sit around for hours waiting. As soon as he got his Ovaltine and Norwegian cheese on rye crisp, he would lick his fingers and leave in a state of almost feline content.

Realizing that not much work could be done until he was so served, we advanced the tea hour to conform with his arrival. The capitalist and the anarchist got on very well, though I don't believe Taylor ever realized that Berkman was the gun-toter who had tried to kill Henry Frick, Taylor's friend. This happened in Pittsburgh, and Berkman spent the next fourteen years in prison for the crime. Whether this was because Berkman had failed in his mission had never been established.

Berkman thought Taylor's ideas for economic reform were pretty naïve, but he was most faithful in accurately recording notes of the conversations. In a nutshell, Taylor's contention was that we would have fewer panics and maybe none at all if company officers and directors were not allowed to traffic in a stock which they were hired by the stockholders to protect. He felt that when these company officers issued false statements, they ought to be clinked; in his opinion they were committing perjury. The law at that time was easy to avoid because one had to prove that the misstatement was willful and the *fraud intended*. Until we could x-ray men's minds it seemed impossible to prove intent.

But Taylor felt that it would be easy to prove that a false statement which either depressed or boomed a stock was intended to shake out investors or to make them buy more; and if such a statement was issued by a company officer who had access to all the inside information, his obvious purpose was to unsettle the market; and if a panic followed, he ought to be punished for it.

To challenge an official statement in those days ran into big money. Youngstown Steel stockholders challenged a Bethlehem Steel statement and it cost the Youngstown stockholders a million dollars.

"Why, Charlie Schwab is such a crook," Taylor told us, "that he milks Bethlehem Steel four times a year. I can give you the day and date he does it!"

He looked at us and asked if it were too strong to call Schwab a crook. As Schwab at the time was in nearby Monte Carlo, losing the millions he had milked from stockholders, neither Berkman nor I thought the statement was too strong.

But publishers did. They felt that the material was dynamite and, though true, would make the depression in America worse instead of better.

In the end, we turned the material over to Franklin D. Roosevelt's campaign committee and in his first campaign for the presidency he used plenty of it. In fact much of it became the basis of the new Securities Exchange Law, and up to 1955 we hadn't had another of those old-fashioned panics.

Berkman was a bit of a problem child too. Kicked out of America, he had walked out of Russia, having small tolerance for either capitalism or communism. In France he got on after a fashion, but every time there was a cabinet crisis, and they came almost as often as the *croissants* and coffee in those days, he would be heaved over the border.

The last time he had worked his way back via Brussels, where there appeared to be a clearing house for just such discredited fugitives. He was told to be at the corner at ten the next morning when a car would pick him up. It turned out to be a Rolls Royce. He was admitted to the back seat where two beautiful women, dressed in the height of luxury, were sitting. When the car reached the border he was told to lie across the seat behind them and not to more than breathe. Their fur coats were then spread out to cover him.

At the frontier the owner told the customs he had nothing to declare and all, including the stowaway, were ushered into France. Well within the frontier, his unidentified friends let Berkman out, warning him not to take a through train, as these were watched. "Take a local to Paris," they warned.

Who they were, he never knew. "I never saw them again," he said.

But rather than have this happen every time France had a change of cabinets, I suggested we apprise the minister of the interior that whatever Berkman's dossier showed of his past, Sasha by now was a harmless, tired, and gentle old man. Anita

Loos, Walter Duranty, and others signed the petition with me. After that Sasha was left alone.

He was living with a German girl but would not marry her, first, because he did not believe in marriage and, second, because if he married her, she would lose her German citizenship and be as easily deported as he had been.

Emma Goldman and Berkman seemed to be as good friends as ever. She lived in St. Tropez and he in Nice, and he would visit her for weeks at a time. Her problem of citizenship had been solved by a young Welsh miner who, reading of her plight, had things arranged so he could marry her and thus give her the status of a British subject. This established, he returned to Wales the same day he married her and never saw her again.

Two other hired hands were odd balls of sorts too. One was addicted to making tasseled lampshades in his spare time and seemed to have a dash of lavendar about him. But he was a most competent typist and worked for us for two or three years. He was British and loved tea parties, naturally.

The other said she was a stenographer and told Alice she would like to work for us because she was sure she could inspire me. Alice by now had learned to take this sort of thing calmly. The Inspiration appeared for work next day wearing a big picture hat with a floppy brim and a fur coat that had lost a battle here and there with the moths. She insisted on working in this ensemble for a while but wasn't making much progress.

"Don't you want to remove your coat?" Alice finally suggested.

The suggestion proved ill-advised, because when the poor thing removed her coat she had no dress under it. Alice gave her a dress and assigned her to make synopses of Shaw's plays, rather than have me look on such a sight for inspiration.

Not only did old ladies from South Africa and retired financiers interrupt us. Harris also would drive up every few days in a

Alexander Berkman and Emma Goldman in 1928.

The Scully *voiture* (the original Rosengart) on the sidewalk of the Promenade des Anglais, Nice. Bending over not to embarrass the car is Arthur Schwartz, composer of Broadway hits. Alice and Frank Scully are in the car.

Michael Powell looking all of his 20 years. One of England's greatest motion pictur
directors today, nearing fifty, he looks just about the same.

At the Riviera studios of Harry Lachman, St. Andre de Nice. Reading l. to r., Frank Scully
president; Leonti Planskey; Lee Murphy, American consul at the Cote d'Azur; Frederic
Brown; Princess Quan Tai; Martin Brown, playwright; Nina Wilcox Putnam; an
Harry Lachman.

taxi asking when we would be getting off another installment so he could get another payment. We'd tell him soon, serve him tea, and get him out the door. All the while the meter of his taxi was running, eating up money he hadn't yet got. Then he and Nellie would drive off into the hills for a two-hour ride while we got back to our ten-hour day.

It was Nellie's intriguing idea that we might work better at their flat, because even to her, six people working in three small rooms seemed a bit crowded. She had also asked us not to overwork Berkman. This request had come, she said, from Emma Goldman. I told her Sasha did as little or as much as he liked. He had been an old printer, and he worked on one of those old-fashioned portable Corona typewriters that had to be unfolded to operate and had only three rows of keys. He banged away on it with terrific speed and was a great help in researching and roughing out material.

When Alice was to pick him up the first time, he said she would know him because he looked like a baby. The only thing he had in common with a baby was precious little hair on his head. He was completely bald, short, wore thick glasses, and must have been about sixty at the time.

When he discovered that for all her years in Norway and France, Alice had actually been born in Pittsburgh, he exclaimed, "Pittsburgh! My home town!"

The fourteen years he had spent in prison there was the longest time he had spent in any one town in America, or even in Russia. It must have produced an odd sort of nostalgia when he thought back to his "home town." Still, I never heard him express any bitterness—about that or anything else. This was confirmed by Ammon Hennacy in *The Autobiography of a Catholic Anarchist*, where he relates how Berkman befriended him when both were prisoners at the Atlanta federal penitentiary for their opposition to the draft in the First World War.

I felt I could leave him in charge of our hillside word-factory while Alice and I worked downtown with the Harrises. They had a beautiful apartment in the heart of town. It took up the whole sixth floor of 9 rue de la Buffa. One huge room, Nellie explained, could be cleared out for a workshop. There we could work from ten to noon, have lunch together, and after Frank had had a little nap we might go on working for the rest of the day.

I tried to convince them that the less they saw of us, the more work would be done. But it didn't quite go down with them, so Alice and I agreed to try their scheme.

Here's how it worked out: We would arrive at ten o'clock in the morning. But Frank, it appeared, hadn't had a very good night and wasn't up yet. He slept in heavy woolen under-clothes and pajamas and sweated through them so they had to be dried and aired on the radiators.

These were lying about, but it was eleven-thirty before he appeared. As that happened to be just the moment for his morning walk to the sidewalk cafe of Frank Gould's Palais de la Mediterranée, it was up to us either to join him or work along on our own. We let him go alone. He would, he assured us, be back in a minute. At twelve-thirty he would arrive and begin shouting impatiently, "Nellie, isn't lunch ready yet?" Then with an air of one who had been patiently waiting for hours, he would call to us to come and sit down.

At luncheon he was always gay. After he had a good *hors d'oeuvre varié,* with a bit of onion and a good stiff dram of Graves wine, I would try to extract from him something helpful.

As he never could remember what happened yesterday, but often seemed alive to what had happened thirty or forty years before, I tried to get him to reconstruct things like the Ireland of his and Shaw's childhood. He would scarcely get on the track before some name would pop up, and Nellie would cut in, take the play away, and silence Harris completely.

She doubtless developed this little habit when she saw his memory slipping. Not wanting her guests to realize it, she tried to fill the gap with her own reminiscences. As she was a charming hostess and the luncheons up to the last were always of the best, it may not have dawned on most visitors that the host had become a stooge in his own household.

After a luncheon of this sort, Harris would take two steps from the dining table to a chaise longue and an open fireplace, and before you could say "James Harvey Robinson," he would be asleep. He would sleep on to three-thirty and then, if the weather were clear, he had to go out for his afternoon drive. This was usually a two- or three-hundred-franc taxi drive around the hills of Nice.

Returning by four-thirty or five, he again became impatient for a drink, and it was rarely tea. After that he would wrap himself up in front of his open-hearth fire and, if feeling well, read something substantial; if not, you would be sure to find him with a French paper-back piece of trash like *La Belle Aventurière*. In fact what he was reading was a better index to his temperature than a thermometer.

Such a day, while not a total loss to anybody wanting to write a book about *Frank Harris en Pantoufles,* certainly wouldn't add much to Chapter XVIII of the *Biography of Bernard Shaw.*

After trying this harmless huddle a few times, we went back to our old vice of working in our sweatshop on the hill. I decided, in the light of what meager material we had, to make it a book *about* a Titan *by* a Titan—a sort of Dempsey-Tunney fight on a literary level. It would be, in brief, a battle of giants, and if the David Harris turned out to be bigger than the Goliath

Shaw, would it matter in the least to the reading public if the material were interesting? The publishers, wanting above all else to have the biography authorized, got a rebuff from Shaw. He warned them that Henderson's *Life* was authorized and he deprecated Harris'.

I argued that it was true Henderson's was authorized, but who read it? For our part I favored a book, unauthorized but *authentic*. A report had got out (at least Shaw said it had got out) that the book would contain fifteen thousand words by him. He was not going to write Harris' book for Harris, he announced, and would have the law on us if we so advertised it.

I had been writing letters to Shaw in Harris' name. They were hardly couched in language of a servant to a master. I knew Shaw was mortally afraid of Harris and I didn't let Harris down in this respect. Alice would take the letters down for Harris to sign. On one occasion the fog cleared and he realized for a few moments that he was playing the role of a stooge in a company which had his name on the marquee as the star. Then he really blew his top. He asked Alice if I thought I could write better than he could? It was a humiliating position for all concerned, but he quieted down after a few minutes and signed the letter. It happened to be one in which I told Shaw that whether he liked it or not, we were going ahead with a biography that would strip him down to his long underwear.

To prevent any further feline sort of vaccilation, I copied all Shaw's letters to Harris that I could find. I sent them to Shaw for final editing for release. Once we had these, I didn't care what he said for publication. Then I took half a dozen of these letters, which went from approving of the biographical project to strong disapproval of it, headed them "Credentials," and let them serve as an introduction to the book. I thought that was very funny, for the letters were no credentials at all.

Despite all these intriguing complications, our word-factory on that beautiful Riviera hill turned out copy at a gay and amazing rate. We managed to get 28,000 words to the publishers within a month of the original rejection of Harris' sixty-five page fragment.

If the publishers voted ours no great improvement over what Harris had sent, I decided I would quit and return the thirty-nine dollars I had got for six months of research. To write another man's book under cover, getting neither credit nor cash, wasn't my aim in life, especially now that I was founding the Scully Circus. The first of our trained fleas from heaven was on his way, and it would be a race as to which would come in first—the book or the baby.

Within ten days after mailing the manuscript, we received a report from the publishers congratulating me on the rewriting job. "With some qualifications," the report added, "the material is well organized, well paced, and well written. If the rest is as good or better, it will be a grand book." Then after a lot of detail, the reader's report added: "Once again let me congratulate you on an A-One job."

It was signed by the same Clifton Fadiman who had written the devastating report on Harris' first contribution, which the old unhappy warrior thought would be his last.

On the strength of this encouragement from Fadiman I decided to go ahead with all possible speed. Of course if I had had the horse sense of a burro at that time, I would have shown Harris the publishers' second report and would have said to him: "Listen, you captured old pirate—new conditions, new deal! If I'm to ghost this book completely, we make a new contract, fifty-fifty, and you pay me back all the money you owe me as of today."

But like most people, I could do only one thing at a time. I let all business details wait until the writing was completed. In the next twelve weeks I turned out one hundred and fifty

thousand words. In the end I felt I was too close to it and asked
the publishers to do the cutting. They, however, after bestowing
their praises, indicated certain cuts, and sent back the whole
manuscript to me for the actual cutting. I slashed sixty-five
thousand words out of the manuscript, and it would be hard to
find the seams.

I then wrote the publishers, explaining what I had done and
why, feeling it was then up to them to keep it confidential or
make it public, whatever would be best from their point of
view. Thus, if forearmed is forewarned, they could not say later
that I had purposely kept them in short supply.

Harris' lapse of memory had led us into an expensive trap
and I felt I deserved a pat on the back for relieving them of
paying a stiff fee for this mental bloc which he had suffered. As
ghost writing did not then enjoy the eminence it does today,
there was some doubt felt as to how this information would be
received by the public.

The publishers did not take too kindly to this enlightenment
and wondered if in the excitement of publication I had not been
carried away with my part in the enterprise. My own view was
that at four thousand miles the excitement of publication is not
too great to an author.

Years later when they signed me to do an autobiography, I
wanted to tell the true story of the writing of the Shaw biography. Clifton Fadiman felt that it would make Simon & Schuster
look like fools if they published my version. It seemed it was
all right for authors to look like fools but not publishers. So I
returned the advance and tore up the contract. (I am known in
the publishing world as the dolt who returns advances.)

I subsequently published some of it in a magazine article. It
made nobody look like a fool. On the contrary, it added a little
hilarity to the duller days of publishing.

After the manuscript had been cut to book-length and was

ready for the presses, I called on Harris and suggested that we work out a more equitable financial arrangement of the royalties. I suggested fifty-fifty, as the standard procedure. Nellie insisted that such a division had never been heard of in the history of literary collaborations. After hours of arguing I got my end up from 20 to 30 per cent. Why hadn't I kept that contract that gave me 80 per cent and Harris 20? That would have been a fair distribution of the spoils.

At this point Nellie begged me not to say how much I had done for fear it would hurt the success of the book.

In other words, I was not supposed to say what I had done, and for keeping quiet, I was to be reimbursed inadequately, because the association with Harris, apparently, would be pay enough. If you can clear up that muddled sentence, you can clear up whatever the Harrises contributed to the biography of Bernard Shaw. But like many muddled people, they, too, got their way.

I went home and quietly dedicated the book to myself, choosing my words carefully. I didn't want any friend of Harris saying later I ever said Harris had written the book. So Harris's dedication, which I wrote, ran:

> I dedicate this Book to
> FRANK SCULLY
> who goaded me into undertaking it
> and then wouldn't let me have a minute's
> peace until it was completed

In this way I did not have Harris even say he *completed* the book—merely that "it was completed."

That's true, too. Between Shaw and me it was completed.

That was the last interview we had with Frank Harris, for though we didn't know it at the time, he was not long for this world. The Frank Harris who could walk twenty miles a day at seventy and run a hundred yards under twelve seconds, who once completed a deal merging Glasgow coal mines which made him 125,000 dollars richer and J. Pierpont Morgan just that much poorer, the Harris who had discovered Shaw, Wells, Bennett, and a host of other writers when he edited *The Saturday Review,* was now a foggy old man of seventy-five, feebly alerted only at the sight of two things: wine and women.

Harris often urged me to drink more whiskey, and when I told him I didn't drink any, he urged me to bathe my stump in it. "Nothing stops pain like whiskey."

Harris' case-history and Shaw's, when put side by side, merely prove that a trencherman and free drinker when opposed by a vegetarian and teetotaller may finish this life in an almost dead heat. (Many people believed Harris was more than seventy-five. Those who knew him better than I did said it was the *third* time he had had a seventy-fifth birthday in several years.)

I recall a party we had for him on his seventy-fifth birthday. He drank anything and everything. Alice and I brought Robert W. Service and Milton Hayes to the party. They looked like identical twins and said that between them they had more successfully copied Kipling than any two poets in the twentieth century.

"Every time I see Kipling," said Service, a charming, modest, and self-effacing author, "I sneak down an alley!"

While we were talking with Harris, his ruddy face suddenly turned green. He ran off to the bathroom. Some minutes later he returned to the party ruddy and smiling again, ready for the next drink.

Even pagan pleasures were leaving Harris somewhat weary. At long last he was worrying a bit about his soul, and I certainly encouraged him in this direction. Monsignor Barry Doyle did too. He lived in retirement at nearby Menton. Every now and then he came over to Nice to give the old warrior encouragement in spiritual matters.

Harris's home was filled with priceless church treasures, some dating from the Fourteenth Century. I often wondered what drove unbelievers into collecting such loot, for obviously the stuff had been stolen at one time or another. Was it proof, too, of the diabolical perversity of latter-day owners? Or were they trying to *buy* their way back to a faith they had lost?

It could be argued that I too was more concerned in those days with material things, though I don't believe out of all proportion to the accepted ethic of the laborer being worthy of his hire.

I have often thought since that schools of journalism would be doing better by their students if they taught them the first principles of collaboration. When young, writers know *how* to write but have nothing to write about. Often they run into a notable who has a story but doesn't know how to write it. Such an association is as legitimate as nurse and patient.

But what do young writers know of contracts? When I first made one, I was a thousand miles from an American lawyer. I asked several nationally famous writers who were wintering on the Riviera what was essential in such agreements. They said a contract had to have a time-clause in it to be legal. So I wrote my first contract and put a time-clause of five years in it. That was for Harris's *My Reminiscences As a Cowboy.*

Around 1952 John Huston, Academy Award winner who directed *The African Queen,* announced he was going to make the Harrisian western next. I remembered that as the wraith-writer I had owned 30 per cent of it. I looked up my contract. I had bilked myself out of owning any part of it five years after writing it. Truly, as Ben Hecht has said, barring J. P. McEvoy, all writers are financial idiots. Fortunately, all of them have Guardian Angels who take care of those who ask for their help.

20

The Circus Starts

•

As for the Scullys we had more important productions in the hopper than the biography of an unbelieving playwright who insulted his times and was well paid for it. The most important of these was our first-born. He was due early in August, 1931.

Prenatally we called him "Skip" and do to this day, though he now is a grown man of six feet-three. He got the name because he was a lively little fellow for months before his birth.

We planned for him to be born in the American Hospital in Paris and had much to do before we could leave Nice for the capital. I say "he" because "it" seemed to me to apply only to inanimate objects and a baby from its conception is a soul, not an "it." Jae Greenberg pushed me into one of those silly bets, arguing that it would be a girl. I accepted, though all we prayed for was a healthy baby.

Shopping around Nice before leaving for Paris, Alice found herself frequently the center of interest. Though a young madonna may be revered almost anywhere in the world, no people seem to have as much love and respect for a little mama as the French.

On one occasion while Alice's car was parked on one of the main thoroughfares it was bumped by another car. The traffic cop on that corner was distinguished by a twirled and waxed mustache. When he saw Alice come out of a shop, he hurried

228

over, and escorted her gently to her car, explaining that it had been bumped and that he had taken all the details of the other car in the event her car had been damaged in the slightest degree. It wasn't an easy car to start; so he handed her his white truncheon which he used to direct traffic, saw that she was safely seated, and then pushed her car till it started. She went around the block and then handed him his traffic billy amid many *mercis* and *au revoirs*.

On another occasion Alice was stopped by a policeman who asked to see her papers. She looked so young that even though she was an expectant mother, he didn't believe she was seventeen. One of her papers didn't seem quite in order. She promised to take care of it right away. He demurred and said it should have been done before.

"But just to show you I'm a good sport and to prove I'm right, I'll call a disinterested party and let him settle the issue," he added.

He called a man whose car was parked right next to Alice's. Given the case, and looking the situation over, this gentleman asked, "Madame, why don't you ask to become a member of the Nice Police Benevolent Society? It'll only cost you ten francs."

The gendarme objected on the grounds that if she did that he would lose the chance of getting a percentage of a fine.

"But you cannot refuse, sir," said the gentleman. "Especially if she asks you, and more particularly in view of her delicate condition."

The gendarme reconsidered in view of her approaching motherhood, shrugged his shoulders, and acquiesced to the request. A policeman had to give any member of the Benevolent Society two warnings before he could issue a citation for a traffic violation.

Another policeman, who also doubted she was old enough to

have a license, met with a laughing response, "You don't look old enough to be a policeman, either."

She took out her license and he took out his police credentials. They found they were born the same day of the same year, congratulated each other, and went on their way.

That Rosengart car had one great weakness. Its wheels were put on in such a way as to unscrew the nuts on the right side as the car traveled forward. On one occasion Alice was taking Alexander Berkman home from his day's stint at Villa Grande Vue. While they were driving along Rue de France, the right rear wheel took off on its own. A trolley was heading toward them, and on three wheels Alice steered the careening vehicle away from a head-on collision, managing to bring the car to a halt within a foot of a telegraph pole.

Sasha was scared stiff but managed to hop out as if the police were on his tail. Police were soon on the scene, because the accident happened right across the street from a police station.

The chief of police had seen the whole thing. He came over, again observing that this deft driver was an expectant mother, bowed, and congratulated her on as fine a recovery from sure catastrophe as he had ever seen.

He then telephoned the garage where the car had just been for a checkup. The chief stood by to see that they did a better job this time. Sasha, never comfortable in the presence of police, was baffled by the politeness. Of course he had never been a mother in France. Nor a father either, as far as I know.

The garage rushed two men to the scene of the accident. Seeing it was that old glorified baby carriage in trouble again, they relaxed immediately. One held up the rear end of the car with one hand, nonchalantly holding a cigarette in the other. The second mechanic put on the wheel. The chief of police warned him to make it secure this time, as any further carelessness might get his license revoked.

Sasha was laid up for about four days after the shakeup, but Alice took the bumps in her stride, and her little miracle just kept swimming around as if nothing had happened.

Alice's calmness in the face of all this excitement suggests that motherhood is a natural function, not a disease, and that expectant mothers need not be treated as invalids. They would be much better off if they went about their normal business, which of course would not include jumping from apple trees or getting into automobile wrecks during pregnancy, since they hadn't been doing it before.

But *after* a birth it was my humorless premise that a little mama should be treated like a Dresden china doll for at least four months. I wouldn't let mine out of the house and not even out of bed for weeks, if she could be kept there.

In Paris this gallantry was even more pronounced, if possible, than on the Riviera. Alice's mother and her sister came down from Norway for the blessed event and all of us put up at the Regents Garden hotel, not far from the Etoile. We picked it because it was near the hospital. It was a serene, well-run family hotel. It had a big garden in the rear, with tables under the trees for outdoor dining. The place was run by Czecho-Slovakians from a once-carefree place, now extinct, called Bohemia. They were a sad and sweet people and insisted that when the baby was born we stay with them until it was time to return to the south of France. "We will take the best of care of the baby," they assured us.

When we would go out to dinner it was always an adventure. It was good for Alice to take promenades, but traffic conditions in Paris never were keyed for flower-pickers from the provinces. One had to look left and right and then could not be sure of a safe crossing.

Taxi drivers, who seemed determined to run down pedestrians, would stop on a *sou,* however, at the sight of an expectant mother crossing the street. The trick was to get on the lee side of *une femme enceinte*.

Skip's birth was the most perfect recorded at the American Hospital. Not a scratch accompanied the labor, and Little Alice was pointed out as a model for all motherhood. Many of her Norwegian schoolmates were in training at the hospital. They all rushed to be witnesses to the *accouchement*. One confided during the delivery, "I shouldn't be here really. I'm on duty in the isolation ward, but I *had* to see how our little *pike* was getting on."

Alice immediately imagined her first-born would show everything from smallpox to cholera on his first nursing. Of course nothing untoward happened.

None of our children would have won any prizes for beauty at birth. In fact most of them looked like pretty sad sacks. They had no hair or eyebrows. Their feet and noses were big. But all of them were amazingly healthy and all were good suckers, an optimistic note for those who were waiting for them to grow up so they could fleece them.

Skip had a huge head. His shoulders hardly extended beyond his ears. But he grew into a handsome baby. He was blond with laughing eyes and a broad smile. Except for the first night after leaving the hospital when he cried for twenty minutes, he was as good as gold.

Our next-door neighbor at the hotel had been living there for years. The next day he complained to the proprietor about Skip's crying. Everybody in the hotel pounced on him.

"What did you do when you were a baby?" one demanded.

"If you had done some crying then, you wouldn't be doing it now," another told him.

We offered to move. But they wouldn't hear of it. "If anybody moves, my friend does," the proprietor said.

The guest suggested that maybe a mattress could be put against the door between the rooms to deaden the sound.

"Sure," said the proprietor, "but on *your* side, not the baby's!"

We had no baby-sitting problems. The hotel maids urged Alice to go shopping; they would gladly take care of the baby in her absence.

Once Alice was caught downtown and couldn't get a cab to take her back to the hotel. It was on the day the Tour de France started and she found herself in the neighborhood of the starting point. This race has no parallel in America. It is a bike race around the country and seems to create more excitement than a world series or a Rose Bowl football game.

Alice pleaded with one cab driver after another, but all shrugged their shoulders and pointed to the bikes and riders gathering for the start of the race.

Finally, in desperation, she went over and appealed her case to a gendarme. He too shrugged his shoulders and explained that you couldn't expect anybody to bother about tourist trade, even if it meant their bread and butter, at a time like this.

"But, Monsieur," she begged, "I have to get back to my hotel. I have a baby and it's now past his nursing time."

"You a mother?" he asked incredulously. "You're nursing your own baby?"

She assured him such was the case.

"Taxi!" he ordered.

No one stirred. He blew his whistle.

"You!" he said, pointing to one with the newest cab.

An argument developed. The driver insisted as a free Frenchman he had a right to see the start of the Tour de France without molestation from foreigners.

Another gendarme a few feet away joined them. On learning

the little mother's predicament, he became even more assertive than his confrere.

"*Allez, donc. Vite,*" he ordered.

The driver screamed his protests, took the passenger in his cab, and honked madly toward the Champs Elysees.

Every time he had to stop for a signal, he leaned out of his cab and told all within hearing about the woman in his cab.

"This imbecile," he shouted. "She gets caught downtown when she should be home nursing her baby, and I lost the start of the Tour de France. *Américaine, naturellement!*"

He raced her to the hotel, ordered her out, turned around, and raced back to the start of the race. . . . Bless his heart. May he and his have been spared the cruel fate that was destined to be the lot of most Frenchmen between those days and these.

I had plenty to do as a new-born father. One job was to cable Jae Greenberg that he had lost a bet, certainly no novelty to him, as the casinos along the Riviera well knew. Hoping to confuse him as to whether the child was a boy or a girl, I cable to Si Seadler: TELL JAE IT'S A GOY OVER AT THE FRANK SCULLYS."

"He doesn't say the sex of that there goy, does he?" Jae asked Si.

"Why, Jae," Si told him. "Don't you know Frank knows enough Yiddish that if it had been a girl he would have said a shicksa?"

Within a few days of this blessed event, however, I was joining Alice at the American Hospital. I simply could not be trusted while she was giving her all for *liberté, égalité et maternité.* One morning I was hopping around our hotel room, not stopping to pick up my trick-sticks for support, when I tripped over a suitcase.

To break the fall I grabbed the foot of the bed. It was a big mahogany affair and so antique that it gave way. Instead of breaking my fall, it broke and fell on me. As it came tumbling toward me, my poor old stump, striving to get away from this new attack, went completely out of kilter and I ended with a screamingly painful dislocated hip.

I was rushed to the hospital, and from that day to this I have never been without pain in the area of the sacroiliac. Sometimes it reaches an intensity that nothing can allay. This goes on for two or three days. Then with lamp treatment, hot fomentations, and every type of manipulation from osteopaths to my children's magic hands, it eases off for a while.

While I was in the American hospital, the proofs of the Shaw biography arrived. I was correcting them between treatments when Paris correspondents called to say Frank Harris had died in Nice.

After a lifetime of pagan revels he was all set to embrace Holy Church as he neared the end. His wife sent for Monsignor Barry Doyle. The Monsignor was sick himself and couldn't get over to Nice till the next day. Harris died waiting.

I was to see this sort of race to catch the last train for Heaven many times in the future, as I had in the past. The world seemed overpopulated with Prodigal Sons, all hoping Heaven would rejoice at their last minute about-face. These death-bed redemptions had been going on since the birth of Christianity and were explained more than once by Our Lord in parables. Even so, we stay-at-homes resented the fuss that was always made over runaways who came home to die after having a grand time violating every commandment while on the road.

We had heard many times about the workers in the vineyard who were hired at different hours and all paid the same at the end of the day, and, like the early workers, we resented this equality of eleventh-hour workers, forgetting that they are taking terrible chances and that millions of them do not make it at all. That the parable was told to illustrate God's mercy, not man's sense of justice, made it hard for us to understand. So many times did Christ illustrate that forgiveness was a most important part of His new commandment that we love one another.

"Has anyone condemned you? Neither will I condemn you. Go and sin no more."

"Much shall be forgiven her, for she loved much."

Harris valiantly defended this side of Christ in tilts with Shaw, who was more interested in swordplay than in peace.

Shaw argued, in effect, that Christ was a hot-headed revolutionary, not the gentle and loving person He admonished others to be.

To Harris this was utter nonsense. A man does not admire most, Shaw's career to the contrary, virtues which are alien to his nature. He admires most what he has a little of and would like to have more of.

That was Harris' faith and could have caused rejoicing in Heaven at this eleventh hour reform of one more Prodigal Son. He might very possibly have earned a baptism by desire.

Alice used to ask me what I really thought of the respective talents of Shaw and Harris. They had little in common, really. Harris loved literature and had many original moments. Shaw hung on to Saint Joan's horse's tail to pull himself up after he had squeezed Ibsen dry. He was a prolific writer, a zestful copycat, but after Harris pulled him over into the theatre, he stayed there, piling up quite a pyramid in that one field.

Harris, on the other hand, was talented in many fields. He began life as a man of action and when he turned to literature he studied hard in both America and Germany. He was a great editor. He wrote excellent short stories. (*Montes the Matador* holds up even to this day.) He wrote commercially successful plays. He wrote some of the best books on Shakespeare of his

generation. His biography of Oscar Wilde is even today one of
the three best in the English language. He did at least six volumes of *Contemporary Portraits,* which are still a help to schol-
ars. His *Life and Loves,* which was suppressed, barring the feeble
attempts to pad and peddle the work with laughable pornographic case-histories, has many fine chapters in its four volumes.
In brief, he left behind several molehills and one dunghill. If
the molehills had all been piled together I believe they would
have proved bigger than Shaw's pyramid.

However, that was not the general view of Harris when he
died on August 26, 1931. His body had hardly been transported to the Cimetière Caucade (Alan Dowling paid for the
funeral) before a wave of venom swept over the press of the
world. Long used to the protocol of either good or nothing of
the dead, I was shocked at how badly the press mauled Harris.
It hadn't done as badly by Frank Munsey, an avowed enemy
of a good press.

It was the intention of the English publishers to submit the
proofs of the Shaw biography to the victim who had so unwillingly sat for the portrait, and Harris' death made it sensible to
do this for all editions. In fact, Shaw asked for the privilege of
seeing the book through the press. This he did in a note he
wrote to Nellie Harris from Malvern, regretting that she was
finished with the strange adventure of being married to Frank.
At such a time he thought there was perhaps not enough money
in the house and he was sending her fifty pounds, which she
could repay later out of the biography's royalties. His press
agents made this *two hundred and fifty* pounds and a *gift,* but
even in its more modest form it was a generous gesture on Shaw's
part.

Shortly after Harris' death, a story appeared in the "Literati"
section of *Variety* saying that now that Frank Harris was dead
I survived as the lone author of the Shaw biography.

Nellie wired from Nice demanding a retraction. Not only did she demand it, she started a barrage of friends, including Emma Goldman, to pressure me into doing it. Failing to get the kind of response she asked for by telegram, she rushed to Paris, and then, finding I was not there, pursued me to London. I was there trying to fit my purse and form to a new artificial dura-luminum leg. In her recent widowhood she had developed an understandable concern about Harris' "honor," which most people didn't believe existed at all. In fact, except for her, I doubt if anybody thought he had any.

She assured me if the story were not denied, his reputation would be ruined, the publishers would suffer vast losses, and all of us would be bankrupt. If I would write the denial, her plea ended, everything would be straightened out and we would all benefit financially.

As plausible as this seemed, I refused to be a party to it. It would have been an out-and-out lie, and while I realized that on high levels of diplomacy, and possibly business, expedient denials are often released on the theory that the end justifies the means, I shared an older moral code. Pilate may have washed his hands and asked, "What is truth?" but simple people know approximately what it is and on this occasion, certainly, I knew what it was.

I was sorry to have had to inflict this added suffering to her loss of her husband, so I took her to lunch at an old restaurant in London where Frank often had gone in his heyday. She later made an appointment to see Shaw. She soon left London for Nice, while I went back to learning how to walk on an artificial leg. The new limb had three speeds forward and one reverse and took longer to make than a Rolls Royce. Herbert Marshall and Walter Duranty had made great progress with these DeSoutter legs, but mine turned out to be a rather expensive failure. Laurence Stallings warned me: "You wouldn't let Paderewski sell you a Steinway, would you? In the next war I'm buying mine from Sears Roebuck."

Shaw completed his part in the biographical project, adding a postscript which I knew all the king's horses and all the king's men could not have stopped him from doing, once he saw the galley proofs. In his postscript he said all the derogatory remarks of Harris had been piously preserved and only the facts straightened. This wasn't quite true. In many places Shaw had added to an opinion another of his own. This frequently had the end of the paragraph contradicting what the opening started to prove.

Those who praised the biography as Harris' finest work, (and critics of this genre went all the way from the *New Yorker* to Tobin and Gertz, who called themselves Harris' official biographers) never once traced the source of Harris' inspiration to me, though Laurence Stallings in *The World* did say it was a nice idea of mine to bring Harris and Shaw together.

The book had a meteoric career. It sold 21,000 copies in its first *day* in London, and in New York within a few weeks was leading both the fiction and non-fiction best-seller list. After about three months it suddenly dived into oblivion, and when we returned to New York two years later, it could be picked up on remainder counters for ninety-nine cents.

It was too bad that poor Harris didn't live long enough to read the reviews. They would have sent him into the next world surrounded by a scent of praise, and that's always welcome whether we deserve it or not.

To complete this postscript to Shaw's postscript, a year after the biography's publication Shaw and his wife left London for Monte Carlo to start on their first world tour. Alice and I met them on the train at Nice. Shaw was dressed in a dark raglan coat, a collar and tie, but no dress shirt. In the adjoining compartment Mrs. Shaw, convalescing from pneumonia, was busy packing their bags. It was about ten in the morning.

As he was sailing on the *Empress of Britain,* I asked him if he wanted to die in a reasonably dry ditch, why he chose a sea voyage that late in life? He grinned his wolfish grin (which was the work of nature rather than any design of his), but said nothing. Then he began fussing about getting ready to leave. I told him he had plenty of time. He was quite sure he hadn't.

"Are you trying to teach me local geography now?" I asked.

He then sat down and asked us how Nellie Harris made out on the book.

"All right," I said. "I was the one who fared badly. I grossed fourteen hundred dollars and had to pay all the help out of that."

"Say, *who* did *what* on that book?" he wanted to know.

"Well," I said, "I did about 98 per cent and Harris 2 per cent. No, that's not right," I corrected. "Remember saying you'd have the law on us if we announced you were contributing 15,000 words to the book? Well, you contributed nearer 25,000. When we got through with the final proofs, my part had been reduced to 76 per cent and yours had been increased to 22 per cent, while Harris still held on to his 2 per cent."

"I don't understand how you had the audacity to try it," he said. "Harris knew very little of my life and you didn't know any."

We talked about some of the details and then Shaw said:

"I will say this for the book. The facts are straight. Any student going to Harris' biography of me, as a source book, can be sure of this."

"Then my husband must have known a lot about you," said Alice quietly, exhibiting a Scandinavian sense of logic which seemed to have eluded both the Master and me. He looked at this little mouse and wondered how she got into the conversation.

He asked about my leg amputation. "Don't feel too badly about it," he commiserated. "I couldn't write better if I had three."

"Numbers don't matter," I said. "A centipede has dozens and can't write at all. The thing that matters is pain."

While we were talking Mrs. Shaw came into the compartment. She was coughing and hoarse. "Now, George," she ordered, "get dressed because we must leave in a few minutes."

He got up to go into the next compartment to take off his overcoat and put on his shirt. As we were saying good-by to him, Mrs. Shaw slammed the door in our faces.

Alice and I looked at each other. We shrugged and laughed in an embarrassed way. "I guess Harris was right about her," I said.

We recalled the hardest job we had was to get an accurate portrait of Mrs. Shaw. Her mere name would arouse such anger in Harris, he couldn't see straight. To him she was nothing but a witch. Nellie would try to add her version. I gave them both, and in the end Shaw added his. But this rebuff sent us back to Harris' version.

In a few moments, however, she joined us where we had walked to the end compartment. She said she wanted to apologize for her rudeness. She thought I was a journalist delaying their departure and had no idea I had written her husband's biography. She added that she was in no fit condition to take such a trip and that she had been down with pneumonia only a few weeks before. (This was years before penicillin, when pneumonia really was something.)

They got off the train at Monte Carlo in good time, he walk-

ing with the spring of youth in his heel and she hobbling behind him, hurrying to catch up with George, her vanishing
genius.

That was the last we saw of either of them. At least in parting they knew the truth of one of the most incredible literary
enterprises of the century. And we parted as friends, which
could hardly be said of our relationship up to then.

21

McCarthy Was a Lady

•

ONE of Skip's first presents was a copy of *Gentlemen Prefer Blondes*. It was inscribed: "To Skippy, his first textbook!" It was signed by Anita Loos, the author.

But that wasn't his first textbook, really. A prayer book was the gift of Mr. and Mrs. George Canty, his godparents. George Canty was U. S. Trade Commissioner abroad. He and his wife were among the few Catholics we knew personally in all Europe. Sophie Pihl, Skip's grandmother, and Maxime Levy, *Variety's chef du bureau,* were witnesses to the Baptism. Maxime gave Skip a silver cup which we have to this day. Skip's male twins can fight it out for the title when old enough to battle for a trophy.

We decided to call Skip "Jed Olaf." ("Jed" had been a sign-off code word between Alice and me for two years. It was a telescoping of *Jeg elsker deg,* the Norwegian version of "I love you," and about all the Norwegian I ever learned.) We felt that Jed would serve him well in America and Olaf in Norway.

But the old French padre, fingering down the litany of saints, could find neither Jed nor Olaf among them. We explained that *Jed* was short for *Jedediah* or *Jeremiah,* and that St. Olaf, while he might not have had any standing among the French, had Christianized the whole Scandinavian peninsula and was in excellent standing in Rome.

243

The old French priest shrugged his shoulders and took our word for it. Priests had to take the word of foreigners for many things in those days. Who knows but what he added a *Jean* or *Pierre* under his breath to assure *le pauvre étranger* some sort of saintly protection?

Years later when Skip learned that he had been baptized at the Church of St. Ferdinand, he expressed surprise. His eyes grew big and he asked, "Is there really a church by that name? I thought it was only the name of a bull!"

Those close to show business asked Alice if she had named him after Jed Harris.

"Who's Jed Harris?" Alice asked.

Amid laughter she was asked, "Who's Ibsen?"

"You must know who Ibsen is," she insisted, "because you used his name, but I still want to know who Jed Harris is?"

However, by the time Skip grew old enough to be confirmed he heaved both names out of his life. He took the name of Thomas instead. To us, however, he still remains Skip.

From the beginning Alice was a wonderful mother, soft on the surface with an unyielding moral code which she kept close to her heart. If her baby cried and stopped the moment she picked him up, she knew he was hamming and promptly put him back in his crib. I had told her he would either be her slave or she would be his. She had to make up her mind which it was to be, and after that her heart would take care of everything else. He would have to grow up and conform to the world, or she would find herself ground to pieces acting as a bumper for him. I told her we could get a dog for him to act that role, but a child's character is not developed by being a mama's boy.

Before leaving for Paris, we had leased a dream house on the Col de Villefrance between Nice and Monte Carlo. The house had been the old *octroi*, or custom's house, on the road to

Mont Alban. It had seven rooms, six balconies, and a tower. All the rooms faced south. The view to the west looked over the city of Nice, the Baie des Anges, Cap d'Antibes, and Cannes. To the east lay Cap Ferrat, Èze, and Monte Carlo. To the north the hills climbed toward frequently snow-capped Peira Cava, five thousand feet high.

Across a ravine from us was a new road called the Moyenne Corniche. All traffic from Nice stopped to look back at the incomparable view. And we, when we were not too busy, looked at the tourists admiring a view which was ours round the clock.

I had a bedroom-workshop at the east end of the villa, with French doors opening out on a large balcony. Alice and Skip shared a large room at the west end with French doors which opened on a huge terrace over a two-car garage. He spent his first months in a *moise*, a basket named after Moses, supposedly in honor of the one that cradled him in the bulrushes. Between our bedrooms was the living room. Alice used part of this for her office. This also opened out on a balcony. This one, however, was covered.

Downstairs were a maid's room, kitchen, living room, and dining room. In the dining room was our only heirloom. It was a provençale buffet of enormous size and centuries old. In the center it had a grandfather clock, which had only five working parts. Makers of this clock discontinued the model 250 years before we got it. They must have been philosophers as well as clockmakers, for they arranged to have it ring every hour on the hour and then, a minute later, to ring again, believing nobody would pay attention the first time. The clock has been through war, revolution, strikes, and incredibly rough treatment and still keeps the best time short of the Naval Observatory.

We transformed the dining room into a guest room and when we had extra secretarial help, used the downstairs living room as their office. We had our meals served either upstairs or out-doors, where we had a large marble-topped table under a rose arbor.

Though we lived on a hillside the garden was level because it was laid out on top of a high retaining wall. In one corner grew a large mimosa tree. Despite the fact that we had a sweep-ing view in all directions, the garden enjoyed great privacy. Di-rectly below us was an olive orchard. Of this we saw only the tops of the trees. To the right, down the old Mont Alban road, perhaps fifty yards, was a chapel. It seated twelve. That was our church. We attended New Year's midnight Mass there and afterward took the padre, who was nearing eighty and retired, back to his *retraite*. He had climbed up there on his own power.

Many of the features of this villa we were to recapture in Hollywood years later when we built our own home on the top of Whitley Heights.

This was not a nostalgic afterthought of someone trying to recapture the idyllic past. We always knew how lucky we were. Hardly a day passed that we didn't find reason to thank *le bon Dieu* for what He had bestowed upon us. We were part of a peasant community, with here and there a glamorous neigh-bor. The butcher, the baker (who delivered the local newspa-per), and the postman came by every day.

At that time the supervision of milk in France, the home of Pasteur, was almost non-existent. We were advised not to trust raw milk for the baby, so we used canned milk. One day, how-ever, a French farmer came along. He had been told we had a baby and explained they had one too. He had got himself a cow and now found he had more milk than their baby would need. Would we like to buy his surplus? It would be fresh and un-diluted, he assured us. From then on he delivered the milk him-self. It would arrive still warm.

Others who passed every day were the Blue Devils, the Al-

pine Chasseurs, who were stationed just above us at Mont Alban. They marched by, their berets tilted on a rakish angle,
smoking, singing, and flirting as they climbed the hill—
anything but the disciplined troops of the flatlands. They were
soldiers of the hills and acted the part.

One time we drove up toward the fort in our little Rosengart. The road got narrower as we approached the gate. Since
we couldn't turn, we continued on into the fort before we were
stopped. We felt we were back in the middle ages, for the fort
must have been centuries old. A guard told us we couldn't go
on. We explained we couldn't turn around either. Whereupon
he called a few Blue Devils who picked up the rear end and
turned the car around with us in it, laughed, and said, "Allez
donc."

Many Americans who visited us would ask if we could find
them a place like our villa. The air of contentment seemed to
capture them completely. And the rent was laughably low. But
when they found we had no electric refrigerator, not even an
ice box, no hot water, no central heating, no vacuum cleaner,
not even a hand-tool carpet-sweeper, and that all our wonderful
cooking was done on an old three-burner gas stove that lacked
an oven, they lost interest. They couldn't think of doing without a washing machine, an electric toaster, an electric percola-
tor, and a radio. And our highly polished red-tiled floors—who
would want them, with only one small stove upstairs and a fireplace downstairs to heat the whole house? Not many besides
us, apparently.

But we had a telephone. What's more, it was an automatic
French type that America didn't have till years later. And it
cost only two cents to call Cannes, and forty cents to call Paris.
The service was no worse than in America. The government
owned the lines but you owned your own telephone. You could
take it with you anywhere you liked. But of course you couldn't

use it in America, because there, under free enterprise, you couldn't even *own* a telephone. You could only rent one from a private monopoly.

Where our narrow road met the new wide highway was a cluster of buildings which included a small general store, a bakery, an outdoor restaurant on a large terrace, and a dance hall. It was all called Moreno's.

The music was supplied by one of those noisy organs normally associated with carousels. People would come up from town on Sunday, *le jour du peuple,* dance, sing, dine, and drink their wine. They usually left before sundown, and on their day there was always sun to go down. No matter how bad the weather might have been during the week, it seemed to be always sunny when the peasants climbed the hill.

For the rest of the week, on our hill, it was quiet. We dined at Moreno's when too busy to do our own cooking. The natives were neither French nor Italian, but Niçois. Their language was nearer an Italian patois than French.

Books were kept by entering what was purchased in a long ledger. At the end of the month we had to go through this book and pick out our items from those of other customers and then pay what appeared to be our total purchases for the month.

On one occasion when all the banks were closed and no American exile could get a dime out of the banks, our credit on the Col de Villefranche was better than the House of Morgan's. We had leased the *octroi* for three years and were able to pay forty dollars a month for the estate, so we were presumed to be quite rich.

We called the *octroi* "Villa Variety." Outside, the place had everything. Inside, it had nothing much but atmosphere. We spent about five hundred dollars on furnishings to bring the atmosphere down to the level of living.

Alice loved to sew but had no machine. We went into Singer's and saw a little hand-operated toy costing six dollars. For a joke I bought it and gave it to Alice. She tried it out. It sewed chain-stitch, which meant that if one stitch gave way, the whole seam would unravel. Alice remedied that by sewing down one side, then up the other, and we never had a split seam after that.

The first thing she sewed was a corduroy dress. She cut it on a bias, with seams all over the place. It turned out beautifully and was a good sample of what the little machine could do. She retired it from service about twenty years later. It had sewn woollen dresses, evening dresses, baby clothes, bed covers, chair slip-covers, and just about everything. One part finally wore out. By then, Alice had heard about electric sewing machines. I couldn't sell her on a new part for the old one. Our kids have had duplicates of that original toy and manage to make them unworkable in a few weeks. This is known as progressive education.

Jae Greenberg had sent Alice a handsome set of three cook books, one of which was *How to Cook a Meal in Fifteen Minutes and Nothing Out of a Can*. The others were more specialized, but in the same vein. The whole menu was laid out—what to buy, what utensils to have ready, and so on: for instance, peel the potatoes, put them on, set the table, cut up the tomatoes. Nothing was left to chance. It also had some good advice, such as: "Use the best plates for friend husband and look your best when he comes home." Though I was home practically all the time, Alice followed its advice. She always spruced up as soon as our work was finished for the day and we got ready for dinner.

In addition to our peasant neighbors we had such nearby friends as Kay Boyle and Laurence Vail, Nina Condron, Alfred Kreymborg, Johnny Weaver, George and Tom Broadhurst, Chauncey and Rita Olcott, Winchell Smith, Lady McCarthy,

George and Böske Antheil, Hutchins Hapgood, Morgan
Burke, Ed Hope (Coffey), Peggy Hopkins Joyce, Michael Arlen, Link Gillespie, F. Scott Fitzgerald, Bob and Rose Brown,
Betty Compton, and visitors like Jack Hylton and Borrah Minevitch.

Kay Boyle and her brood lived just above us on the main road
with Laurence Vail. He had been divorced from Peggy Guggenheim who had borne him two children. These and one of Kay's
children by a previous husband, as well as one by Vail, were all
living together. Later Kay and Vail married, and Peggy Guggenheim came down from Paris to be a bridesmaid. I believe,
for the record, I was penciled in as the best man. Alexander
Berkman thought it was disgusting and wouldn't attend the
wedding or the reception. He didn't believe in matrimony, remember.

Someone explained to him that Kay Boyle was thinking of
going to Austria and to America for a while, and that unless
her children were legalized, they couldn't even get passports.
Oddly, the record of one of their children read: "Father, Laurence Vail. Mother, unknown." Kay insisted she was quite well
known, but the French authorities held a different view.

In addition to writing a Willa Cather kind of prose at that
time, Kay Boyle would type the manuscripts of Laurence Vail
and play hostess to all sorts of visitors, from Philip Barry to
Caresse Crosby. She even found time to knit little sweaters for
our Skip and often came down to play with him and have a chat.
She never seemed harried or hurried. She was a sweet and wonderful neighbor.

Nina Condron, a fine Irish poet, must have felt this too about
Kay, because she spent most of her time with her. She once explained to us that she had barely known her own mother. "She
spent practically no time with us children," Nina explained.

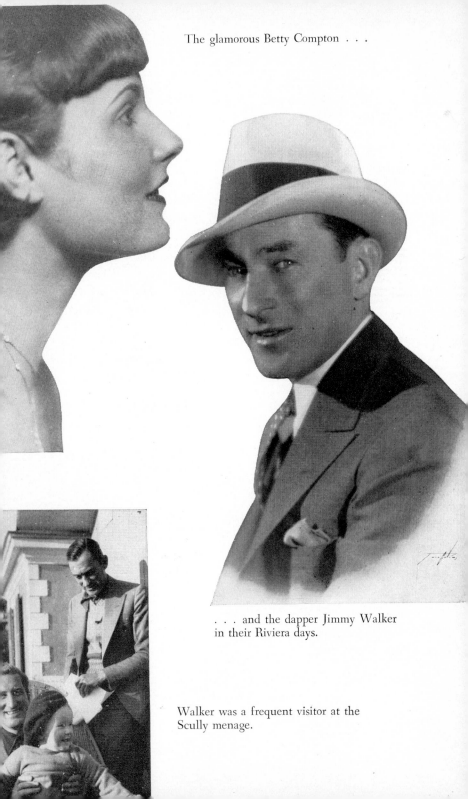

The glamorous Betty Compton . . .

. . . and the dapper Jimmy Walker
in their Riviera days.

Walker was a frequent visitor at the
Scully menage.

Rex Ingram on the *plage* at Nice with two beachcombers, one being the author.

Mormor Pihl, Norwegian grandmother of the Scully Circus, with Skip and Patt.

The author and Patricia in a hairpulling match. He at least had some. The Scully babies never did.

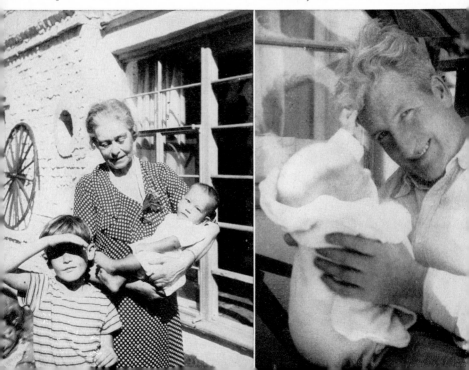

"She was away from home most of the time, lecturing women's groups on child-raising."

Down the road from us lived Raquel Meller, the Spanish chanteuse, who in 1926 opened on Broadway at twenty-seven dollars and a half for the first night and grossed twenty-seven thousand dollars the first week.

We bought our eggs from her. The reason we did so was that our little country store had two baskets for eggs. One was marked "Fresh." Until all those in the basket so marked were sold they remained "fresh." That sometimes took weeks. They were never moved down to the not-so-fresh basket.

Raquel Meller's eggs, on the other hand, were freshly laid the day of purchase. She was a charming butter-and-egg gal. She had a beautiful villa which looked down on St. Jean du Cap Ferrat, where Somerset Maugham and Nina Wilcox Putnam both had houses.

Villa Variety was a busier and gayer word-factory if possible than Villa Grande Vue or Villa Paulette. In our first year there we had four books in the hopper. *Fun In Bed* was going through the final editing. Negotiations on the life of Chauncey Olcott, which had been on and off for three years, ultimately became a positive project while we were at Villa Variety. *Sandrik, Child of Russia,* began its career there and was eventually published in 1933 in New York and London.

We also ghosted and published *My Monte Carlo Indiscretions* by Lady McCarthy. Her "indiscretions" consisted chiefly in wearing short skirts and showing her legs a few years before society began going around the Riviera in bikinis. It was our first adventure as a publisher and we showed a profit of 386 dollars, a high, many thought, for 1931 in the publishing world!

People would stop for tea or a short visit while going from

Cannes to Monte Carlo, or when coming back. That was the way we met Betty Compton for the first time. She was living at Cannes and, being starry-eyed hillbillies, we knew little or nothing of her romance at the time with James J. Walker, the mayor of New York. She came once with Arthur Schwartz, who brought us a huge packet of press clippings from New York. They were not about himself or his shows but about our books. He was convalescing from too much *Bandwagon*. He had known Betty Compton in New York but was rather unnerved at being asked to escort her about the Riviera. On another occasion she appeared with a handsome giant who was the ace stunt pilot of France.

Though there were conveniences we didn't have, there were more wonderful things we did have. Alice had never kept house before, but work was the thing she feared the least. She never knew or cared about the "inconveniences." "For instance," she used to say, "what better way is there to clean a rug than to take the whole darn thing and hang it over something and shake it or beat all the dust out of it?"

Under my study was the rose arbor. People coming in would lean over the balcony and comment on the fragrance of the air. It was only cleanliness, sunshine, and flowers (but is there anything better?)

All the curtains Alice hemmed by hand. She also hemmed the towels, tablecloths, and napkins which she had bought in the Basque country. They were made of pure linen and were so indestructible that we still used them twenty-five years later.

"I was such an ignoramus," Alice now confesses, "in regard to cooking, that I didn't know about the lack of an oven."

While we lacked refrigeration, we did have a cellar which was hewn out of rock. It could be entered from the garden side and was always cool and dry. We kept certain foods there and if we had meat which was not being used that day, we took it across the road and put it in the refrigerator at the general store. Our butter was kept in a clay olla. Thus it was always solid but never hard.

Our peasant neighbors were quite disturbed by Alice's handling of Skip. First, she didn't swaddle him. Peasants used those long white strips of white damask-like cotton. They were woven showing two pigeons flying with a banner between them on which was written "Mon Petit Ange" or another design with "Mon Petit Chou." The bands were about six inches wide and a yard and a half long. These they wrapped around the babies from under the armpits down their feet. The binding was supposed to straighten their legs.

Then, she gave him oatmeal and tomato juice. They held it was crazy to give a baby food of that sort.

"I must explain that until I had Skip I didn't know upside down on a baby," Alice said. "I was living in a foreign country and had nobody to advise me except Evelyn Currey. She gave me a book before Skip was born. It is called *Doctor Chavasse's Advice to a Wife*. It used to send Frank and me into howls of laughter. Every chapter opened with a poem, explaining what glories and joy a wife was to her husband. I got the idea that I couldn't go into labor if I didn't have a four-poster bed to hold on to. We still read it—for laughs. I really raised Skip on a ten cent U. S. government pamphlet called *Infant Care*. And I followed that to the letter, and after we straightened out his lack of assimilation of sugar, he began to blossom into the healthiest, happiest baby for miles around."

We marked with joy each ounce Skip was gaining, and one day I took over the weighing while Alice had been banished to bed for forty-eight hours to get some rest after a minor operation. We had a new little maid at the time. Her name was

Antoinetta. She was seventeen. Italian, she had escaped illegally over the mountains from Italy after her father had been scheduled for the castor oil treatment from Mussolini. They stopped him on the way to church. He asked if he couldn't go to Mass first. They let him go. After Mass, he took to the hills, crossed the frontier, and waited for his wife and children to join him. They settled outside of Nice, growing carnations.

Antoinetta and I were bathing and weighing Skip. I was wearing my new artificial leg. I got up to mark the weight increase on Skip's chart, then planned to sit down again.

But Antoinetta had pulled the chair away from under me. I fell and broke my hand in four places. It was Carnival time, and short of her own head being broken, nothing could have kept Antoinetta away from the Carnival. Then too it was Thursday, her day off. I believe she had started on the previous Tuesday, but being a child of nature with no sense of time, she didn't remember that. All she remembered was it was Thursday and it was Carnival time.

So off she flew, leaving her lord and master groaning with a fractured hand. This was indeed lamentable because, though no acrobat, I walked on my hands because I used elbow crutches of my own design, which put all the weight on my hands. The little mama who had been ordered to bed for two days to allow her operation to heal had to jump out of bed and become nurse, nursemaid, housekeeper, and doctor, for it was Carnival time and you couldn't get even a doctor for the next two days. Alice spent the next forty-eight hours soaking my hand in hot water and wrapping it in fomentations. In trying to favor my painful hand I strained my right hip and stirred up a new sciatic attack. Between the two, I was laid up four months.

Antoinetta was a character. Alice gave her some money one time to go down to the market and buy some vegetables and

fruit. After several hours she came back. No food. She bought
a dress instead—for herself.

Our only wedding gift, that little goldplated alarm clock, disappeared one day. She had accidentally cooked it with the spinach and didn't have the heart to tell us.

One morning after her day off, the doorbell rang early in the
morning. Alice went to open up and let her in. She was only
twelve hours late. At the door lay a beautiful bouquet of carnations, but no Antoinetta. She left them as a peace offering and
then ran off.

She was followed by a chef who had to have all sorts of costumes to fit his labors. He lasted about a week, told us he had
the inside story of the Lindbergh kidnapping, and tried to get
the American Embassy to give him free passage back to America. The Sûreté Général sent an agent to see me and between us
we agreed the informer was strictly a free-loader. He was an
Alsatian who talked French with a German accent.

After that, Alice decided she was better off with no help.
This didn't work out too well either, as she had a baby to take
care of, my secretarial work to do, or part of it, and had to play
hostess on almost a moment's notice. I said I always worked
with the hope of being interrupted, and one day Major King,
a friend from London, high in the brass of United Artists, took
me unexpectedly at my word. I invited him to stay for dinner.

To this day I forget that the little woman ought to be consulted about such things before the invitation is extended. Alice
and I often laugh about how badly this sort of unrehearsed
hospitality frequently works out. On this occasion she decided
to make an apple pie, for dessert, and then remembering she had
no oven she took it across the road to the restaurant for them
to bake it.

Knowing nothing about apple pies, these peasants proceeded
to pile fresh bread on it after taking it from the oven. The pie

arrived on our table looking as if it had got in the way of one of the tanks of the Blue Devils.

Everybody laughed except Major King. He looked at it sadly and said he wasn't crazy about pie anyway.

22

When Irish Eyes Were Troubled

•

Almost from the beginning of our marriage Alice learned to slow down to the pace I had set as the secret of one man's survival. The girl who ran errands with the grace and delight of a faun had matured into a beautiful young madonna. She accepted a way of life which was not that of the general run of young mothers. It never occurred to her to hire baby-sitters so that she too could have a night out. Night life was not for me. Therefore it was not for her.

I did things temperately. She learned to find joy in doing things that way. Others might fly from ecstasy to anger all in one day, but we decided that the little things which most people allowed to develop into quarrels and even crises did not seem to us worth all that commotion. We saved our feelings for things that mattered: admiration for each other's growth, for one thing.

We were serious about many things but not about the things most people feel are serious matters. We had no Joneses to keep up with. But our souls, we felt, were badly in need of repair.

We believed in temperance in *all* things, even in restraint on occasion, instead of free-expression and contraceptives. Frankly, I don't believe Alice knew anything about such things. In fact before Skip was born I had to sort of sit by the fire and figuratively knit baby socks to let her know she was going to have a baby.

This virginal innocence, I know, would be rated by most people today as a sort of fatheaded ignorance, but it is a beautiful thing to encounter and, once met, gives you an inkling of how beautiful it is in its final form of the Immaculate Conception of the Blessed Virgin. People who don't believe those things, whose innocence departed before they reached their teens, have been robbed of the finest flowering of love.

After five children and a quarter of a century of marriage, this spiritual quality somehow still hovers over the Scully Circus. It emanates from Alice. If we ever have a saint in our family, this reformed Lutheran will be it.

She, more than I, believed that people were basically good and that ambition and greed—actually forms of intemperance—made them bad or brought them to bad ends. We tried hard to love our neighbors and to purge ourselves of old racial prejudices. In this, Alice was more alert than I and would show a hurt surprise if I gave vent to an old bias against any group. It was all right apparently for me to say that the Scandinavians were the most civilized people on the face of the earth, which I did many times, but it was not all right for me to denounce my old *bêtes noires,* the Germans. It was hard to restrain hatred of Italian Fascists right across the border and German Nazis just beyond them. I suggested we take a trip to prove or disprove that certain people have goose-step virus for which there is no vaccine short of what is done when cattle go down with the hoof-and-mouth disease. She said we would sometime.

To her, quite rightly, this was temper, not temperance. Once she told me that a sad day in her life took place long before we were married. She had been sent to get a box for packing my portable typewriter. One lid was made to be used for a table across my knees when writing in bed. The price agreed on was three dollars. The pirate, taking advantage of her youth and innocence, charged her six. I was boiling mad at both her and the chiseler. Adding fuel to the fire, she then mixed some hot compresses, dipping one in boric acid when I wanted it plain. She handed it to me. I heaved it at her. She ducked and it hit the wall.

That was the first and last time I blew my top and she must have suspected that it was the dying ember of a violent Irishman, because it was before she returned home to Norway and if she had had any doubts it wasn't the end, I fear she would never have come back. I don't recall that either of us ever said we were sorry. I know I didn't.

Being human as well as holy, she felt on occasion, like all young brides, that home and mother might be easier than living with a genius, junior grade. But when she thought about all the trouble she had taken to get married and all the trouble going back to Norway would involve and how little she viewed the prospect of happiness with anyone there, she told me she went down the road to the little chapel and said some prayers of thanks instead.

The beautiful plans we had made when we married didn't quite go the way we laid them out. They went *better* than we planned, for we asked for what most people would consider very little. "Man proposes and God disposes" is usually interpreted to mean that man has terrific ambitions and God bridles them. That wasn't our conception of the phrase at all. We knew what we wanted. We got more than we wanted.

How could we say that, when within a few months of our leasing our grandiose villa I lost my job? *Variety* began to feel the pinch of the depression and Sime was not one to ask people to take a cut. It was all or nothing with him. If he couldn't pay forty dollars a week for Scully's European Runaround, he wouldn't pay less. So he dropped the feature until such time as his exchequer would show a more favorable balance.

Normally, this would have depressed a family terribly, and millions of families in those days had to sustain such a loss. But I had had so many real troubles that the loss of a job bothered me much less than the loss of a pencil. I just *knew* God would provide if we showed a disposition to meet Him halfway. Sometimes, it seemed, He took care of us when we showed no disposition at all to go out of our way to take care of ourselves.

I realize this violates a basic credo of a hustling society, but I can't help it. That's the way it was. I rarely asked for temporal help anyway. When we heard people now and then complaining that they asked God for favors and He never even answered them, we usually said, "Oh, yes He did. He answered you. He said 'No!' "

Alice and I shared this faith, and the proof that we were right in doing so came right there on that Riviera hill. We lost a job and did better for it. We entered more profitable collaborations —one with Chauncey Olcott and the other with Olga Tchirikova, and our *Fun in Bed* was heading for best-sellerdom.

Sandrik Tchirikoff was a boy of ten when I first met him. His father was a charming ne'er do well, but his mother was a beautiful girl with serene spiritual qualities and a strength of character rarely found in this world. Her name was Olga Tchirikova and she had written in Russian the story of their lives from the time Sandrik was born as an exile on the island of Lemnos off the coast of Greece to their eventually finding a home of their own at Menton on the French Riviera.

She addressed Sandrik directly throughout the narrative. He was the seventeenth descendant of Tzarewitch Berkai, the first converted Tartar prince. Sandrik was the godson of Grand

Duke Alexander, who was living his last critically ill months under the Tchirikoff roof when I first met them.

Born in a hospital tent on Lemnos in a violent rainstorm shortly after the counter-revolution of General Wrangel had failed, Sandrik began a life that consisted of moving from one evacuation camp to another. Finally in Constantinople they got an opportunity to go to Menton. Dreaming of comfort and sunshine, as only refugees can, they found their new home was a cellar. But they worked hard to set up a business and home of their own and finally succeeded.

It was a great story of motherhood under extreme hardships. Olga had been born in luxury, her son in poverty. Their journey together till they reached a reasonable physical comfort to match their amazing peace of mind—which they always had—made this, to me at least, a great human document and one badly needed at the time, especially in America where adversity seemingly was so rare it appeared impossible for anyone to take it in good grace.

Sasha Berkman read the manuscript for me. He said it was written in a beautiful but old-fashioned Russian prose. The quality of the mother, he said, was superb. He, however, didn't want to meet her, being even more allergic to White Russians than to Red ones.

Knowing no Russian, I decided that Olga Tchirikova, Alice, Harry Galland (a young University of North Carolina graduate who was our secretary at the time), and I would talk the book out and would try to come as close to her experiences and intentions as possible. We worked under our rose arbor mornings and sometimes journeyed over to her place at Menton, dining on Russian dishes while the cook, who had already completed his part of the meal, would sit outside and play sad tunes on his balalaika.

One evening she told us about her marriage. It very evidently was a matter of convenience, not of love, but she and her husband always showed great respect for each other. In a refugee camp which was worse than many of the others, Nicolai had asked her to marry him. She had consented on condition he could get her to a place where the living conditions were less gruesome.

Now, twelve years later, they had a most harmonious home and still treated each other with, if anything, greater respect than when they married. Some friends had once asked her how they could do this if it hadn't been love to start with? "How could you be happy?" they pursued. "We were too busy, and still are, to be unhappy," she said.

In Russia they had been a family of great wealth and luxury. Years later she met some wealthy Americans in Paris who had just bought some Russian silver and other beautiful items. They asked her if she would like to see them and perhaps confirm their authenticity. She went to their hotel and recognized the silver as her family's, but she never cracked a sound about it. Instead, she assured them that they had made a lovely choice and that the pieces were indeed authentic. I thought such a story belonged in Sandrik's book, but she fought not to have it included and she finally won her point.

Though a soft and beautiful woman, Olga Tchirikova, like Alice Scully, had a hard and unyielding inner moral core. As George Gobel used to say 'way back in 1955, "You don't hardly see women like them no more."

We spent most of the winter and spring on *Sandrik* and took the manuscript off with us for a final writing in the Tyrol in the summer of 1932. It was published both in London and New York the following year. It got good reviews but didn't do too well. Still, I remember it as a rich experience shared with beautiful people.

Our soothing relationships with the Tchirikoffs didn't rub off, however, on the Olcotts, though they lived only a few miles apart. Chauncey was ending his days a retired millionaire as a result of having sung Irish songs (written mostly by a Jew, Ernest Ball) in romantic plays for Irish servant girls.

We had been discussing the writing of Chauncey's life for several years, but I made it quite clear to them that the last Irishman I had dealt with was Frank Harris, and that since then, publishing friends had taught me about "overhead."

The Olcotts seemed financially able to carry such an overhead (which I put at about three thousand dollars), having about the swankest apartment in Monte Carlo, a house in Sutton Place, New York, and an estate at Saratoga Springs. But Mrs. Olcott seemed quite sure she could charm us into working for nothing.

"The book will make us all millionaires," she kept telling us. It seemed to me these people were singularly unobserving. The harbors were full of yachts and not one belonged to an author. She used every device to avoid paying that overhead. She wined and dined us as if we were royalty, but she wasn't putting down any money for the bricks, figuring, I suppose, that we could build simply with straw. This went on for about three years. It began before I had even met Alice and was going on two years after we were married.

I find all sorts of notes taken by Alice. On one occasion Chauncey dictated to her at a sidewalk cafe for at least two hours. On another occasion we came to the apartment in Monte Carlo for luncheon. Chauncey was indisposed, having eaten too much lobster and drunk too much champagne the night before in the company of Marc Klaw and George Broadhurst. Mrs. Olcott "entertained" us herself with a long account of herself and her healing hands.

She wanted to know what sort of car we drove. Alice told her it was a little four-and-a-half-horsepower car. Rita was an exceedingly well-nourished dowager at the time. In a tired voice she said, "We have a Rolls Royce. But we have to change gears too."

She wanted to know what kind of accent Alice had. I told her it was a tiny bit American but mostly Norwegian.

"Oh, I had a great-grandfather, or something, anyway it was a long way back. He was married to a Danish princess," she said. We looked on this as rather ambiguous name-dropping, whereupon she continued, "Is it true that Danish people never lie?"

As Norwegians are slightly allergic to Danes in the mass, particularly after having lost Greenland to them, a war of words in which Alice's eminent Uncle Johan Mellbye to his dying day never admitted defeat, it didn't seem like a remark a Norwegian would affirm.

I said I thought Danes were like other people. "Some told the truth, some didn't; and sometimes the ones who usually told the truth sometimes didn't, and those who usually didn't tell the truth sometimes did."

This left all hands bewildered, including me. But I wanted to get the conversation away from Alice, Danes, Rita Olcott, and everybody but Chauncey.

"What's the religion of your country?" she asked Alice. Alice explained it had been converted from paganism to Christianity by St. Olaf. In those days everybody was a Catholic, of course, and remained so until the Reformation when practically the whole country joined the Protestant sect of Martin Luther.

"Still, there are more Catholics now in Norway than there used to be," Alice said. "Visits to Lourdes and Rome and such places have opened the eyes of many Norwegians."

Rita then told us something of their tours and how they had had a private audience with the Pope in Rome. Indeed most of her experiences were among the princes of the Church, rarely among its lowly.

Chauncey, she said, had worked very hard until about four years previous to our meeting when he fell ill during a performance and lost much of his memory. She added some trivial things about his popularity, told us he had worked thirty years with the same manager and had started many children in the theater, some of whom later became famous—among them Mary and Jack Pickford and the Gish girls. Incidentally her own career was not slighted in telling us an item here and there about Chauncey.

Recently we found two pages, typed single-space. They were notes which Alice had made the day after her first meeting with Mr. and Mrs. Olcott in Monte Carlo. Reading the notes over twenty-five years later, Alice and I howled with delight at her English of those far off days. Here, exactly, is the way Alice reported the incident:

"Mrs. Olcott told us that she was very interested in medicine and that she had cured her husband by faith and her hands. He was 2 minutes without a pouls and she prayed to her niece who had been a noun and stroke him with her hands and he lived up. Of this she became quite famous and she got thousands of letters asking her to cure that person and this and she had quite a hard time sending back money orders which were sent to her."

Considering the hard time we had to get Mrs. Olcott to pay any part of our collaboration, then or any time later, I can well believe it took a great deal of effort for her to send back money orders after being acclaimed and publicized as a faith-healer.

That "noun" of course is for "nun" and "pouls" is French for "pulse." Alice said, translating it recently, "The phrase undoubtedly means that Mrs. Olcott asked her niece to pray for the success of her mission. She then stroked Mr. Olcott with her hands and he returned to consciousness—which of course might have happened if anybody touched him while he was sleeping. I wasn't there. I don't know. Miracles happen. Maybe this was one."

She remembered her hands were photographed by many photographers and subsequently sculptured in pink marble. In this form, pictures of them appeared in papers all over the world.

She showed us the view of the Riviera from their apartment. The dazzling casino, all of Monte Carlo and the port of Monaco, lay at their feet. Under their feet was a huge rug of *petit-point* which must have taken years of other unsung magical hands to make.

Then she showed us a room which I believe was Chauncey's. Everything came from the period of Louis XIII. By now Chauncey had recovered and joined us on the tour. She said she didn't like antiques much except for that period. Wherever we turned, she did the talking, and if we asked Chauncey anything, all we got was "Yes," "No," or "I don't remember."

We stayed for cocktails and were then importuned to stay for dinner, as Chauncey had recovered from his overindulgence. He sang ever so softly during the dinner while Rita chatted on and on, dropping high society names like mail down a chute.

I couldn't help thinking that here again were Gentiles using vain repetitions. Chauncey, like Frank Harris, had become a muted prisoner in his own household.

Mrs. Olcott didn't quite claim she sang all his songs. She didn't even claim she wrote them, but she did claim to be the inspiration of the best of them and the author of at least one of his plays. Though I was to write his life, only her name would appear on the title page. For this she was willing to pay a thousand dollars extra. It was certainly obvious that by this time around the Olcott home she had become the prima donna and he a tired old super carrying a spear.

He was grateful for the opportunity to escort us alone to the private elevator which led to his garage, and he continued with us outdoors to where our tiny dusty car was parked. We begged him to go in, as the night was cold, but he held our hands and bid us a gracious goodnight, a gentleman to his aging finger tips.

The most regretful part of all this was that as a result of Mrs. Olcott's vacillations and interpolations, we never got Chauncey's story as Chauncey would have liked to have it written. He had none of her social pretenses and was indeed grateful to God for the good fortune that had come his way. He had owned his own company lock, stock, and barrel, and when he retired, the road just about retired with him. He took about two million dollars out of the theatre and died, as he said, with no consciousness of guilt barring his way to his soul's salvation.

After his death we finally got to writing his story, but by then it was wholly through his widow's eyes. It was a long, slow job. I called it *Irish Lover,* but it subsequently was published under the title of *Song in His Heart.* Though I owned half the rights, Mrs. Olcott quietly sold these to Charlie Rogers for a picture, and he in turn sold the package to Warner's for a million dollars.

For once in my life I decided to repair an injustice. This was a reversal of my general philosophy of life. There being only twenty-four hours in a day, I had long ago decided that if you spend tomorrow going backward you can't spend it going forward. To spend a year trying to get money fairly owed you might cost you more than spending the same year creating something new. But in the Olcott instance I felt that people with their kind of money should not be allowed to keep piling it up at the expense of people like us. There seemed to be good social reasons for a suit.

I wanted to include Rita Olcott, Charles Rogers, and Warners in the suit, but my attorneys argued that Warners had bought from Rogers in good faith and therefore should not be considered culpable, even if their title were obviously faulty. Our course was to sue Rita Olcott instead. She avoided service and finally the attorneys got court permission to plaster the notice on her Sutton Place house, but by various devices she kept getting delays and continuances up to the time she died.

It was established that the book rights were sold to Rogers for 25,000 dollars. Of this Rita Olcott had got half. I was entitled, as the person who actually *wrote* the book, to 50 per cent of what she got. Her estate asked if we would settle for four thousand dollars, which we did. Warners grossed more than three millions on the picture.

It was the first and last time I ever went to court about a thing like this, and I'm not particularly proud of having broken an otherwise perfect record of treating injustice as little more than ashes in one's eyes on a windy day.

23

Fun with *Fun in Bed*

•

Aɴ ᴏʟᴅ specialist in public relations, now kicked upstairs to the basement of *belles lettres,* I felt the urge to do something funny and exciting to stimulate curiosity and possibly increase the sales of *Fun in Bed.* I remembered that Nina Putnam had brought over some furniture from Colonial times to decorate her villa at Villefranche. Among the things was a four-poster bed. This gave me an idea.

I went down to the old town of Nice and bought a volume which was printed in the 1770's. It had a blank page. I tore it out. Then I studied George Washington's script. After mastering his signature, I purchased an old gold coin, a Louis as it was called, such as would have been in circulation in Washington's time. Then carefully imitating Washington's script, I wrote:

"I have had much fun in this bed and following the customs of Molière, am leaving a pourboire."

I wrapped the gold coin in this message. I figured if I reported I had found it they would guess the tieup immediately. So I took it to George Antheil at Cagnes.

He and J. P. McEvoy were going to write an American opera around Mac's *Mister Noodle,* the story of the rise and fall of a comic strip artist, and George himself had talked me into working with him on a musical version of Voltaire's *Candide.*

269

(Whatever became of those projects?) I had taken Otto Kahn over to the Antheils for luncheon in the hope of interesting him in backing the *Candide* show. The banker was kindly disposed toward young talent in those days. So all of us were rather clubby at the time.

I told George he probably would be getting a call from some French journalists about Washington and the gold coin. "Brush them off," I told him. "Tell them you have it but that you're a busy composer and can't be bothered with nonsense like this right now. If they insist, show it to them and then tell them to be off about their business."

Then I had the French newspapers tipped off about Antheil's loot. They rushed from Cannes and Nice to Antheil's place. One carried a camera to photograph the documents. Asking how the objects got there, it was explained they had been found hidden in the mattress of an eighteenth-century bed which had been shipped from Connecticut to Nice.

Antheil played the character part perfectly. He made a brusque admission that he had the note and the gold coin and then closed the door on them. They pleaded with him to let them see the message. He finally did. They asked if they might photograph the message and the coin. He let them do it. Then they asked him to let them see the bed. With this he blew his top and told them to get lost and quit bothering him.

They printed the story and the photograph of the amazing document. When the American newspapermen in Nice saw it, they telephoned the news immediately to their Paris offices. One of them, George Axelson of the *New York Times*, was asked by his Paris manager, "Sounds like a publicity plant, doesn't it?"

"For whom?" demanded Axelsson. "For Washington?"

So his boss accepted the story and cabled it to America.

The French press didn't let it stop there. They began a great inquiry. Did Washington actually know Molière? Was the word *pourboire* commonly used for "a tip" in the eighteenth century? Were the Americans so dirty they didn't clean a mattress in 150 years?

I had hoped that when the story reached America it would start a whole epidemic of mattress-ripping, particularly in those places where George Washington was supposed to have slept. In fact I sent a duplicate of the document and a gold coin to Dick Simon, suggesting that he have it slipped in a mattress in the Newburgh headquarters of Washington. I arranged for another friend to find it there. But Dick Simon had lost some of the dash of his youth and was afraid to go along with the gag.

The biggest laugh in connection with the exploit was the story in the *New York Tribune*. Their copy reader, not wanting to offend the fine sensibilities of the paper's suburban readers changed "I have had much fun in this bed" to "I've had a good night's rest in this bed."

That killed the gag. Instead of a free ad for *Fun in Bed,* it was a piece of posthumous publicity for Washington and Molière, neither of whom needed it.

In time I told the newspapermen all about how I had conceived the publicity gag, and everybody had a good laugh. I don't know whether it ever sold a book or not. Stories like the nurse who came into a room, saw a sick priest laughingly reading the book, and rushed out shocked to report the scandal to her superiors, probably sold more books than my elaborate Franco-American joke.

John Emerson and his wife, Anita Loos, had told us about a health resort in the Tyrol mountains that had done wonders for Emerson's throat. He had lost his voice years before, but this treatment, they assured us, had restored his speech.

The place was called Bad Reichenhall. It was a few miles west of Salzburg. I decided to take the cure to arrest an increasing sinus and throat infection. We planned to take the rough draft of *Sandrik* with us and complete it between treatments. These took about six weeks.

What to do with Skip became a problem, not from our point of view but from the point of view of friends who thought we were acting too much like gypsies and not enough like a nice bourgeois family. By now he was the happiest and healthiest baby on the Riviera. His hair was as blond as wheat straw, his cheeks a rosy red, and his body tanned all over from sunbaths. He looked good enough to eat, like peaches and cream. It got so we could not take him to the old town when we went shopping. Natives would cry in ecstacy at his blond beauty and often snatch him from Alice's arms and run up and down alleys proudly showing this miniature Viking from the North to our olive-skinned neighbors from the Mediterranean.

Evie Currey begged us not to take him on tour through Italy, Austria, and Germany. He would be subject to all sorts of possible infections, she argued, and he might even be kidnapped. The Curreys were not leaving town. Their grown daughters had gone to Gibraltar for the summer. Evie and the Colonel therefore had a practically empty villa. Why not leave Skip with them since they had nothing else to do?

He was just about a year old at the time and was so easy to take care of that we were not keen about giving him up even for a few weeks. But Mrs. Currey stressed the health-hazards of a long trip. We finally agreed to leave Skip behind with her.

We asked her, however, not to let him get overweight. It would be as bad for him to get too fat as it had been for him to get too thin. In church he was so good that natives would come up to us afterward and remark on what an angel he was at Mass.

We instructed Evie to cut out his evening meal as soon as his weight reached twenty pounds.

Before we delivered Skip to Mrs. Currey, however, we ran

into a character who was driving a horse-drawn fiacre around Place Massena in Nice. He was standing in the driver's seat. (The driver had been reduced to a passenger.) He was dressed in San Tropez pants of Copenhagen blue, a dark blue sweater of a marine, and a naval officer's cap. He also was sporting a beard. He snapped his whip at us and cried, "Hi, kids!"

"Borrah!" I replied. "Borrah Minevitch!"

"Hop in," he ordered, "and I'll drive you around town." We tried to, but the driver was sitting there.

"Move over, *cochon*, I mean, *cochier*," he corrected. The driver moved over to make room for us.

While we drove around town, Borrah explained that since I had last seen him he, too, had become a father. To a little girl, in fact. Her name—will I ever forget it?—was Lydia Ellen.

Unfortunately, in New York Borrah had made a bet with Sam Rothapel, known in show circles as Roxy. If it were a boy, Roxy would have to take a trip to Africa and if it were a girl, Minevitch would have to go.

Why Africa? No reason. Just to make it harder.

Roxy was opening a new theatre and planned to introduce Minevitch and his Harmonica Rascals as the opening attraction. He intended to build these mouth-organists into a complete symphony orchestra. But since the opening was months away, Roxy insisted that Minevitch make good on the bet. When Borrah demurred, Roxy and others, London-bound, kidnapped him, only to learn when they were on the high seas that Minevitch had been born in Russia and they hadn't bothered to get him a re-entry permit. When he landed in Europe, however, Roxy took care of that and then told Minevitch, "Now kid, you take that trip to Africa, bring me the canceled press clippings, and be back in plenty of time for your opening."

As the Riviera's grief commissioner without portfolio, it was only natural that Borrah should come to me with his problem.

He wondered if I could help him get some publicity out of the deportation. This didn't seem much to ask. I blithely said, "Of course."

Minevitch proceeded to charter a yacht, planning to sail from Cannes to Corsica and then to Tunis, feeling that if he merely set foot on African soil, that would satisfy the conditions of his bet with Roxy.

I gathered all the correspondents together and invited them to a going-away party aboard Minevitch's chartered yacht in the harbor of Cannes. He had re-named the yacht the *Lydia Ellen*. The child wasn't even there. She was in New York. But her mother and father were there, posing for all sorts of pictures for the news photographers.

Alice embroidered the name Lydia Ellen on a little sweater of Skip's. He wore sailor pants and a gob's hat and was given the honor of breaking a bottle of champagne across the *Lydia Ellen's* bow at the christening. He was so brown and healthy that any change in his routine made him smile more, not less.

The going-away party became pretty rowdy. Minevitch had too much liquor on board and the newspapermen proceeded to push each other around. I began to wish I had never become master of these bacchanalian revels. Somehow I got them all back to dry land, and Minevitch set sail for Africa. He was to cable us from Corsica and later from Tunis.

For several days no word came from him, and the reporters became alarmed. They began to dog my steps for news. I suggested we go down to the American consul to see if he could trace the whereabouts of the ship. The consul said he couldn't help unless French authorities reported a wreck or something.

I hired a private plane and cruised up and down the coast looking for some sign of the Minevitch yacht or wreckage. I saw nothing.

The correspondents kept sending out stories, but the Paris news bureaus had been warned by New York to cut down on cable costs during the depression—anybody planting or sending in phony publicity stories would be fired. Everything we did, Paris checked to see if we had actually done it.

After three days of fruitless search I received a telephone call. *En fin,* it was from our wandering Borrah. But he wasn't calling from Corsica or Tunis; he was calling from Monte Carlo. Somewhere along the line he had got the idea that he could get just as much publicity if he sneaked into the harbor of Antibes, tied up there, and then, incognito, went over to Monte Carlo and tried to recoup his investment at roulette.

By this time all the reporters were in up to their necks, and since it was one of the worst years of the depression, all of them felt the hot breath of dismissal. I promised to help as best I could.

Each day they would meet at a little cafe in Nice and plot a way to recover from their plight. I decided to take Minevitch completely in hand, but when I sought to call him back, the bird had flown. A few days later he called from Paris, saying he was in hiding there. He had picked one of the best-known hotels to hide in. He then said he guessed he would go to London for a few days to prolong the secret of his whereabouts.

"Listen," I screamed, "you can't go anywhere without detection. Now you have police hunting for you. You better get back to that yacht and make good and keep out of the way of any gendarmes on the way back from Paris to Villefranche or wherever you scuttled that yacht."

Minevitch said okay, and that he would be calling later when he got back to where he had left the yacht.

Instead of doing this, he went to a little town not far from Marseilles and hired a fisherman to row him out of that port and into another. There he waded ashore and asked a gendarme the way to the post office. At the post office he wired the American consul that he was safe.

Then he wired me a nice cock and bull story to the effect that the crew of his yacht kept cruising up and down the Mediterranean at a thousand francs a day, and when he saw they were not doing anything but eating up his money, he dived overboard and had a fisherman row him into the town near Marseilles. I gave the wire to the correspondents. They checked with the consul. That got everybody off the hook.

From the south of France he went to Paris and then to Cherbourg to catch the *Bremen* for New York. Apparently he was still wearing the gay fisherman's garb and beard which he had worn when he left Cannes aboard his chartered yacht.

He arrived in New York a hero in his own eyes, but he was clinked and held at Ellis Island. The re-entry papers Roxy had fixed up for him were missing. Minevitch had packed them in his trunk. On purpose? Why not? This of course gave him a new fanfare of publicity. In the end it was all straightened out, but he didn't go into the new Roxy or the Capitol or wherever it was with his eighty-piece orchestra of Harmonica Rascals. The deal was all washed up by the time a tired Borrah got back to New York.

He got booked instead into Loew's State, where the management ordered him to shave off his whiskers. He wouldn't do it, claiming they were now part of the Minevitch Story. He went to court. He got an injunction, thereby winning his point. Then, to further confuse everybody, he went to the barber's and ordered his beard shaved off. Naturally he got all kinds of publicity.

A year later I met him in New York and was amazed to hear him tell me the whole story as if it had all happened, including the pirates who had kidnapped him on the Mediterranean. To his dying day he probably believed it did.

This, in a terrifying way, happened on June 26, 1955, near Paris, while I was correcting the proofs of *Cross My Heart* at Desert Springs, California. Years before, Borrah had returned to France and had become a Francophile. He had produced pictures abroad and had bought an old mill in Mereville which he refurnished and renamed *Moulin de Minevitch*. It became a rendezvous for visiting V.I.P.'s.

Three weeks before his death, he married Lucille Watson Little, artist and former wife of Deems Taylor. Abel Green, editor of *Variety*, flew over from New York to be his best man. More than forty French and American notables attended the wedding.

On the Saturday night a few hours before his death, Borrah had a dinner date with Frank Folsom, president of R.C.A. He never kept it. He suffered a cerebral hemorrhage and was rushed to the American Hospital at Neuilly. There he was reported dead on arrival. He was only fifty-two. R.I.P. to his gay, sweet soul.

His madcap adventures had enriched my life but had exhausted me, too. After I was through with his 1932 Mediterranean adventure, I felt I was back in Arizona with that Cherokee Indian who sold me a piece of a lost gold mine I had created out of whole cloth myself in the first place.

24

Viva Vino Santo!

•

IT WAS a beautiful summer's day as we headed toward the Italian frontier in our Rosengart, ultimate destination Bad Reichenhall, Germany. To get there we would have to cross Italy and a part of Austria. Long acclaiming myself as president of Gate-Crashers International, Local Number 7 (the lucky one), I never seemed to learn that the quickest, although the dearest, way to move around the world was to have your papers in order.

America at that time was charging ten dollars for visas to visit the United States. In reprisal, foreign countries charged us ten dollars for visas to visit them. As a thousand Americans traveled abroad in those days to one foreigner making a tour of the United States, the trade balance in visas was all on the side of the foreign exchequers.

I had found that one could clip nine dollars off that charge in many countries by asking for a transit visa. In a tour of Europe, one could save fifty dollars by this method.

According to a transit visa, however, one was supposed to pass through the country en route to elsewhere in twenty-four or forty-eight hours. But after one passed the frontier, who counted the hours? I've stayed for months in countries on transit visas. In those days customs officials never bothered to check passports going out of a country, only coming in. It was a racket, anyway. Englishmen could travel anywhere, visas to all countries included, for about two dollars. Their passports seemed to last forever. Ours lasted two years. Then the stickup started all over again.

Some persons like red tape. It makes them feel that what they are doing must be dreadfully important to require such scrutiny. To me this is one more proof of how hard it is for liberty to live unless the bureaucratic weeds are constantly trimmed back and even cut down now and then. Not being strong enough to cut them back, I have followed the practice of walking around them.

I've known many who crawled on their bellies across frontiers, sometimes taking several nights to do it. Some took bullet holes with them. Once in a new land, they went to places where faked passports from their native land were sold, and were thus guaranteed some measure of freedom for a while. France was full of such émigrés.

Going from France into Italy in those days, especially at the Riviera border, was not an easy, breezy transition either. Frontier guards bristled and took it out on tourists, the Italians more than the French. Mussolini was brandishing his state capitalism around, a sawdust Caesar of a balcony empire. He was all for discipline—for everybody but himself. The Fascist symbol of the old Roman Empire was everywhere, and the private lives of the top-level Fascists were about on par with those of the dissolute patricians of pagan Rome.

As Alice knew no Italian, I briefed her on the short ride to Ventimiglia where our old friend Dr. Serge Voronoff was still making a fortune out of transplanting monkey glands into the old goats who still pranced around Riviera casinos and villas, shining with sex appeal and loaded with silver dollars. We didn't stop to pay him a visit.

I told her all she needed to know in Italy was *"Quanto*

costa?" (How much?) and *"Troppo!"* (Too much!) With these two phrases she cut the cost of our tour of Italy practically in half.

Her first surprise, however, was at Ventimiglia. We were stopped for customs inspection. At least four varieties of guards stood at attention while Alice was ordered to lug her biggest suitcase into the customs house. She tripped and stumbled over the bag.

Not a hand offered to help her. They all saluted and let the flower of Norwegian womanhood get up on her own. Whatever her feelings may have been previously about a country bogged down with military trappings, this first proof that an officer is not necessarily a gentleman cured her forever after of confusing the two.

Ever the informal gypsy, I had no papers to speak of. I bought a transit permit to drive through Italy. But instead of driving steadily on to the Brenner Pass, we decided to mosey around Italy awhile. We bathed at Alassio and spent the night near Genoa.

In Milan we viewed the Duomo and decided to take a picture of it. No parking was allowed in that area, so we called over a traffic cop and asked him what about it? He said he would let us park and take pictures of the cathedral provided we first took pictures of him. This we agreed to do. We took his name, number, and address. It certainly must have surprised him when later from Germany he actually received the pictures as proof that some of the best-kept contracts are those which are never written.

We discovered that every time we asked for directions to a certain town, all we got in return was *"Sempre diretto"* (Straight ahead).

We also made another discovery—never clutter a request with a lot of polite and badly mangled Italian. Don't say: "Please sir, if it pleases you, will you direct me to the ancient and honorable city of Milano?" All you needed to shout was *"Milano?"*

That did it. Even a peasant understood that much Italian.

We stayed one Saturday night in Pavia. Is there anything like an Italian town on a sunny Sunday morning? They are all so gay and holy. Girls who are not twins dress up as twins. Peasants who wear shoes to church take them off on the walk back to their farms. Those better off repair to sidewalk cafes for a Cinzano after Mass.

Alice and I were sitting outside one of these cafes and I was remarking that Mussolini had not misappropriated the loan he got from America to build roads. The main highways at least had been improved.

At the sound of his name I felt rather than saw three persons slide up behind us on the inside of the cafe. The windows were open. Alice noticed them at the same time. Two were officers. I decided we would get out of the place. Snooping, which couldn't be shelved even for Sunday mornings, was not my idea of sunny Italy.

Though it was off the main road to the Brenner Pass, we decided to go to Venice for several days. This was in the nature of a honeymoon. We had never considered our short hop to Cannes as worthy of the name honeymoon. Venice was more like it. Before driving to Venice, however, we spent the night at a hotel called Albergo Tre Re—the Hotel of the Three Kings. In days of old it actually was the hotel of kings traveling from Vienna, Venice, and Milan. It had retained its beautiful simplicity through the centuries. The rooms were like whitewashed cells in a monastery, but the furniture was of the most exquisite mahogany—all of it. The kitchen was huge and had a gallery of hundreds of copper cooking utensils.

Alice was dispatched to make the arrangements. She asked, *"Quanto costa?"* The manager said, "Twelve lire." Alice thought he said, "Twenty-two lire." She would have said *"Troppo"* if he said "Two lire." He offered to throw open a wine cellar which could be used to garage the car for free. For eight lire he would give us a chicken dinner, and by that he meant a whole chicken. In those days eight lire amounted to forty cents. It became such a convivial party that he trotted out some new wine. It was so rich that it had us all reeling, the proprietor included, before the chickens could be caught, killed, drawn, and roasted.

We got to bed early and observed that the gates were closed by dark. It was a moonlight night. Characters began crawling out of the woodwork and congregating in the enclosure below. Soon they began a *boule* tournament. This was a game of rolling balls toward a small circle and then trying to knock the nearest ball away from the goal. It was accompanied by a great deal of shouting, handclapping, and bravos. It went on till midnight.

Nevertheless, refreshed, we came down from breakfast in the morning to continue our drive toward Venice. When we backed the car out of the wine cellar it, too, almost reeled. In fact for the rest of that day every time we breathed, the car didn't smell of gas or the air of the great Lombardy plain, but of the fragrant aroma of new-made wine. We decided that the three kings must have lived very well—especially for sixty cents a day.

In Switzerland I had read Hilaire Belloc's *The Road to Rome,* as delightful a travel book as was ever written. Didn't it inspire me to want to do likewise? Apparently not. Why didn't I care about visiting Ireland, or Norway, or Rome, or the Holy Land? Or even Lourdes? Something obviously was wrong with me.

Alice didn't push it either because she knew we were always close enough to Rome to run down there any time. Besides, we had to get on with our work in the Tyrol and then get back to our home and family. She had been to Lourdes and the seed of faith planted there, though it lay fallow a long time, ultimately flowered. But at that time she was a Lutheran who had accepted the conditions of a mixed marriage but had not been fired by any precept or example of mine to become a Catholic.

Still, she had better reasons for going to Rome than to Lourdes. For one thing her great-grandfather was buried in Rome. He had been Norway's greatest historian and, though a Lutheran, had had access to even the back files of the Vatican Library. To see the grave of such a distinguished ancestor might have been reason enough to visit Rome. But she was a resolute person. We were passing through Italy on the way to a health resort. When we did what we started out to do, she felt we had to hurry back to her first-born.

When I think of the sacrifices many people make to visit Rome, I still can't believe we made so little effort. We were sure it would always be there. We seemed to think we would too, and would get around to a meeting in the not too distant future.

We never did. Instead we became a part of the highest mountain in the world, the mountain of pilgrims who never made the pilgrimage.

I took Alice for rides in Venetian gondolas instead, even going as far as the Lido. After a week we left for the mainland and proceeded sorrowfully toward the Brenner Pass.

Just before reaching the Brenner Pass, we stopped at a little hotel in the Dolomites. I looked around Cortina d'Ampezzo, hoping to see Dr. Vittorio da Putti who had a clinic specializing in heliotherapy. I met instead an Italian who, like us, had the heart of a gypsy.

When he found that our papers were not in order, he told us about a friend he had at another point on the frontier. He

was sure this friend could fix it up for us to go out that way
without trouble. In fact he drove with us fifty kilometers to the
border, introduced us to his friend, exchanged money for us,
and arranged for us to go out that way the next day. Not a lira
of graft was involved. This route, however, would have required us to go to Vienna and then cut back toward Salzburg.

We changed our minds the next day and instead of cutting
over to the friendly frontier, we moved straight ahead toward
the Brenner Pass. Every few miles we were stopped by some
character in uniform.

About ten miles from the frontier I had Alice go in a little
mountain inn and change to her "frontier dress." This was a
dazzling creation of soft red wool, cut with a V-shaped bodice
and adorned with silver buttons. It was a frock designed by me
and made by her. She looked stunning in it.

At the frontier itself we were confronted by such a variety
of *soldati* as would be found in a Hollywood back lot when
four different musicals were being filmed at the same time.
There were Alpinistri, Carabinieri, Fascist militia, and some
uniformed derelicts left over from the Napoleonic invasion.

All of them agreed that we had no credentials worthy of the
name. They had a hard time keeping their minds on the papers,
however, because Alice's dazzling dress kept distracting them.
Finally one officer, pulling himself together, indicated that one
of the documents said that if we had any trouble we should
have wired Rome for an extension.

"Where does it say that?" I demanded.

They pointed out the paragraph.

"Surely," I said, "it says it in Italian, in German, and in
French. But it doesn't say it in English, does it? And they took
my English pounds."

At that time the English were in good favor in Italy and
I decided that for the moment I would waive all rights as an

American of Irish descent and broaden my *a*'s till we got past the frontier. One officer said to the other, "That's right, it doesn't say it in English. He has a point there."

"Okay," I said. "You work it out while I go over to the rest room."

I left Alice behind to mop up.

Her flaming red flannel dress which was cut like a form-fitting military uniform to the waist, and then flared out in a skirt like a skater's, really had them unnerved. It was what the style-makers called ravishing. The only trouble was that Alice had an antipathy against wearing flaming red woolens in July.

When I came back, the victory was not quite complete, but very near it. The guards were sighing like a lot of Romeos.

"You know," I said softly to two of the officers, "I'm traveling for a news syndicate. Il Duce has circulated a lot of propaganda to the effect that it is very easy to travel by automobile these days. But my papers don't believe it. What I'm looking for is material to show how *hard* it is to travel this way. So you see, you guys are really my friends. You're giving me just the material I need. Thanks a thousand."

With that, one officer looked at the other and almost immediately they reached an accord. They ordered the rest of the guards to push our car across the border and bowed to Alice as if she were the Greater Garbo.

Into Austria at last, Alice and I laughed and felt like free people again. There were no uniformed characters crawling over each other on the Austrian side, and we were treated with a warmth and hospitality that we had forgotten existed since we had left France.

In Bad Reichenhall we carried on the treatments and worked mornings from eight o'clock to twelve without a break. On such a schedule we finished the polishing job on *Sandrik* in six weeks and were free to travel around afternoons.

We visited Berchtesgaden, a mountain stronghold between Reichenhall and Salzburg. At that time it was a peaceful hill town where women made the prettiest of formfitting sweaters, usually black with red and green collars and cuffs. Lanz of Salzburg featured them.

About the time we were there, Gottfried Reinhardt offered to drive Otto Kahn to Berchtesgaden from Salzburg, but Kahn refused, having vowed never to set foot inside Germany until Hitler was no more. This was in 1932. How many people recognized Hitler as the world's Number One Menace as early as that? He was a clown to most cultured Germans. He couldn't even speak good German.

The only obvious flaw in life as we lived it at Bad Reichenhall was the appearance of Prussian troops that came down for maneuvers. The sight of their gray uniforms changed the natives from free-going, smiling peasants into grim humorless realists. They explained to us that they hadn't seen Prussian troops since the end of World War I. "It seems the trouble is beginning all over again," one said.

Even the girls in the *Bierstüben,* who are not above harmless flirtations normally, served the soldiers in silence. When the troops paraded, their band playing, not even the children stood on the curbs to watch them.

In the town at the same time was the first brown-shirted Nazi we had ever seen. He was literally the village idiot. Everybody laughed at him, as kids do at a clown at the circus.

To us who had just come from Italy, this was a bad sign. It showed us how hard it is for the human race to protect itself from new forms of attack on its liberties. The Tyroleans concentrated all their fears on the gray uniforms of the Prussians. These had been a familiar menace to them. They didn't realize that that village idiot in the *brown* uniform was a *new* menace destined to overshadow all previous menaces. A boy of sixteen could have obliterated that menace in 1932. But by the next year this plague had grown to such proportions that it overwhelmed Germany and Austria and not many years later looked as if it were going to overwhelm the world.

When our suspicions were confirmed by 1933, it convinced us that life as we knew it was destined to be a dead chapter in the life of all Europeans, and we prepared reluctantly to pull the Scully Circus out of Europe and to try replanting it in less restricted soil.

It was a sad decision to make. Both in Italy and Germany we had found the people, as distinguished from their rulers, easy to understand and to love. Wherever we went, kids and grownups gathered around our quaint little car and soon we were kidding about it as much as they were. The churches and chapels were full of pious souls, many of them poor. To see whole communities stop while a funeral went by, the men removing their hats and all blessing themselves while saying a prayer for the deceased, was to see people who knew what was important and what wasn't.

In the Tyrol the natives greeted us as we passed by with a warm and loving phrase. It was *"Grüss Gott!"* (God's greetings to you!) How much more beautiful than "Heil Hitler!" In those hills ruins of the bombings of the First World War could still be found in great numbers. Even many churches had not been rebuilt. But the people managed somehow.

Austria seemingly had come out the worst, and Austria, as far as we could see, had learned its lesson best and wanted no more of power politics with the devil in the driver's seat and good souls taking the hindmost.

The *gemütlich* quality of these people cropped up in the most unexpected places. We advertised for a typewriter. Along came a man wheeling one in a baby carriage. We looked at it and decided to take it. The man pushing the baby carriage turned out to be the mayor. He said he had been wheeled about in the carriage when he was a child.

In lower Bavaria too, despite the fact that it was the starting place of Hitler's mad schemes to liquidate all but his blood-letting pagans, there were plenty of good people. Before he liquidated himself, Der Führer had destroyed five million Jews and six million Catholics, not to stress many more millions who were just good people of no particular faith beyond a love of liberty and neighborliness.

Yet in Munich in 1932 you saw little of what was going on underneath the surface. We asked a policeman if he could direct us to a modest-priced hotel.

"And do you know where we can find a really good cheese cake?" I added.

"Käsekuche?" he asked.

I nodded.

He smiled and gave us directions to a place at the far end of town. We were heading that way anyway, having decided to return home by way of Lago di Garda rather than the Brenner Pass.

The next morning at a traffic intersection we were stopped by a *Polizei's* whistle. A cop came over to us and smiled. "Did you get your cheese cake?" he asked. "And was it good?"

He was the same policeman who had directed us the night before. He had been transferred to another end of the town the following morning. We told him everything was wonderful. He wished us *Grüss Gott* and off we went toward the frontier, never to return to Germany. It was a pleasant memory.

In a town called Riva at the top of Lake Garda we stayed overnight at a small hotel and noticed a wine freely advertised as Vino Santo. This meant either "wine of health" or "sacred wine." We asked the price of it and the proprietor said twelve lire. That seemed a lot of money, so we ordered a quarter of a litre, which worked out to twenty cents for about a pint. We didn't drink it at the time but dropped it under the seat of the car.

Driving down the west shore of the lake, we passed the point where D'Annunzio had been exiled by Mussolini to spend his days on a wooden ship which projected into the lake.

It was a beautiful sunny morning. Suddenly the right rear wheel of our car sounded as if it had exploded. We stopped and got out and discovered that one of the spokes of our over-sized baby carriage had come loose and torn its way through the inner tube, practically destroying the tire.

We had a small jack which, even so, was too big to get under the axle, and when stretched to its limit was too small to raise the wheel so that a new tire could be put on. An able-bodied man could lift the car, it was so light, but neither of us was able-bodied. So we built up a base with rocks and things, hoping for the arrival of a Good Samaritan to give us a hand.

Finally a large car drove up and stopped. Here, we felt, was our Good Samaritan. The Germans all drove large cars in those days. This was a German. He got out of the car, bowed to us crawling in the dust, walked across the road, took out a camera, photographed us in our misery, saluted, smiled, got back in his car, said *"Guten Tag!"* and drove off.

I swore like a blue streak—a habit Alice has since helped me break.

When Alice and I got back in the car we could hardly say a civil word to each other. As usually happens in such cases each party silently blamed the other for the accident. At this point Alice began complaining about her throat. I took her temperature. It was 104 degrees.

"May I have a little of that wine?" she begged. I reached for it. She took a swig. "Mmm," she said, "good."

She took another swig. "It's warming my throat. It's doing good."

She kept telling how much better she was feeling, and after a few more miles I took her temperature again. The fever had gone!

I was convinced that the sacred wine or wine of health, however the phrase translated, could certainly perform minor miracles.

We stopped at the south end of Lago di Garda to see if we could buy some more. There was no more to be bought. It was, as politicians say, a local issue. It seemingly was such a delicate wine that it got "car sick" at the mere thought of being transported.

The rest of the trip was a series of little accidents on a par with the torn tire, and every time a frustrating thing reared its ugly head, we dowsed it with Vino Santo.

On the last day, hurrying along the Italian Riviera in the hope of reaching home before sundown, we even passed up eating. As hunger gnawed at our vitals, we each took a teaspoonful of Vino Santo. Within seconds we felt as if we had just got up from a seven-course dinner!

There was still a little left and we agreed we should save it for the frontier guards. "If it looks like trouble, I'm going to ask them to have the dregs of this wine," I said. "I know to your Scandinavian sense of honor that sounds like stooping to bribery, but I'm too tired to care right now."

The car was bogged down with small purchases and the officials could have saddled us with custom duties and perhaps a confiscation here and there.

This time the Italians waved us out of their country as if we were plague-ridden. The French guards were down to one. It was getting late. He wanted to get home too. He asked us if we had anything to declare.

"Nothing to declare," I said.

He looked at our passports. A picture of Skip dropped out. He picked it up and smiled.

"Yours?"

We bowed proudly.

He stuck his head in the car, got a whiff of the miraculous wine, and smilingly ordered, *"Allez donc, mon brave!"* which roughly translates, "Okay, old-timer!"

We were back in free France at last.

We talked about that wine for months but could never find a priest or any connoisseur who had ever heard of it. We began to believe we had dreamed it.

Then one day, while lunching at the Reserve de Nice we happened to mention it to Conte Mario del Turco. The wine, it appeared, was not unknown to him. "In fact," he said, "the madre wine stock from this Vino Santo came from our vineyards in Tuscany. In the Tyrol these stocks developed a grape and a wine that really did perform miracles, but the wine sours and loses all its miraculous qualities in a matter of days if transported so much as fifty kilometres from its source."

He later tried to send us some and, as he foretold, in transit it had lost all its powers for healing and most of its bouquet as well.

25

"Your Baby Is Dying"

•

Is THERE any feeling of elation quite equal to being released from bondage at a frontier? Especially if you're heading for home? Prisoners on being paroled must share it. Discharged soldiers, too. Penitents who have made a good confession and have had their sins forgiven them must know the feeling best of all. Everything seems to move faster afterward.

We hurried through Menton, Monte Carlo, Beaulieu, Villefranche, and even Nice, hoping to get to Skip before sundown.

Evie Currey's villa was at the Fabron end of Nice. We didn't quite make it before dark. By the time we arrived, Skip had been put to bed for the night and it seemed sensible to acquiesce to her pleas that we return around ten the next morning when she would have everything ready for us to take him home. All we saw of him that night was the outline of his little head in a darkened room.

We went home, disappointed, to Villa Variety, unpacked, and tried to recapture some of the elation we had felt on crossing the border into France. It was good to be home, but without that gorgeous little brown bomber with the blond hair and blue eyes the place had a funereal feel about it.

The next morning we were on the *qui vive,* anxious to get our family together and to get back to work. We arrived at the Currey villa at ten. There in the shade, wearing a sunhat, sat a pale, fat little child, his eyes like slits. It turned out to be our Skip.

He didn't look at all like the Skip we had left six weeks before and he didn't act like him. He turned away from us and crowded against Evie Currey. Six weeks away and he didn't know his parents from two fence posts down the road! So much for the natural instincts of babies.

Evie's idea of a beautiful baby had won over ours. She believed the more rings of fat a baby had around its wrists and ankles, the prettier it was. She had piled food into Skip until he had gained eight pounds in six weeks. We feared fat because it doesn't all go to wrists and ankles. Some of it surrounds the bronchial tubes, and Skip was wheezing as proof that his air space had been cut down too much.

We thought the sun had been doing wonders for his general condition when we left. Evie was afraid of it, so she had kept him in the shade with a hat on. We had always encouraged him to go to anybody who held out arms to him, believing babies are timid enough without encouraging their shyness. He had lost this friendliness, too, apparently.

It was quite a revelation to see how two schools of thought, both believing they were doing what was best for the child, could produce such opposite results in such a short time. We couldn't blame her. She loved Skip and she loved us. We took our crying little stranger home with us, all of us obviously disappointed and heartsick.

Not many days later Skip's wheezing increased and he began coughing. We called a baby specialist. It was a drizzly, cold afternoon, but the doctor told us to bring the baby down to his office. He said he was tired and didn't feel like coming out in that sort of weather.

Alice told him not to bother. She would not take a sick baby out in that weather either. We called Dr. Bernard instead.

Though he lived at the other end of town, the Fabron end, and was a general practitioner, not a specialist, he came right over. He diagnosed the case as broncho-pneumonia. He telephoned the Children's Hospital and reserved a bed. Then he helped us bundle up Skip to take him to the hospital.

There Skip went through more tests. It turned out he had diphtheria as well as broncho-pneumonia. "We have one chance in a thousand," said Dr. Bernard. He asked us to give him *carte blanche* to do whatever he saw fit.

The hospital was a few blocks from Dr. Bernard's home, seven miles from ours. It was run by Sisters of St. Vincent de Paul, the nuns who wear those huge starched white bonnets that look like swallows in flight. We sought a private room for Skip, but the nun who had charge of the babies' ward assured us that he would get better treatment under her care in the ward. She must have had thirty babies, all under a year old, in her safekeeping.

Dr. Bernard told her and us that from this moment on Skip was his baby and that she was to call him any time during the day or night. She called him as many as six times in twenty-four hours. In all, Skip stayed in that hospital, hovering between life and death, for eight weeks.

He suffered one crisis after another. The diphtheria vaccine seemed to set up a toxic condition which left him with asthma after the pneumonia crises had passed.

Dr. Bernard was so sorrowed by all this that he advised us never to have fewer than three children. "Something might happen to one," he said, "and in any case you don't want to raise a lone child, do you?"

He was a warm, tall, Norman, with a soft reddish beard, very matter-of-fact in speech, and he spoke excellent English. As the years went by, we realized that this was the soul of France. In Abbé Van den Daele, the Curé d'Ars, and Dr.

Bernard we found what we loved and admired; others found it in Voltaire, Anatole France, and Clemenceau.

At the hospital, visitors were not allowed after seven in the evening, and incoming calls were not received till the next morning. So we took to driving around the hospital each night; when we saw a light in Skip's corner, we felt comforted and knew he was still alive. We dreaded that night when we would drive around and find the light out in that corner.

We learned that one time the Sister had worked forty-eight hours without getting off duty. We asked if we couldn't put a special nurse on to relieve her at night. She assured us that wasn't the solution. "His condition changes so rapidly from minute-to-minute that a stranger might fail to heed the changes and he would be gone," she said. "Last night he actually did die, and I kept breathing my air into him while stimulating his heart. That got him past one crisis—it's the only way I know to save his life."

She was a small slight old saint, perhaps fifty, who obviously had worked hard all her life. She would pin up her tremendous white starched hat so it would stand straight in the air. This way at least it was out of her way. If it weren't for her and her love of God and therefore for the least of his children, a little stranger, the son of foreigners, never would have made it.

During this period, Alice credits me with the best piece of acting she has ever seen. We were lunching with friends at Villa Variety. Skip was scheduled to come home the next day. After six weeks the battle appeared to have been won. The telephone rang, and since it was right next to me I answered it. The call was from Dr. Bernard.

"Your baby is dying," he said.

Skip had suddenly suffered a critical reaction to the horse serum in the diphtheria shot.

The shock was so unexpected and so devastating that I was

trying desperately to disguise it lest I pass it on to Alice, who might not be so able to take it after all she had gone through. I told her as calmly as I could that the call was from Dr. Bernard and that he wanted her to go over and visit Skip right after lunch. As the lunch was just about over anyway, we excused ourselves and hurried off to the hospital.

It was obvious Skip was more dead than alive. Alice kissed the palm of his hand. That brought a small remembrance and he smiled. Then he went back to battling for air again.

We, in turn, went back to making the rounds, driving around the hospital at night. It was around the time of the kidnapping of the Lindbergh baby. As we drove around in the dark, we consoled each other. "At least we know," I said, "where our child is. We know he is getting the best possible care and the rest is in God's hands."

After a few days Skip passed the crisis and in two weeks we were able to take him home.

Dr. Bernard told us he must never eat horse meat. "This allergy probably will never be cured," he said sadly.

We assured him we didn't intend to feed anybody horse meat.

"Then don't eat beefsteak in France," he warned.

He never sent us a bill for Skip. I noticed that mine never included those scores of calls he made on Skip. We tried to broach the subject many times. He always shook his head and smiled. "I told you he was my baby while he was in the hospital, remember?"

Another stalwart of that time was Maria, the peasant woman who did our laundry. She lived across the road a little up the hill from us. She would come down the road trundling the laundry in a wheelbarrow. She took it to the public washing troughs, a cold-water, hand-powered, open-air laundromat which was just below the chapel.

There were two basins into which spring water was piped.

They were hewn out of gray rock. One of the basins was for the soapy water, the other for the rinse. The water was ice-cold, and there were no facilities for hot water. The front edge was slanted up to form a type of scrubbing board. The peasant women had a paddle. With this they whacked the clothes.

Maria would then wheel the clothes up to our house and hang them in our yard. She was a tall, strong woman with a queenly posture. She had two older children and was very evidently going to have a new baby. Alice asked her when she expected it. She didn't know. "When it comes, I'll be ready for it." She went on picking up clothes, washing them, and earning a little extra money for the baby's arrival.

Three days after this conversation, her baby arrived. It was a little girl. Four days later Maria came by for more laundry.

Her husband was a little shrimp with a strong will. He obviously was head of the family. He insisted she was to nurse the baby whenever the baby wanted. "Demand-feeding," it's called. She preferred to follow the custom of the time and feed the baby on a clock schedule. But she obeyed her lord and master.

At times she would take care of Skip when we had to go out. She had him for the afternoon before he went down with diphtheria and pneumonia. Alice rushed over to Maria and asked if she might take her and her baby, then about six months old, down to the hospital for a checkup, since it was common knowledge that diphtheria was a communicable disease. Maria stood there like a queen and told Alice she was not afraid. The baby appeared healthy and she would accept it as healthy.

"Let me know if you change your mind, will you, Maria?" Alice asked.

Maria smiled but stood like a statue representing faith. There wasn't going to be anything wrong, that was all there was to it.

"Many a time when I have been afraid I could only think back with admiration of Maria," Alice once said. "Many people could say she was foolish, ignorant, and all that. But she had experienced sickness, and even the death of two of her children, so she knew what it was. She could have been afraid of hospitals, as many were, but she certainly wasn't neurotic, and she proved she was right. And maybe it is strange, but of all the people we know who have had the advantage of education and the conveniences of civilization, I don't remember anybody who gave me such a sense of strength and courage and goodness and trust in God as Maria—unless it was Abbé Van den Daele."

The Abbé was a regular visitor and the source of our spiritual strength during those dark days. Though retired, in a way, from the actual hard work which had been his lot in the wilds of Canada, he liked to do some missionary work—just to keep in practice.

He would come up for luncheon about once a week. "On condition," he said, teasing Alice, "that you have either poached egg on toast with spinach, or a hamburger." Of course he wouldn't mention grapefruit. He craved them. But they cost about fifty cents apiece at the time. We always got some for him and he made no bones about how delighted he was at the sight of them.

He was very tall, thin, with white soft hair, very clear pink skin, and the bluest of blue eyes. He would come in his priestly robes, which in France is usual, wearing a very flat black broad-brimmed derby, which also is part of French clerical garb, and wheezing from the walk from the bus to our house.

His hands were big and gnarled from hard work and frostbite he had experienced through years in a much more severe climate than he was enjoying in Nice. He belonged to the Oblate Fathers and seemed to get his converts by the best method—fine example of what faith can give a person.

He and I would have lively conversations on religion, and I suspect it baffled Alice a bit to see that faith could be such fun. When we first met, awed though she was by such a character as I, the big strike she held privately against me was that I was a Catholic.

"I was not broadminded on the subject," she confessed. "I had all the arguments of a prejudiced anti-Catholic. While Frank was in the hospital I tried several times going to the Episcopal Church in Nice. The Lutheran Church to which I belonged seemed too far away. But whenever I felt really miserable I found myself in the Chapel of Sacré Coeur, where Abbé Van den Daele would see me and smile and bow to me in passing. He grew on me. His fatherly interest was something my heart was starving for.

"When I was a child we used to play games, some of which turned out pretty morbid. My father would take short trips and ask me to come along. One time I didn't go with him because I claimed I was too busy. While he was away, we played a game in which I was a little girl whose father had died. That was the last time my father asked me to go with him. Within a week he was dead.

"That cured me of playing games I wouldn't want duplicated in real life. For the next fifteen years and until Abbé Van den Daele came along, I felt this fatherly loss continually. The Abbé seemed to supply the needed sublimation.

"When he and Frank would discuss the verities, I wanted to join. But I could not find a point of entry. One day I said I'd like to ask a few questions about Catholics. They wanted to know why. I told them it was quite possible that someday I might want to become one myself. Frank objected. He said converts were humorless people and he felt that such an added cross would be too much for him to bear. The Abbé said I shouldn't consider such a drastic step merely because my husband was a Catholic. I'd have to have deeper personal reasons than that."

Later she said she definitely wanted to become a Catholic and if we wouldn't help her she would go somewhere else for instructions. This shocked the old Abbé and brought him to heel.

After that she was allowed to join our discussions. One day she brought a story to one of our seminars that was a dilly. She got it from the life of the Curé d'Ars, whose photographs so reminded us of Abbé Van den Daele. A rich lady wanted the Curé to help her procure some relics. She sent an emissary, being too busy to go herself. "Tell her to make some relics herself," the Curé told the emissary.

From the first we have tried to teach ourselves and our children that if a thing can be done, we can do it. If saints can come out of this vale of tears we believe we can do it too. It's amazing how much one can do by trying. Before you know it you've accomplished it, life is over, and somebody is collecting your relics! This, at any rate, is our objective. How close we will come to it, of course, God only knows.

It's heartbreaking, and wonderful too, to see a little baby making a long uphill fight—armed with nothing more than love and his own will to live. Even after we got Skip home, life was touch and go for him for a long, long while. At the slightest sniffle we knew that whatever we did we would be battling for his life in twenty-four hours. This happened at least eight times in ten months. To ward off pneumonia, we would wrap him from head to foot in hot, wet fomentations. As all struggling only made matters worse, we wrapped him inside these steaming compresses as if they were strait-jackets.

We tried music to see what this would do to soothe him in a crisis. Some music drove him wild; other music helped. The songs of Rodgers and Hart, and Schwartz and Dietz seemed particularly to soothe him. Larry Hart had given us a complete set of his songs as a wedding present and they now were serving as lifesavers.

Oddly, Al Jolson drove him crazy and we soon got rid of his records. Indeed, I was so fearful as to how badly Jolson had scared Skip that, years after he was well out of the woods, I dreaded taking him to see a preview of *The Jolson Story*. But by then either Jolson's voice had mellowed or Skippy's allergy had been so dissipated he showed only pleasure at Jolson's singing.

But the thing that calmed him most when life hung on by a thread was a frail little thing of Arthur Schwartz's called *I'll Always Remember*.

Tom and Iva Broadhurst visited us often in those days. They had retired from Broadway. They were much older, but we enjoyed a wonderful warm friendship. Tom hoped that the next Scully baby would be a boy and would be named Tom, after him. It didn't quite happen that way, but years later when Skip took a name for confirmation, not knowing the Broadhurst wish, he took the name of Tom.

Skip's greatest disappointment after an attack was that he would tumble and sprawl when he tried to walk again. This made him weep bitter tears. He remembered he could walk before. What had happened to his legs?

One visitor would walk with him, encouraging him as if he were a friend who had imbibed too freely. "Come on, Skip," he would say, "I'll take you home to your wife. You shouldn't have taken that last one for the road. Come on."

Skip would stumble and stagger and hold on to his friend's hand.

The friend was Jimmy Walker.

26
Lord Jim Dandy

•

Tʜᴇ role of father-confessor to knights in tarnished armor was becoming mine more and more as time went by. I seemed to catch the great ones either when they were old, in ill repute, or on the downbeat. This dismal design, like Hollywood type-casting, showed up again in November, 1932.

J. P. McEvoy had just come over for a short trip and was returning to New York on the maiden voyage of the *Conte di Savoia* as one of George Peck's press guests. He wasn't the happy, carefree Mac we had known in Paris. The sweep of the depression had caught him in its net, too. *Americana*, a revue starring Jimmy Durante and Ruby Keeler (and bothered by Al Jolson who was enamoured of Miss Keeler and subsequently married her), had failed to come off with the usual McEvoy success. He had dropped close to 100,000 dollars on it.

Meanwhile his children were gadding around Europe and America. He seemed determined to conceal from them, his daughter Dorothy particularly, that he was not a coupon-clipping millionaire but a genius who had his ups and downs. We argued that they should know the facts of life, as he had known them and as we had known them.

Even at that moment we were making a lark of penury. We would hunt out the cheapest restaurants in backstreets. We made a specialty of those not costing more than twenty-five cents for a good luncheon, a penny extra for a napkin.

302

While we were sitting on our balcony after breakfast one morning we were interrupted by the arrival of a cable. It read:

FRANK SCULLY, VILLA VARIETY, OCTROI, NICE.

TALKING OF YOU TONIGHT AT SEA ON THE CONTE GRANDE WITH GREAT LOVE AND AFFECTION. SOME OF US WILL BE SEEING YOU SOON.

BETTY COMPTON, JAMES J. WALKER, NAT FERBER.

Two I knew. Walker I had never met.

Mac suspected it was an overture to my writing Walker's biography. He seemed to feel it would be an excellent subject if honestly told. I reminded him that *Variety* had recently carried a front-page story that the *Post* was offering fifty thousand dollars for it, however told.

Beyond the vague outlines of his career as a playboy and a politician, nobody could have known less about Walker's private life at that time than I did. He had made a tour of Europe the summer before and had been warmly received everywhere. He seemed to be America's answer to the then Prince of Wales —gay, handsome, charming, a ladies' man and, additionally, a wit, which could hardly be said of the Prince of Wales then, now, or at any time.

I had heard that he had got into some sort of trouble and had been forced by an old pal suddenly grown stern, Governor Franklin D. Roosevelt, to resign as Mayor of New York because Judge Seabury had found many things wrong with his administration of the municipality. There was also a report that a "Madame X" was mixing up his love-life.

"Madame X," of course, was Betty Compton. We had met her several times during the spring previous to the arrival of this friendliest of cablegrams.

Later that day a postcard arrived. It had been mailed from

Gibraltar. It showed the *Conte Grande* at sea. There was a cross over one cabin. "Mine!" wrote J. J. Walker. A steerage porthole was also marked. "Mine," wrote Betty Compton. "Ha, ha!"

It was clear these people thought I was as familiar with the details of their love-life as they were. Such candor, especially when detailed on a picture postcard, just about knocked my surviving pin from under me.

Nevertheless, if they were now prepared to Tell All, and respectable magazines and publishers were anxious to pay for these confessions, who was I to wonder about the changed literary tastes in America? After all, since I had swallowed a camel like Frank Harris, why should I now strain at a gnat like Jimmy Walker? If I were asked to be my brother's keeper, did I have to act as his judge and executioner as well? Since by now I had come to the conclusion that all money was what the Russians called "dirty paper," what was wrong with earning some of it and having Maria wash it so that all of us could use it for legal tender to pay our bills?

Did the cable company balk at transmitting Walkerian messages paid with such tainted money? Did International Tel and Tel turn over to charity the 25,000 dollars the company had received the previous year from Mons. Walker and Mlle. Compton as payment for their sweet talks between New York and Cannes?

Even when I dug into their story I found only one hotel that didn't seem particularly pleased to cash their kind of money. As for lawyers, doctors, dieticians, and the like, these had no qualms about such payments. So why should a character like me feel particularly debased and ashamed by such a transitory association?

I had long formed a habit of being myself and trying to let others be themselves. I didn't conceal my belief that I thought my way of life was better and that a holy family was the happiest family. But beyond that I didn't go unless asked. I felt sorry for Walker. I felt sorry for everybody who was in a mess, and he *was* in a mess.

He was a Catholic who had brought public scandal on the Church. He hadn't lived with his wife presumably for several years. But they hadn't been legally separated either. The writer of a song entitled "Will You Love Me in December as You Do in May?" Walker's answer to his own question seemingly had been "No." He had been running around with other women for years. Now he appeared to be caught in the tightest web of all. He had fallen in love with one of them. She had become his mistress and, as has frequently happened in history, the one-time master had become the slave. His unwillingness to give her up had ruined his political career and was having religious repercussions involving his soul.

Flattered by the cablegram, Alice and I went down to meet the *Conte Grande* when it put into the Port of Villefranche. Nat Ferber, like J. P. McEvoy, had come over planning to return to New York a week later on the maiden voyage of the *Conte di Savoia.*

By the time the *Conte Grande* reached port, Walker looked as world-weary as a lunger working on his last cough. He was a ghost of the buoyant playboy of the rotogravures. He weighed 125 pounds, about the same as Betty weighed, and they were dressed in mackintoshes of identical cut and material.

"Jim!" called Betty. "Come over here."

He moved through the maze of customs inspectors, hotel guides, taxi drivers, *porteurs, marins,* and trunks, pulled a languid hand from his mackintosh and shook mine as we were introduced.

"Hello, Frank," he said with the simple, easy air of an old and tried friend.

As such intimacy fetches me very easily, I found myself doing all I could to help a fallen idol.

Thus I met the once Beau Brummel of American politics, appearing like a wraith out of a chilly haze that had suddenly turned the usually sunny, sleepy port of Villefranche into a picture version of the London docks. Unshaven and pallid, he had pulled his mackintosh up to his chin and his hat down over one of a brace of bloodshot eyes.

The Riviera correspondents were anxious to grill him as soon as he cleared the customs. He was equally anxious to avoid them. He had a call to make to Paris and he wanted to find a hideaway as soon as he got that off his chest. I told him to go to our villa just up the hill, as any telephone call of his would surely be tapped in a hotel. He could, I pointed out, go from our place to a retreat like the Hotel du Cap on Cap Martin. I added that I'd give the newspaper men some sort of story to mollify them.

I led the reporters into a little *bistro* and gave them a yarn to the effect that a magazine had offered fifty thousand dollars for Walker's life story. It was the story I had read in a three-week-old copy of *Variety*. They picked the yarn up on the first bounce and cabled it back to America as news.

After we had cleared all wires, Alice and I mounted to our villa expecting to find the Walker party there. What we found instead was a setup of movie cameras, portable soundtrucks, and arc lights all over the place. Some of the lights were even parked in our garden. Dumbfounded, we could only assume that a newsreel crew had tapped the telegraph wires and were waiting for Walker to walk into a close-up.

I breathed the well-known sigh of relief on learning that it wasn't anything of the sort. A. E. Dupont, the German director, was doing a picture called *The Marathon Runner*, starring Brigitte Helm. He had chosen the location without knowing who was living in the villa, never suspecting that it was an old friend of his. When he found out, he was so delighted he moved the arc lights and the mucky boots of his technicians into our living room.

Fortunately for the Walkerian peace of mind, Lord Jim had got out of there before the cameras arrived, or he never would have believed I was on the level with him when I sent him to what, up to then, had been one of the few cloistered retreats on the Riviera. He was, I hoped, reposing at Cap Martin.

Alice reminded me that Hotel du Cap Martin had burned to the ground a few months before. Thus I had sent Walker to a hideaway that no longer existed and in consequence had successfully lost him!

Well, he would call in his own good time. Not too soon, I hoped, for I had a polishing job to do on *Sandrik, Child of Russia*. While he seemingly had found an escapologist's haven, it soon became evident that mine had been invaded and would soon be ravaged. Correspondents began ringing my telephone to learn of Walker's whereabouts. This was not unusual. They often called me when they couldn't locate a celebrity. I was like St. Anthony. I had got a reputation for finding things, and people often thought of me in no other connection. "What's the name of H. G. Wells's villa?" "Do you know where Kipling is stopping?" "We have a query from London that the Dolly Sisters cleaned up at the Cannes casino. Where can we reach them?"

This sort of thing didn't lessen with the arrival of Jimmy Walker and Betty Compton. He may have thought he was out of politics after twenty-three years of it and as a private citizen was entitled to live his own life as he preferred it, but that wasn't the press view. He might not have understood why he could not sneak into the Monte Carlo Casino and sneak out again unobserved. Was he such a dunce that he didn't know

he had to surrender his passport on entering, that it was duly
listed and was therefore a matter of public record? Did he not
know that every foreigner had to have a *carte d'identité* from
the police, and that this too was available to any reporter having
the energy to look it up? Apparently not.

Had I told reporters, "Try the Carlton in Cannes," I would
have spared myself nothing. Another call would surely have
come saying, "They're not there." To suggest the reporter try
Lord Derby or Michael Arlen or somebody else would not
relieve me of further interruptions. Only accurate information
would. So I went about it as any good reporter might have
done. I called the Italian Line and in the most Walkerian
manner demanded:

"Where did you send my luggage? I have lost a trunk."

"Who is this talking, please?" they naturally wanted to
know.

"Who do you think is talking?"

"Valkaire? Shimmy Valkaire?"

"Where the heck is my baggage?"

"Why, Monsieur, we sent them to Hotel du Cap."

"Hotel du Cap, where? Martin?"

"No, Antibes. We sent them in care of the *concierge*. I'm
sure if you count them you'll find all your trunks."

"All right," I said. "I'll have him check them again, and
call you back. Good-by."

If I could run Walker down that easily, imagine what French
reporters, supported by *concierges,* cops, and the *Sûreté Générale,* could have done if they only had put their minds to it.
So the next time Paris called wanting to get hold of Walker, I
told the correspondent, "Try Hotel du Cap d'Antibes. Jeannette
MacDonald is there too, if you're looking for her."

About a week after their arrival, Betty and Jimmy dropped in on us for tea. He had picked up ten pounds and that awful pallor and those bloodshot eyes that were outstanding charac- teristics when he stepped off the boat had given way to a bit of tan and a yeasty bravado which was more like the Walker we had read about. He had on one of his trickier costumes. No- body, you know, could wear such sissy clothes and look so masculine in them as Walker. He had a way too when he sat down of pulling up his trousers and twisting them inward so the outside seam lay on his knee. Thus he kept his creases with a razor edge long after his valet had returned to America.

One day he was a symphony in brown, the next in blue, and one costume I remember particularly consisted of flannel trou- sers of baby-blue with coat and shirt to match.

His conversation was full of ephemeral wisecracks and only the beauty of the view seemed to silence him for a moment. He had a habit, conventional enough, of thinking a thing out by brushing a hand over his hair. But he did it in an odd way— with the *heel* of his hand, not his palm or his fingers—as if the hair were pomaded and he didn't want his fingers greased by contact with it.

This may have been true, for he had a slicker's haircut and an impeccable part always. These touches, added to those sharp- printed features of his, as if a Hollywood beautician had made Lincoln over nearer to a flapper's ideal, gave him the air of a mime with a mind. And that, I suspect, is what he always wanted to be—an actor-manager, but given to song and dance rather than the idiom of Shakespeare.

In any case song and dance was what we tried to cure him with. Being frugal peasants ourselves, we decided to celebrate McEvoy's departure and Walker's arrival with a combination cocktail dance and supper at Moreno's across the road. The place was never used except by the peasants on Sunday afternoons. As ours was on a Thursday evening, we naturally had the place to ourselves.

One long table was laid out with all sorts of liquors and glasses and *pan bagnat* sandwiches, a generous Niçois idea of what more refined bars call "appetizers."

Over in the corner was a huge mechanical piano which played so loudly that when the literati gathered, nobody would go into a long spiel as to why his last book was a hit or a flop. There was nothing to do but to drink and dance, and most of them voted it the most hilarious party ever pulled on the Riviera.

The party, like all parties, suffered from one of two *faux pas*. Tolly Taylor got hold of Walker's ear and began bending it about the perfidies of Wall Street. Walker kept reaching behind him for his glass of scotch and soda, still feigning attention to Taylor's exposé.

People were coming in and out. We had hastily invited perhaps a hundred—everybody from Michael Arlen to Alexander Berkman.

Suddenly Iva Broadhurst loomed before me and pulled me over to one side. "Rita Olcott is furious," she whispered. "She has made an entrance three times and nobody has noticed her. She begs you, please, to introduce her to Jimmy Walker."

It never occurred to me that at such a Bohemian shindig people would stand on protocol, and I thought surely Mrs. Olcott must have known Walker from New York. After all, he had been one of the honorary pallbearers at Chauncey's funeral. I shrugged my shoulder and did as requested.

As I made the introductions, Mrs. Olcott reached out her hand and with a pose reminiscent of dowagers and their lorgnettes said, "*Mayor* Walker! You will always be *Mayor* Walker to me!"

I had previously introduced her to Betty Compton but in her haste to meet Jimmy, Mrs. Olcott had cut Betty dead. She then gave all of us a sweeping invitation to luncheon at her place the following Tuesday.

Afterward when Betty and Jimmy repaired to our villa, Betty kept repeating, "The witch! The stinking, fat old witch! I wouldn't eat at her place if it were Buckingham Palace."

"This dame!" Jim cried, referring to Betty Compton. "She either loves people or she hates them. There's nothing in between."

We compromised. We didn't go over to Mrs. Olcott's for luncheon. Betty cut her dead instead.

The only other kickback came from Alexander Berkman, the eminent anarchist. He wouldn't come because he didn't want to meet a "crooked politician." Others, equally radical-minded, were above such nonsense for the moment. Walker, realizing that he was in hostile territory, was at his best.

Laurence Vail's son, Sindbad, refused to shake hands with Walker, having heard what a terrible person he was. Kay Boyle, trying to overcome the embarrassing moment by shaking hands with Walker herself, remarked. "My, what warm hands you have!"

"They got that way," said Walker, "from keeping them in other people's pockets."

It took Kay five days to get over the shock of his candor.

But a week or so later Walker was again his old defeated self and the gnawing that was going on in his vitals began to work toward the surface. He began to think cautiously and soon to act that way, and before the winter was over it was obvious that a change of scene hadn't effected a cure. At best it had been a shot in the arm.

It didn't take much to discourage him. That fifty-thousand-dollar offer for his memoirs had been withdrawn before he left New York and without that to buck him up he had no incentive to write.

"As far as I can learn," reported one scout from Fourth Avenue where publishers gather like bees, "far from a fight for Walker's story, the stampede is all the other way. Editors are wary of him. They don't believe he will tell the whole story and anything less would hardly add to the volumes on political economy which crowd the shelves of the public library as it is."

Nevertheless, we did receive an offer from the *American Magazine*. They would pay five thousand dollars for an article entitled "Why I Couldn't Be a Better Mayor." I thought it was a handsome offer, and it would give him an excellent chance to state his case.

But quick as a flash he said, "Why should I write myself down as a heel? The best you could get out of an article along those lines is a suspended sentence. I did nothing that required me to cop a plea. Tell them we'll give them a piece entitled, "The Kind of Mayor You Didn't *Know I Was!*"

We never got an answer. Apparently they thought they knew the kind of mayor he had been.

From our first meeting to our last, our relations were harmonious if a bit indefinite. Except for not wanting to get down to cases, which is quite understandable, we got on excellently.

It took us weeks to agree to a financial working arrangement. And when we agreed and wrote it down, he looked at it and suggested a more generous arrangement. Ultimately he dictated a fantastic letter to Alice. In it he released to me everything of his of a literary nature, and if I felt I couldn't use all the money it brought, he'd see what he could do about absorbing what I couldn't use.

After signing this letter, he called the next day and said not to use it. "It will make editors think we do not believe the stuff is worth much," he explained. "What I am trying to do is to protect you from attachments. I am in a complicated financial position and have judgments against me. If you and I form a partnership, creditors can easily attach money due to us. So it would be better if you took it all and then gave me my half on this side of the ocean. But I have to think of the proper wording to protect you and still not make the stuff seem too important to creditors or too unimportant to editors."

He never got around to thinking of the right words. We worked on the literary projects instead. This was Scully all over. I rarely seemed able to make a proper business arrangement before getting completely enmeshed in a literary commitment. Yet somehow we managed to live well—as well at least as the lilies in the field, and they, Our Lord had reminded us, were arrayed in a glory Solomon couldn't match. So we didn't mind really. Theoretically, Walker was broke. Theoretically, he was living on the bounty of Betty and her mother. I doubted he would be tagged as a mendicant. He played golf, dressed well, and lived well. He didn't eat too well, however, for he had to take spinach pills and watch his ulcers.

How anybody could remain so cheerful with a squeamish stomach forever sniping at his happy disposition was a mystery to me. I think I admired this trait of Walker's more than anything else. The thin man, it was generally believed, was a victim of pulmonary tuberculosis, as well as an emaciated bankroll. This folk-lore was further strengthened by the fact that one of Jim's brothers had died of T.B.

The truth was Walker had suffered from stomach trouble for years. This and a trick heart were his chief physical infirmities. His lungs were all right. He claimed to have cured the ulcers by diet alone, without recourse to surgery. If this were true, it's surprising that his weight didn't shoot upward. As it was, no matter how much he loafed or how much he ate, he couldn't get above 135 pounds. As most persons touching sixty find it all too easy to put on weight, I rather suspected his ulcers were still at it, though his heart may have had something to do with his penciled physique.

One day, apropos of nothing in particular, he said, "A lot of things that happen to us are outside our control, but a beard is a man's own fault." He had hardly said it when in walked Dr. Bernard. He was French enough to own a beard.

"Let him examine this trick ticker of yours, Jim," I suggested.

Jim looked at him, at us, shook his head, grinned, and then decided to take the whole thing as a joke. He stripped to the waist. Dr. Bernard pulled out several special gadgets to double-check on his findings. When he had completed his diagnosis, he told Jim he had this and that and should do this, that, and the other thing. His heart was so-and-so and he ought to eat such-and-such. Then he examined me, took a look at Skip, said "Au revoir!" and left.

Jim sat there in a daze.

"That's funny," he said as he wiggled his shirt into his trousers. "You know, I once went to the Rockefeller Institute about this heart of mine. I had to go every day for a week. They took x-rays, cardiographs, blood tests, and just about wore me out before they arrived at their diagnosis. Well, this guy has come out with the same answer in fifteen minutes!"

"That's what I always say," I said, "a beard is a guy's own fault."

Laughing, we went into the next room for tea. He always enjoyed this except for the cakes, cookies, scones, and pastry that went with it. As Betty's problem was to keep her weight down and force his up, she had developed a habit of looking enviously at some heavily sugared piece of French pastry and then saying, "Try that one, Jim."

Left to right: Frank Harris, Frank Scully, M. Lincoln Schuster, Nellie Harris on the French Riviera in 1930.

Philip Eliot, Nina Wilcox Putnam (his wife) and Alice Pihl (before she became Mrs. Scully) at the new Monte Carlo "rubber beach" (1930).

Director Harry Lachman and President Scully of Lachman-Putnam Productions watching Mickey Powell
parachute from the sky on to the
back of a camel in Nice (1927).

Betty Minevitch, "Skip" Scully and
Borrah Minevitch before the "ill
fated" cruise of the *Lydia Ellen*.
Photo taken in the harbor of Cannes
(1932).

He would affect a frenzy of revolt against being constantly
ordered to eat cake merely because Betty liked it but couldn't
eat it without running the risk of going the well-nourished way
of the first Mrs. Walker. In the end he would eat it. Then he
would call for more tea.

When we finally got him down to work, Betty and he would
appear at our place promptly every other afternoon at three.
This meant driving over from Cannes—about twenty-five miles
away. We would talk things out and Alice would take notes.
Betty's contributions didn't simplify Alice's work, though they
often clarified one of Jim's stories. She had a clearer, sharper,
and of course younger mind and seemed to remember many
incidents better than he did. At the time she was twenty-eight
and he was fifty-eight.

He would compliment Alice on her note-taking. How she
could keep all three of our stories straight when frequently we
were all talking at once was a mystery to him. "Court reporters
would collapse under such an ordeal," he assured her.

After the break for tea, we would return to the story conference. This would go on till about seven or eight. Then we'd
quit, giving Alice all the next day to transcribe the notes and
resuming our huddles the day following.

Now and then, too tired to think about preparing a meal, the
four of us would dine out. We usually picked a place nearby and
not too expensive. I think the gayest times we had cost the
least. The cocktail party at Moreno's set us back twelve dollars,
and a visit to da Boutteau's ran to about five dollars for the
four of us.

27

Walker Dines Out

•

Iᴛ ᴛᴏᴏᴋ us five years to find da Boutteau's; so tourists couldn't be expected to find it overnight. It was in the old town of Nice, back of the cathedral. It was something like Le Tour D'Argent outside of Paris, only so much different that the comparison begins and ends with that "something." In Boutteau's you dined in the kitchen. You walked among the pots and pans. You lifted a lid here and there and you said, "I want this, and I want that." Pointing was good manners.

Then you said with a wink, *"Et deux bouteilles du vin sans etiquette."*

That wasn't the "wine without manners," as it seemed to read, but the "wine without a label." The boss returned your wink, made the sound of a bottle popping, and life got gayer from that moment on.

In the end, after wining and dining as you never had dined before, you figured your own bill with the aid of one of the coatless waiters, only to find that a banquet for four set you back less than the cover charge at any glittering gyppery in New York, Paris, Berlin, or London.

But first you had to find the place. I piloted at least seventy-five people to this hideaway in my time, and to a man they all came out beaming and made over. Some had to be restrained from whipping out their hunting knives and cutting out chunks of atmosphere to take back home with them.

The night we took Walker and Betty Compton there, we had been at it from three in the afternoon till nearly eight at night.

"Let's knock off," I said.

"And go home," added Jim.

"No, let's go to da Boutteau's," I said.

Betty looked at me in doubt. So did Jim. Da wasn't on any recommended list they knew of.

"Anything like La Poularde?" Jim wanted to know.

"Or Caramello's at Cap Ferrat?" questioned Betty.

"No."

"Or the Colomb d'Or at St. Paul?" tried Jim.

"No," I said. "Better."

"Where is it?" asked Jim.

"Down in the old town of Nice," I said.

"All right," said Betty. "Let's go."

"Not with my stomach," said Jim.

So naturally we compromised by going to da Boutteau's.

We started down the hill from our villa into Nice. Near the Municipal Casino at Place Massena, we turned into the old town where the streets were so narrow you could almost touch both walls by stretching your arms a bit. In and out of these winding alleys we honked till we came to the cathedral.

The spot looked like a bad print of New York's old Five Points. We parked by backing our car against a couple of garbage cans and, *voilà, en face* was da Boutteau's!

The place was perhaps twelve feet wide and fifteen high. It had an unreal air of antiquity about it, and I could see that Jim was ready to scram if anybody so much as lifted a pewter cup.

We couldn't get in the main door because the place was so

crowded that tables had been placed against it. We had to go down a side alley. That door let us practically into the soup tureens.

What a scene! Old Provence at its gayest! Chattering diners. Steaming dishes. Red and white tablecloths. Room perhaps for twenty persons and thirty already dining there, da Boutteau among them. Waiters wiggled around the tables in white aprons and shirt sleeves and waistcoats. Customers bent over steaming pots.

The ceiling was hung with everything from dried gourds to a red umbrella. The clock was a frying pan with its business end used as the face of the clock. These are common now. They weren't then. Wisecracks in Niçois decorated the whitewashed walls. Some official body had awarded da Boutteau a diploma for his cooking, and with Heaven-sent humor he had hung it on a wall upside down.

It didn't look as if we'd get a seat for weeks. But one sniff, and the Walkerian nose knew it was among the aristocrats of the supper table. He was reluctant to leave.

I spotted da Boutteau himself. He looked like any other waiter—in the same sort of apron, shirt sleeves, and waistcoat as his hired hands. He was giving a client a musical program by rubbing a thumb on the seat of a chair and then on a wall and a window. Both of them thought it better than chamber music and were laughing their heads off. Da Boutteau saw me and waved. He came over.

"Quatre places," I said.

"Four," corrected Da, whose English didn't go much beyond that. It didn't need to. The family's clientele for sixty odd years had been almost wholly French *gourmets*.

"Upstairs?" suggested Da.

"No, no upstairs," I said. "Here."

"All right," said Da. "Take my table then. We are about through."

So we took the family table, which just about sat us on the stove.

"You order," said Jim suspiciously.

The menu came. On the cover was a cartoon of a tourist driving from Paris and passing one *hôtellerie* after another, even when the chefs stood outside and tried to stop him with a gun. Through Fontainebleau he drove, Dijon, Lyon, Grenoble, and on and on, till he spotted da Boutteau's. There the artist had him driving right into the front door, a beaming smile on his face, home at last!

On the back of the card were songs in Niçois, a dialect like no other known tongue. Inside was the menu; and in that, paradise.

"You order," repeated Jim.

"Okay," I said, *"Salade Niçoise, poulpe à la sauce Niçoise."*

"What's this pulp?" said Jim.

"Oh a sort of lobster à la Newburg. You remember Newburgh? Near Albany?"

"Nuts to both of them," said Jim. "What else?"

"Corsican lamb. Or broiled pigeons on toast, smothered in green olives."

"What does the lamb Corsica *cost?*" asked Jim.

"Three francs."

"Twelve cents?"

"Yes."

"I'll take the homing pigeons."

"Well, I'll try the lamb *and* the pigeons," said Betty, who was never known to pale at the fury of a quail.

"And just a variety of vegetables," I said.

"And for dessert," suggested Alice, *"Sabayon* and *café filtré."*

"God help you if I get poisoned here," morosely remarked Walker.

"The wine will stop that," I said.

"It better."

"Oh, Da!" I called. "Two bottles of wine."

"Chablis? Chateau Neuf du Pape? Graves Superieure? Bordeaux Blanc, 1926?"

I shook my head to all of them.

"*Sans etiquette,*" whispered Mme. Scully softly.

"*Deux, sans etiquette!*" Da cried. He made a sound like the popping of a champagne cork again.

Meanwhile the *salade Niçoise* was gathering force. Sliced tomatoes, chopped anchovies, onions, black olives, green olives, tuna fish, cucumbers, green peppers, and celery were mixed in a big bowl. At the side, some chopped garlic.

"No garlic," I said.

"No *garlic?*" asked da Boutteau in blinking doubt.

"He can't take it," I explained, meaning Walker, though the fact was I couldn't.

"*Eh bien,*" sighed Da and went on with the dish. In a bowl he flipped what seemed like careless quantities of olive oil, mustard, wine-vinegar, chopped anchovies, salt and pepper. He whipped this up and then poured it over the other items as a salad dressing.

It was the most colorful, beautiful hors d'oeuvre ever you set your eyes on. One mouthful, and everybody was swooning with delight, and when it was gone, we all were dunking the peasant bread into the sauce at the bottom of the bowl.

Da Boutteau began dusting off the wine.

"Try this," I said.

"What is it? No label? No dago red for me," Jim growled.

"The boss's pride from his own vineyards in Bellet," I whispered.

"And this?" said Jim, pointing to a dish covered with native reddish sauce.

"Oh, that's the sort of lobster. Try it."

"Swell! Sort of lobster, eh? What do you call it?"

"Poulpe."

"Say," cried Betty, "this lamb is delicious, Jim. Try some. I'm on a diet, but I *have* to have another helping. It melts in your mouth."

"You mean *your* mouth!"

"Anybody's," corrected Betty.

Jim's stomach began saying yes to everything. He was wining and dining like one of the old kings of France.

"What does that sign say?" he asked.

"It says, 'Da Boutteau doesn't give a darn—he closes on Sunday!' "

"That's nice. Church-goer and wine-grower."

"After Mass he spends most of Sunday among his vineyards high in the hills back of Nice. This wine without a label is his own. He's very proud of it."

"Why doesn't he go to America?" said Jim. "Let's set him up in New York."

I turned and asked him why.

"He says he can't cook without wines," I translated. "He says not without *good* wines." (America was in the last throes of Prohibition at that time.)

"Who wants *crêpes suzette?*" cried da Boutteau above the din of the little room. "*Oui ou non?*"

Most of the remaining guests shouted "*Oui!*"

"*Eh bien,* I'll make some then," he said, disappointed. Apparently he had hoped to get out of making them.

At the end of the meal of meals, with almost everybody else gone, he furtively brought us a guest book to sign. I had been there often and had never seen it trotted out before. Since da

Boutteau didn't really know who we were, it seemed better to let flattery take its course. Jim put on his glasses, inked the house pen, and wrote: "This place puts the Ritz on the fritz. Subpoena me any time. Everyone else has. [Signed] James J. Walker."

"And I'm beginning to care for this place in a big way!" scribbled Betty, buoyed up by her second portion of Corsican lamb.

We then tore an old canceled stamp from an envelope and asked the *proprietaire* for a piece of string. With these we made a seal and otherwise decorated the page to make it look like a document.

Da looked on smiling, in an embarrassed way, not quite sure whether we were giving his place a big hand or playing it for laughs. When we were through, we called him over for the reckoning.

No bill came. Instead, Da pulled a chair up to the end of our table and tore off a corner of the "tablecloth." It turned out to be paper printed to look like red and white checkered *provençal* tablecloths. Jim grinned, but it was old stuff to me; it was the only accounting system Da used.

All of us began to figure the bill.

"How many *salades*? Two?" asked Da.

"Four," we corrected.

"*D'agneau roti?*"

"If you mean that Corsican lamb," said Betty, "I had two myself."

"Three altogether," I said.

So we continued down the list. If you forgot anything, it was your own fault. Da Boutteau had no means of remembering it. "How can I with all these customers?" he pleaded.

The dearest thing was the dessert. The *sabayon* was made by whipping the yolk of eggs in sugar and cognac and then heating the mixture—a long, slow job. It cost twenty-four cents, or *twice* what the lamb, pigeon, and other delicacies cost.

Each meal set us back about eighty cents. I took the modest tab, which probably started the rumor that Walker was flat broke.

I didn't go in to da Boutteau's again till Dick Simon came hurrying into Nice. Da saw us, signaled to me, and brought over the guest book. He opened it to our page and showed me a clipping of a picture which he had pasted in there. It showed a group of us. He pointed to Walker.

"Val-care, non?" he asked. *"Shimmy Val-care?"*

"Yes," I said, "that's Walker. That's Jimmy Walker."

"He like?"

"Crazy over your place."

"And the *poulpe à la Niçoise?"*

"Well, I tell you, Da. I haven't had the courage yet to tell him it was *octopus*. You see, M. Val-care has a weak stomach."

"Eh bien? And you?"

"I know, but it took even me years to get over the idea. No, it's better for all concerned, if M. Val-care orders again, to tell him it's a *sort of lobster."*

"I unnerstan'," said da Boutteau.

"And the *vin sans etiquette?"*

"Made him feel like his first day in New York's *Hotel de Ville*. His first day as mayor."

"A good feeling," agreed Da. "Me, every time I drink it, it makes me feel I'm in love for the first time."

"What a wine!" I said.

"Pas mal," modestly appraised the artist who made it.

28

Exit "Madame X"

•

IT's a mystery how any serious work could be accomplished in such a lotus-eating atmosphere. Nevertheless it was. I took afternoon siestas as part of my rebuilding, but I began the day around 7:30 and Alice, with a convalescent baby, was up and on the job even earlier.

Walker, never an early riser, used to golf mornings at Biot, a little town famous for its pottery. Martinelli, the old Metropolitan Opera star, was its mayor.

After an evening such as we shared at da Boutteau's, it was a little hard to get down to brass tacks again. I could see Walker was reluctant to kiss and tell, Tammany boys being about as bad in this respect as gangsters. However much they might despise each other privately, they stuck to the code publicly. Loyalty oaths meant loyalty to each other.

I finally talked Walker into writing a series of letters to celebrities, believing we could interpolate some revealing personal history along the way. The line between gilt by association and guilt by association is often very narrow. In politics the difference between a hero and a heel is frequently a matter of timing, not of morals. In Walker's opinion, Roosevelt, by becoming righteous at the right moment, climbed upward over Jimmy's astonished body. Walker felt that Al Smith, too, had used him to Smith's political advantage. Of Farley, however, I never heard him say an ill word.

324

After Walker had been discredited at home, anybody in the Roosevelt administration would have done well to have avoided him. But Farley, while Postmaster General, went out of his way to visit Walker in Cannes.

"Let's try some letters," I said to Walker one afternoon. "I know there's an old saying, 'Never write a letter, never destroy one.' But we don't have to mail these. They can be contrapuntal exercises to warm you up for the real thing."

"Sort of 'Letters I Forgot to Mail?'" said Jim.

"Yes," I said, "sort of."

He liked the idea immediately. "Okay, let's start on one to F.D.R.," he said. "Then we can try one to Al Smith, then to Marie, Queen of Roumania, then to Gene Tunney, then to Bernard Shaw."

"Fine," I said. "Let's try Roosevelt first."

As soon as New York and London learned what we were up to, Walker's stock climbed as if the year were 1928 instead of 1933. We received offers running as high as sixty thousand dollars for the first serial rights on these letters.

I wrote about five of them from material Jimmy and Betty supplied. They thought they were great. But the letters never came back to me for final typing. They joined the letters Jim forgot to mail.

One day I found out where the bottleneck was.

"Say, why don't we do a book about Betty first?" Walker asked. "Everybody knows my story, but nobody knows hers. And hers is far more interesting than mine."

My response to this had all the enthusiasm of a mute, inglorious Milton. In brief, I said nothing.

After all, how can you tell even a second-hand prince charming that nobody's interested in his girl except himself. You can't say: "I've got sixty thousand dollars in my hand if I deliver your story and even half of that, sight unseen, if you'll sign a contract. But nobody has offered so much as a dime for hers."

So you say instead: "All right, we'll knock out a rough draft of hers—a couple of chapters, maybe, and a table of contents, and a synopsis—ten thousand words, let us say, and send the blueprint on a shopping tour. Then we'll go back and finish yours. By the time we've finished your story, offers will be coming in for hers and we can go on with hers."

Both agreed that was a sane solution. Thus we swung from "Letters I Forgot to Mail" to "Ex-Madame X" and sadly filed away forty thousand words of his story. All of us retreated backstage while La Compton took the spotlight.

Once she got it, the famous Compton elbows kept her there. Being a person of much stronger will than Jim, Betty kept me at her yarn day and night. We simply couldn't get back to his after that. He soon found himself being driven harder to help out on her story than I ever pushed him to work on his own. He revolted a few times, but the revolts were easily put down.

"I come over here for a rest," he once cried, "and I'm pursued everywhere. I lock the door and through it I hear: 'Jim, listen to this chapter Frank just sent over and let me know what changes you'd suggest.' My Godfrey, am I never to know peace and privacy again?"

He never was. Her car had blocked the road and none could move till we pushed hers out of the way. When an offer of twelve thousand dollars came for her life story, all of us were forced to work harder to earn it than we would have had to do to earn sixty thousand for his.

Despite his protests to the contrary, it was clear to me, if it wasn't to them, that of the two evils he preferred sweating over her story more than he did working amiably on his own. It all had its roots in the same sorry soil. By working on Betty's story he was able to defer telling his own, and by embossing her story

with his fine Gaelic hand he was able to have things said
which he didn't have the courage to say himself.

In time he saw that this would open him to the charge of
hiding behind her form-fitting skirt. After that, he began editing the heart out of her story. In brief, having killed his own
by his delays, he now began to kill hers. In the end he succeeded. Suggestions that certain chapters be altered to conform
more nearly to the known facts met with arty opposition. The
piece was to stand as written; not a comma could be changed.
That was Betty's ultimatum to the publishing world.

That wasn't Betty, of course, but Jim. She had a lot of courage and if left to herself would have come out with a straightforward story of their life together. But watered down by his
hand, it soon became clear that instead of a banquet we were
being asked to dine on a tasteless literary *lapskaus*.

One of the parts they worked hardest to conceal was why
Betty suddenly married an assistant director at Paramount in
Astoria. She honeymooned with him to Cuba and just as sud-
denly divorced him and returned by way of Miami to New
York, and to Walker.

They attempted to clear up this mystery and, whether true
or not, their explanation was at least plausible. It seemed that
Tammany, feeling that their whole house of cards would tumble if this dame were not eliminated from Walker's life, came
upon an even more shocking twist. It appeared that Betty was
going to have a baby. The Tammany boys whisked Walker
down to Long Island and then told her, thanks to this indiscre-
tion, all was off between them. She took an overdose of sleeping
tablets and when she awakened, found herself being married
to a relative stranger in the apartment of a Tammany judge.

Thus escorted aboard a Cuba-bound steamer, she became so
sick she had a miscarriage. This in turn washed up all the
Tammany reasons for marrying her off to an obscure bachelor.

She rapidly divorced the stand-in in Mexico and returned to Hizzonor the Mayor. At least this is the sordid story they gave me.

Other old friends assured me that Betty could not have had children. This, however, turned out to be untrue. Later, after she divorced Walker and married another man, she did have a child. In fact, she died from the effects of that childbirth.

There was no reason to doubt the story they told me. Since it couldn't be printed then by editors who apparently knew it before I did, they said good-by to the money they had advanced, leaving me holding a bag which, on examination, might reveal a footnote to the Life of a Ghost, if I ever decided to write one.

Walker's divorce from his wife and subsequent marriage to Betty Compton in Cannes completely knocked the X out of *Madame X*. By then editors were stampeding away from Betty's story as they had earlier from Walker's. She and he were only too glad to forget their scarlet past. They wrapped themselves in a cloak of respectability and tried to hide from photographers on their wedding day.

We didn't go to the wedding, but it was reported that in a fit of anger he started after a photographer. Now, no man minds being photographed on his wedding day if his conscience is clear. After all, it's not like a mugging in a rogues' gallery. Or in Walker's case, was it?

This, to any amateur psychiatrist, was the tipoff to what was eating him. He didn't want to see proofs of what he was doing. He never meant to quit the Church. He never meant to divorce his wife. He never meant to marry a divorcee. Yet he did all those things, and here were the pictures and documents to prove it. He had excommunicated himself.

After the marriage, they left the Riviera for suburban life in England, where Jim lived as a remittance man on his mother-in-law's beneficence in a Surrey manor she had bestowed on the "happy couple."

This lasted for a few years. Many people, of course, were out of work in those days, but Walker had not been off a public payroll for thirty years. He began to discover what everybody else knew—that you spend lots more money when unemployed than when employed. He made overtures to get a 25,000-dollar income tax rap squared. New York's cloak-and-suiters offered him a job as arbiter of their labor disputes. This was a way out. He grabbed it.

What had driven him from home in the first place was "an acute consciousness of lost honor," the same disease that made such a wreck out of Joseph Conrad's *Lord Jim.* Walker didn't want to return to the scene of his greatest triumphs and his bitterest defeats, but he had to in order to make ends meet.

The Pagliacci of politics was not returning to the New York of Central Park Casino, Broadway openings, night clubs, and ticker parades. He fitted New York of the boom days like one of his own Friedman-tailored dinner jackets. He had the heart of a hoofer and the manners of a Ruritanian prince. Indeed, I used to think his defeat was brought about because he didn't know how to change his act. While his tap dance in a top hat was a delight at dawn to workers bound for their labors in 1928, it was no delight to those laborers, no longer employed, in 1931. Had he gone pious, like the Prince of Wales, displaying a sober side to the peasantry that paid his keep and saving his lighter moods for Biarritz and Cannes, he might have lasted out a second term. He might—giddying thought—have even become President of the United States.

For his private life—which he said he was willing to match with anybody's (a large order)—apparently was not much worse than that of those who ruled America in Harding's day. And, publicly, he was one of the few persons in political life you wouldn't be ashamed to introduce to your friends—anywhere.

Roosevelt had that same urbanity and personal charm—and Walker and Roosevelt had once been great friends. This was easy to understand, for they were a lot alike, though they came to their ways of thinking from different ends of society. Walker was of Broadway, with the airs of an aristocrat; Roosevelt was of the aristocracy, with a hankering for the idiom of Broadway. (Witness his use of "chiselers," "tough guy," "hard-boiled," and the like.)

For a while in his exile, Walker was bitter against Roosevelt. Ingratitude about summed up his grievance. "I made Roosevelt," he used to say. To your surprised look, he'd add, "Well, I made Farley, and Farley made Roosevelt. Ergo, I made Roosevelt!" Plato couldn't have summed it up more briefly.

But Al Smith he found it hardest to forgive. Smith, in Walker's opinion, had joined the opposition in the showdown and had decided to make the world safe for hypocrisy.

They all knew that Walker's first marriage was a failure long before he ever ran for mayor, Jim insisted to me. From Roosevelt down, they knew about Betty Compton and that Jim was footloose long before he met her when she was an obscure chorine in *Oh Kay*.

So their raising of outraged hands when Seabury found that Walker had a female banker left Jim in a state of defeated fury. And when Roosevelt and Seabury ordered her to be billed as "Madame X," their idea of gallantry infuriated her as well. For they failed to realize that when a philanderer of fifty falls in love with a show girl in her twenties, you're not doing either of them (in *their* opinion) a favor by billing the lady as an "unknown woman"!

Walker's own version of just where in his career he bilked himself out of office bears out the contention of this study.

Others may not agree with this opinion, for a thousand different observers have a way of pointing to a thousand different things which may have caused the fall of an idol. And none of them may be wholly wrong. But, after all, the man's own opinion ought to be considered too.

In Walker's case none of the things on the record brought about his downfall. What caused it was a simple emotional gesture which happened only a year or two before his eclipse. But it illustrates, to me at least, how impossible it is to tear up the roots of a lifetime, and it explains, moreover, why he could find no peace of soul in divorcing one woman to wed another.

The average person raised on Henry-the-Eighth sort of personal history might have come out all right by doing what Walker did. To have resigned a post you are about to lose anyway, to have divorced a wife you hadn't loved in ten or twenty years, to have married instead a girl you did love, and to have gone off with her to another country to settle down— all these things to most persons would have seemed like a sensible solution of a complicated problem.

But each of these steps in Walker's life couldn't have been a solution, because of his mystical Shanty Irish religious roots. He could not get away from the good old religion; his effort to do so trapped him in the end. He traced his own fall to one of those unaccountable acts previously referred to.

In the police parade in the early 30s, on a hot May day, the line stopped for a moment's rest at 49th Street and Fifth Avenue. One block farther on, on the steps of St. Patrick's Cathedral, stood the Cardinal and his entourage. Walker turned to Grover Whalen, who was then his Commissioner of Police as well as his social arbiter, and asked if he should make any special recognition of the Cardinal as they passed the Cathedral.

Whalen didn't think he should, beyond the ordinary cour-

tesies, and Walker was fully prepared to pass the Cathedral,
bow to the Cardinal, and continue leading the parade up Fifth
Avenue. But as the parade started anew, the Cardinal moved
forward from the shadow of the Cathedral to the edge of the
steps. The brilliant red of his robes caught Walker's eye, and
before Jim knew what he was doing he was running up the
steps to greet a Prince of the Church in a manner familiar to
all Catholics. He knelt on one knee, kissed the Episcopal ring,
and when he realized that he'd let an old religious emotion
overwhelm his latterly developed agnostic sense, he tried to retreat to his place in the parade. But on one side of him a score
of cameras had photographed his obeisance to the faith of his
fathers, and on the other side a score of cameras had photographed him as a hypocrite.

What went on in the mind of the Cardinal at this sudden
gesture of humility and faith, no one knows but the Cardinal,
but those around him felt that the Church was being used as a
stooge by a backslider. All of them resented an act of faith by
somebody whose private life, they knew, was violating that
faith at every turn. And in the Bible-belt of America the
photographs were used as proof that the Mayor of New York
was a Papist of the blackest sort.

As for Walker, he could never explain why he did it except
that now and then his mental processes went berserk and he
did something by pure emotional reflex. But this particular act,
which probably not a thousand people remember, Walker never
forgot.

The Princes of the Church didn't forget either, for when
Marty McCue, a Shanty Irish politician of no great ability,
died, the priest who celebrated the Solemn High Mass took
occasion to preach a sermon. He told what a fine family man
McCue had been, how faithful he had been in his duties to the
Church, and then went on to give Walker the works.

At that Solemn High Mass were Al Smith, John Currey, old John McCooey, and about all the Democratic leaders of New York except Walker.

To them and to Walker that sermon was the end.

Whatever transpired afterward, with all the ramifications of the Hofstadter investigation and Samuel Seabury's search for wrong-doing in Walker's administration, Walker himself could never get over the fact that he had stepped out of his way to affront those to whom he previously had turned for spiritual guidance.

As nothing plagues us through the years like our own *faux pas*, it may be true that it was this incident which really finished Walker, but he kept making magnificent misses all along the line and finally chucked himself out of office about a month before the end.

When he went to the Albany hearing, he still thought his debonair act and his Tammany palm-slammers could turn a flop into a hit. He was still wisecracking to the very doors of the hearing. When, however, he got into the witness stand and Roosevelt began making him play the role of stooge for a change, and he saw further that he was going to be thrown out, he held a hurried conference with his counsel and they decided to pull a fast one.

They had to all intents and purposes decided to throw in the sponge. Walker wrote an eighteen-word resignation and issued a three-thousand-word statement damning the whole Roosevelt procedure. This made it look as if the whole thing were over, but it was not as simple as that. What they were working toward was this: By resigning, Walker had taken the thing out of Roosevelt's hands. It was then the intention of his council of war to renominate him and have him run on a vindication platform. He would of course be re-elected and Tammany would have given Roosevelt the old runaround.

There was nothing the matter with the idea except that over in Europe lay the love-interest of the plot. And since it had cost Walker and Mlle. Compton a fortune in telephones and cables for the year or so they were separated, it seemed cheaper for him to hop a boat and make a personal visit.

As always, when Walker made these trips—whether they were to Florida, Bermuda, or Europe—the press was told that he was on the verge of a breakdown and that his physician had ordered a vacation, preferably a sea voyage.

Well, this sea voyage took him and his secretary, George Collins, to Naples on the *Conte Grande*. They had booked to make it a round trip, planning to get back to New York just in time for the Democratic Convention when Walker would arrive and stampede the delegates to the *status quo ante*.

Betty hurried down from Paris to meet him in Naples, and then George Collins got sick and instead of Jim taking the *Conte Grande* back, he decided to take the *Rex*, which was making its maiden voyage.

One of the turbines of the *Rex* broke down in the Mediterranean and the ship had to put in to Gibraltar, while mechanics hurried down from London to repair the damage.

Walker walked the bridge like a Napoleon at Elba and in the end, seeing his crown slipping from his grasp, deserted ship, hurried across France, gave Betty another good-by in Paris, and then caught the *Bremen* from Cherbourg, still hoping to reach New York before the Democratic Convention was over.

As a footnote to irony, it should be stated that he arrived later on the *Bremen* than he would have on the *Rex*, which after its turbine was repaired made fast time to New York.

But in any event he was too late, and the delegates, after waiting for a stampeder who never came, turned to a fat, family man—in Walker's phrase "the hardest-breathing man in

New York"—who had been sleeping away on the Surrogate bench, and picked him as their candidate for mayor.

A Democratic nomination in those days was equal to election, and as the man they did choose had about one-tenth the popular appeal of Walker, it is easy to believe that Walker would have won if his heart hadn't yanked him across the Atlantic just when he was most needed in New York to direct the strategy of his own battle.

As proof of this, he received a reception which topped any he had ever given other visiting celebrities. At least five thousand persons went down the bay to meet him, and all the Tammany leaders who had nominated O'Brien in Walker's absence agreed that if Jim had been present at the Convention, nothing could have stopped his renomination.

This may have been their diplomatic way of easing him out of the picture. That may even have been their intention in the first place, but the fact remains that if Walker's back hadn't been turned they couldn't have done it so easily, and the further fact remains that he turned his own back.

Thus, one way or another, he had bilked himself out of a job which he wanted to keep till the end of his second term and then retire in his own way. As it was, it amounted to being thrown out on his ear, and his personal pride couldn't permit him to face that. So he took another steamer back to Europe, this time with Betty who had come over from France to join him. Trying to laugh it off to the last, they wrapped themselves in blankets and sneaked aboard ship like Arabs in the night.

He thought by marrying her he would be making an honest woman of her. He didn't realize what it would do to him, one whose Irish roots went down into a soil so deep they could never be rooted up. As long as they lived in sin, to use an old phrase, there was hope that Walker could break the spell and thus effect his own reformation. He couldn't be a communicant while living that way, but divorce and remarriage was another matter. This was an open defiance of Church laws and the sanctity of the marriage sacrament. Excommunication was the inevitable sequel.

The result of all their hush-hush was ludicrous. Reporters took up the challenge and began to dump Walker's apple cart every time he set it up. Though he was an honorary citizen of Cannes, he couldn't close the mouth of every civic employee. Thus his "secrets" were public knowledge almost as soon as he formulated them. The press didn't have to bother me for inside stuff this time. They got it right off the record.

Two correspondents from Nice, one from the AP and the other from the Hearst string, tried to get the Mayor of Cannes on the telephone. Failing, they drove over to Cannes. They walked into the *Mairie* and asked where the marriage banns were posted.

"Down the hall," a clerk told them.

They walked down the hall, took a wrong turn, and opened a door. There sat Jimmy and Betty with the Deputy Mayor. Walker was furious. The reporters just laughed.

They broke their story that night about the marriage banns and the next day the banns were posted. As there normally was a ten-day interval between the posting and the marriage, the reporters decided that April 13, 1933, would be the day.

I doubted this, as April 13 that year was Holy Thursday. Whatever religious scruples Walker had overcome, I was sure he could not quite defy his past beliefs and marry during Holy Week. In this I was correct, for the marriage was postponed until two days after Easter Sunday.

On a rainy day, April 18, they sneaked in the back entrance of the *Mairie*, still hoping to keep their splicing a secret. With them was Mrs. Compton, Betty's mother, a French doctor, and an American lawyer.

This was where we got off. By this time Alice had become a Catholic; so there was small chance of our giving aid and comfort to what was, from a Catholic point of view, the culmination of a private frailty into a public scandal.

In the marriage chamber, however, besides the invited witnesses, and unknown to the Walkers, were two reporters. Outside were news photographers, newsreel cameramen, journalists, and a sound-truck. As the Walkers came out, photographers attempted to snap their picture. A general roughhouse ensued. Some claim Walker struck a photographer; others that the photographer threw a nitrogen bulb at Walker. Anyway, it was a nasty mess and Beau James dropped from being considered the best sport in the world to a dog whose ancestry was anything but thoroughbred.

The poor guy, I thought. His misplaced gallantry was giving him no peace. No groom smashes cameras on his wedding day unless there is within him a dreadful sense of guilt. His case was really for Freud.

He had to admit a few years later that in fighting a thousand years of Irish faith he was poorly equipped. He was no Robert Ingersoll. He was a weaker Charles Stewart Parnell. His Betty Compton was a stronger Kitty O'Shea. That gesture of obedience and humility, which Walker showed for a minute on the steps of St. Patrick's Cathedral during the Police Parade in the 30's, was the real Walker. The rest was tap-dancing on the piety of his ancestors. It was to entertain non-believers who would desert him as soon as he was stripped of his power.

That a divinity shaped his end, rough hew it as he would, was the best part of the Walker story. How lucky he was, God only knew. He must have prayed many times for forgiveness.

His story had become another in a long list of Prodigal Sons. He certainly had had a close shave. But he died repentant, in a state of grace, one more lost sheep for whose return to the arms of the Good Shepherd was always a cause for rejoicing in Heaven. He never was really bad. Only weak.

But he must have done a mighty good deed for somebody sometime, and that somebody must have prayed often that he be rescued from the eternal penalties of his own persistent follies.

I was to see these last-minute rescues happen so often in my lifetime, especially among smart Irish kids, that it did more than anything else to put the fear of God in me, too.

After all, I began to figure, I might not be so lucky. I'd better stay closer to my guardian angel and the saints whose names I took and whose lives I was expected to follow. And, most of all, I had better remember the Queen of Angels had the clearest understanding of all.

She knew all about the ignominious things that could happen to the best of Sons. She had seen hers crucified for the sins of mankind. She would never turn a deaf ear to anyone who asked for her intercession. Her Son Himself had told the parable of the Prodigal Son. That showed He knew how weak we all were; and if we ultimately righted our own craft and expressed sorrow for having offended Him, His mother's pleading for one more son of one more mother would not be ignored.

By now the principals of the Walker Story are awaiting Judgment Day. All we can do is to pray for their souls and ask them to do as much for ours.

29

The Conversion of Alice

•

THE mystery that may never be solved was why my little Alice wanted to become a Catholic. Why didn't the easiest way of others rub off on her? What had happened to the old theories of environment and heredity? Had they died with Darwin? Unbelieving hobohemians on every side seemed to be doing well. Some of them were fallen-away Catholics. Why should she try to go up, if the chances of coming down were better than even?

She saw me covering a story of a young Englishman, a lapsed Catholic named Richard Corbett, who had murdered his French mother because he couldn't bear to see her suffer any longer from an incurable disease.

"If God decided the end had not yet come, why should one of His children presume to know better?" the prosecution argued. H. G. Wells, who certainly thought he knew better, and Sir Arthur Conan Doyle attended the trial—both pro-euthanasians. To them it wasn't matricide. It was a mercy killing and therefore, in their eyes, justified.

The French tried Corbett and exonerated him—all in one day! The jury debated the case only twenty minutes and freed him.

Not long after this experience I went up to a man in Monte Carlo to ask him a few questions, and two guards escorted me to a west-bound bus. Who was he? The British had knighted

339

him; the French had made him a Chevalier of the Legion of
Honor. He had been running around with a Spanish countess
for years. She also was a lapsed Catholic. He couldn't marry her
because her husband had gone insane and Spanish laws would
not permit a divorce under such conditions.

Known in all the capitals of the world, he nevertheless
couldn't be sure his mistress would not be snubbed in any of
them. So he bought Monte Carlo to make sure nobody could do
that to either him or his mistress.

And who was he? Sir Basil Zaharoff, the tsar of the merchants
of death. Where he was born, what his citizenship was, nobody knew. I was on the hunt to find out. Clipping bureaus
would not even mention his name when telling me that they
kept no clippings on the gentleman referred to in my letter.

I wanted to write of his life in the idiom of Chicago gangsters,
for, stripped of all the spurious honors that he had bought in
one way or another, he was simply a racketeer on the highest
level of world politics.

Among people like these, messed-up Catholics in the main,
how could Alice see the truth of a faith they had all befouled?
The dampening effects of bad environment met a sharp exception in her case. Far from being demoralized by such people,
she became more convinced than ever that her happiness lay
in trying to emulate the lives of the saints of the Church
Militant, not the lives of the deserters who had gone over the
hill.

A practical little person, with an amazing skill at doing anything from repairing a faulty electric switch to correcting a
faulty child, she was a profoundly spiritual person as well.
These two qualities, practicality and spirituality, became the
keys to her character. They soon began leaving their marks
on the whole Scully Circus.

She grew. She grew physically one inch with each baby,

and she grew spiritually by following the Do-It-Yourself vogue a generation before it became a vogue. Was this the Curé d'Ars' influence? Indeed, in all matters she was humble enough to follow instructions. To this day she is the only person I know who reads all the instructions connected with a gadget before touching it. As a result, with her at least, few things break "by accident." Under her care household conveniences last for years.

I admire this because I am the sort who wants to "cut to the chase." As far as I'm concerned, we can read the instructions later. I play too much by ear, and as a consequence those things I play by ear I play badly. I don't like to read instructions and like even less to play the role of an instructor. Teachers, I knew only too well, have to bone up too.

Jimmy Walker found it hard to face the facts of his faith. To a lesser degree so did I. I was being tapped for the greatest of all teaching tasks, the role of missionary. I dreaded the role. I had seen converts and, barring possibly the late Walter Hooke, Chairman of the New York Boxing Commission, converts seemed a humorless, driving folk. Still, if Madeleine Hennessey Hooke could make her husband a gay convert, perhaps I could do as well with Alice.

In addition to Abbé Van den Daele, we had another force offsetting the bad example of such fallen-away Catholics as Jimmy Walker. That superior moral force was another peasant woman like Maria. Her name was Thérèse.

These two peasant women were the soul of nobility. Maria had a faith that nothing could disturb. She acted as if it were no more for her to have a baby than to have a tooth pulled. She was a Gibraltar in a quaking, cowardly world.

Much like her was Thérèse. Thérèse was perhaps thirty-two, tall, with a nice figure, fine features, and beautiful eyes. She had a lovely mouth but her teeth had been neglected. Everything else about her was beautiful. She assured us we would be very happy with her once we knew her. She asked for 350 francs a month and would like one day off a month.

The reason she wanted this day off was because she had a boy in a religious orphanage school at Juan Les Pins and could see him only on the first Sunday of the month.

Her manners and speech were so gentle that just talking to her seemed to bring an added peace to the villa. From the first, she cooked most exquisitely. She even served tea in such a dainty manner that Jimmy Walker looked up and later felt impelled to remark on her gracious and soothing qualities. She loved Skip from her first day with us. Her older boy, Joseph, was her pride and joy. He saddened her, though, because he had top honor grades in everything but one subject. She didn't understand why not in *every* subject.

She asked that she be allowed to do the marketing down in Nice because she could get much better things for less money than Alice, a foreigner, could, and besides, since Alice was having another baby, she wanted to do everything she could to spare her.

She even tried to give back the money she saved by shopping for us. It was common practice for the sellers in the markets to give 10 per cent back to the shoppers if they were buying for somebody else. That was their commission. They would even, if a lady and her maid went shopping together, take the money from the lady and hand the 10 per cent to the maid.

On Sunday Therese would get up early, go to Mass, then to the hairdressers. After that she would do the marketing and have a beautiful breakfast ready when we returned from nine-o'clock Mass.

She took over the running of the house and would only listen to us when we were having guests for dinner. Any plans for her comfort or leisure she ignored.

She had one big fault. She loved us too much and lived our life, not her own. At vacation time Joseph was invited to come and stay with us. He was a wonderful boy and sought in all ways to make his mother and us happy. He loved to run down the hill—a mile—to get a morning paper for me.

I can see now that Abbé Van den Daele, Thérèse, and I acted the eternal triangle, but with a new twist. More and more, Alice found herself bumping into one of us while seeking a spiritual solution for her life. There was no earthly reason against her conversion and countless heavenly reasons in favor of it. But she practically had to force the Abbé into taking on the task.

Her instructions went on quietly, weaving a strong thread through the tapestry of an otherwise demoralized design for living. In fact, almost to the day Jimmy Walker was breaking all ties with his faith and marrying a woman who had been his mistress for five years, Alice was taking his place in the long line of practicing Catholics. It was a line that went back unbroken to the Last Supper. It had met thousands of tests in 1900 years—everything from persecutions by Roman pagans to Hitler's blood baths.

As always, we found it difficult to procure sponsors. There were nearly thirty million Catholics in America and more in Europe, but I seemed singularly unfortunate when it came to having them as friends who could be called on to act as godparents. The Abbé found them for us. The man was Prince de Béarn et de Chalais. He had been in the French Embassy in Washington for years. He was also a Prince of the Church and a man of substance. His family had owned great vineyards in the champagne country of France. He was also an official at Lourdes. Her godmother was the Princess.

"Much as that was a happy day, the happiness of the decision has multiplied itself as time went on," Alice has since confessed. "It has been a constant wonder to me how the Catholic Church makes allowances for human frailties. It actually moves with the times, keeping up to date in the strangest ways."

In discussing this side of our lives together, Alice has always thought that I skimmed over too lightly what it must have meant to us. It wasn't merely a matter of a church wedding and some baptisms. It became a part of our daily lives. She felt this religious side was of such importance that it influenced our everyday way of living, thinking and acting.

That was true. But religion was such a private affair in those days and of course, generally speaking, still is. I'm an extrovert on most things and certainly have never hid what I was but it didn't seem to me that signposts were needed.

The task is to make those few good hours on Sunday last all week. In this respect Alice is a much more active Catholic than I. She frequently gets up and goes to early Mass during the week and is home before the rest of us have even got up.

She has always looked fresh as a blooming rosebud. She wore no makeup and immediately on arising she bathed, dressed, and combed her hair. She never left her bedroom without being fully dressed—and rarely, unless quite ill, appeared in the living room in a dressing gown. Slatterns did it, and even women who thought they were ladies did it, but to Alice it was a lack of self-discipline. Women who had disciplined themselves would never do it, she insisted. She tried to instill in our children the importance of disciplining themselves in small things like this, as a practical application of one's faith. Personal daintiness, modesty, neatness might have seemed to them minor issues, but she felt that when a major issue did arise, these small disciplines would make it easier for them to meet the major issues, and temptations.

"This may seem remote to many people but to me it is a part of right living," she would add. "Saints were not made from lack of temptation, but from the way they resisted temptation."

I remember her discussing discipline from another direction. "Throwing bricks in the general direction of a piece of land you own will not build a house. It has to be done by plan, brick by brick. It requires persistent spiritual strength, not much, just a little, but persistent, to make the difference between a good life and a bad one, a saint and a sinner, Heaven and hell."

As I sat there and watched her being received into the Church, I could not help but think of these things. I thought back, too, to the Chapel of St. Mary's in Tucson, when Bishop Gercke received Francis Perry Elliott. As the sun moved westward it finally lay like a halo on the old author's white locks.

But here this March day there was not much sun. And it was not an old man who was bracing himself against the Vatican wall for strength to die in a state of grace, which he did. Here was a young and beautiful mother, in her twenties, not much older than the Blessed Virgin was when incredible things came to her. A long life, in all likelihood, was ahead of her.

The Chapel of Sacré Coeur was a ruins, really, and the Sacrament of Baptism was administered in the vestry. But it was the same in its essentials as if it had been administered in St. Peter's in Rome, on the River Jordan, or in Tucson, Arizona.

Two days before the Baptism we had lunched with Otto Kahn, and he had paid a tribute to the Catholic Church and the fact that it was a going concern in those days of general collapse, for just then all America was paralyzed by a nation-wide banking panic. I thought at the time that a terse explanation as to why the Catholic Church, in the face of a world all at sea, was still a going concern was because it knew where it was going.

The fact came even more forcibly to me as I sat in the little Chapel of Sacré Coeur as a witness to the Baptism of Alice Pihl Scully. It's a long ritual, the Baptism of an adult, for every step in it has a meaning, and neither the meaning nor the form ever varies.

That her spiritual growth could take place in such a bohemian atmosphere—an atmosphere of people who were sure of nothing but their belief in unbelief—was astonishing. It was going on at a time when examples of Catholics who had fallen away were coming more and more into our lives. Their tangled lives were sad to us, however gay they might have seemed to others. At least four of them had complicated their lives, and knew it, by marrying, or planning to marry, in violation of the laws of the Church, and all of them were deferring as long as possible the final break with their faith. They feared that their inner lives and their outer actions could never permit them a moment's peace.

It had never occurred to any of them that it would have been a little bit less difficult if they had adhered more rigidly to the simple commands of the Church. If they had gone to Mass every Sunday, that might have solved everything. As it was, we couldn't help them much, though they were all well worth the helping.

Part of this was due to the fact that I have a fixed dislike for being my brother's keeper. In Alice's case I leaned over backward. I tried not to give her any encouragement beyond what one's everyday acts might do in that direction, and I know many times she must have felt discouraged that I seemed to take so little interest in the spiritual problem she had to solve. But to me this is the most personal matter in the world; no one can save our souls for us but ourselves. Anything we do of enduring value must come from within.

Frank and Alice rejoin old pal Jim Tully in Hollywood.

Fanny Holtzmann wrote Scully a fan letter; a lasting friendship resulted. Twenty years later, they celebrated its inception in Las Vegas.

Cardinal McIntyre of Los Angeles gives his blessings to the author of *Blessed Mother Goose*.

Monsignor Hagearty brings Scully a diploma as a Knight of the Order of St. Elizabeth. Ann Blyth, movie actress, is the witness.

Like that banker I knew in Prescott, Arizona—the one who had wandered around and tried everything. Finally he lost a huge fortune and thought that with it he would lose his mind. Catholicism saved him that, at any rate, and afterward he couldn't say often enough that he never wanted the money back except for the good he might do with it and, since he might fail even in that, he guessed he didn't want it back at all.

I had read enough of the writings of converted authors whose conversion seemed to give them no lasting peace, since they couldn't stop writing about it, and resolved never to become equally garrulous myself. While I firmly believed Catholicism was the solution of most people's woes, I refrained from telling anybody in particular that this was his answer, unless he asked me, and few ever did that.

And so as I watched Alice's baptism I had a feeling that this was the will of God and none of my making. Certainly of all the people there I was the most moderate believer. The Abbé was sanctity itself, and the two witnesses, Prince and Princess de Béarn et de Chalais, went to Holy Communion every day. They led an active as well as a religious life, a sanely balanced way to live.

Alice is so sensitively made that quite simple things make her quiver, and this experience was moving her to the point where she might easily have fainted. Fortunately before this point was reached her witnesses were called up to stand at either side of her so that she could hold the hand of each.

There they stood: Alice bareheaded in a brown corduroy dress of her own making and a gray fur coat, her little Highlander hat in fur and corduroy having been removed halfway through the ceremony; at her left, the Prince, a well-built man of fifty; and at her right, the Princess, a beautiful woman a few years younger. When the long ceremony was over, Alice went to make a general confession, and her witnesses repaired to the big chapel to say some prayers for all of us, while I knelt there too and said my rosary.

On this baptismal occasion, there were only four or five persons present. The whole ceremony took a good deal more than an hour, and when it was over we repaired to a Russian restaurant for a gorgeous luncheon. We invited the others, but they wouldn't think of breaking in on our happiness. It was like honeymooning all over again.

Our luncheon started with a lobster salad and went into fried chicken and ended on apple strudel with cream. It seemed just perfect. In this world, at least, surely the more innocent needs of the flesh are not incompatible with a soul that has been fed on the riches of the Church.

Afterwards, happy and strangely free from the worries of a world which had lost its way, we returned home to our little villa on the hill, where little two-year-old Skippy greeted us with his broadest grin and happiest embrace.

Alice wanted to know a dozen times if I weren't happier now, and I couldn't answer "Yes," because there honestly was no change for me. She was what she was. And I, in my hazy, lazy way, had always been of one mind with her. With her, I had reached other things that endure. For thirty-eight years I had got on without them. I had no wife, no home, no children. I was all right. At least I thought I was. But now I knew differently.

So what? Well, the "what" is that previously I had been a failure in every direction, and if some measure of approval has come to me in this greatest of all gambles (arranging words on paper), maybe it was a Heaven-sent pay-off for facing life's responsibilities instead of dodging them forever.

We had agreed that it was crazy to marry and to have kids with conditions as they were—that is, if you're hell-bent to live only for conditions; but if conditions are something you don't care more than sixteen fairly long hoots about, then marrying and having kids to trot behind you to Mass in this year of grace is the only thing to do.

The rest of the world may not agree with this, but my answer to the rest of the world is: *we're happy*, which is more than can be said of most of those who laugh at our simple formula for a perfect life.

The mystery remains. How could a rose like Alice grow in such eroded soil? Was I a compost that helped?

Does such a violent figure of speech err on the side of exaggeration? I'm inclined to think so. I prefer to view her as the one, in a relay race, who was handed the baton when our team was far behind, mostly because of my faltering steps. Afterward she made up so much yardage that we now have every hope of winning in this race to save our immortal souls.

30
Return of the Native

•

In the summer of 1927, while lunching with Somerset Maugham at his villa on Cap Ferrat, we were discussing taboos and fears men had and whether logic or superstition motivated their fears. I admitted I was mortally afraid of New York.

"It's the town that broke me down," I explained. "When I came to Europe I had a chance to travel deluxe from New York. I turned it down, preferring to go by way of a slow steamer from Galveston, Texas. That's how much I feared even a few days in New York."

He told me of a man he knew in China who had a similar dread of Shanghai. For business reasons, he often had to go from one suburb east of the city to another place west of it. By direct route the places were only a few hours apart. But he would spend days getting to his destination by a route that avoided crossing Shanghai proper.

He asked when I planned to return to America. I said I doubted I ever would, unless the political pressure of Europe pushed me into it.

By 1933 I seemed to have overcome that earlier phobia. Besides, political pressure from the east seemed to be giving the needed push. Others may not have felt it much. Maugham himself didn't feel it until 1940 when he got out by the skin of his teeth as the Nazis and Fascists proceeded to take over most of France. But we had felt it in the summer of 1932.

I had other reasons of course. I naturally wanted to show off
my bride, now the mother of one-going-on-two. I thought perhaps a personal interview with editors and publishers would
straighten out the Walker-Compton literary fiasco. I had a new
Fun in Bed book to do. I had details of *Sandrik* to attend to.
Besides, if I had to go to New York, I liked it best in summertime—most of all on a Sunday morning in summertime.

Then, too, Barry Fox, secretary to the director of Cornell
Medical School, and long privy to my aches and pains, felt
there might be some modern techniques that could eliminate
the screaming sciatica in my right hip. Since it was suggested
that I have my tonsils nipped again, what better men than at
New York Hospital?

We had promised Skip's grandmother that she could have
him for a year between his first and sixth birthday. Dr. Bernard held the view that a change in climate might knock out his
asthmatic attacks altogether and thought Norway would be ad-
mirable, since the change of climate would be so marked.

All these reasons convinced us that a trip to America for
three or four months would be a sound calculated risk. We
would stay until our second child was born. (It turned out to
be Sylvia Frances Scully, Smith College, Class of 1955.) Then
in the fall, if the political situation had bettered we would
return to Villa Variety.

While we were debating the pros and cons, the Italian Line
made an announcement that settled everything for us. They
said the S. S. *Rex* would put in to the Port of Villefranche
bound for New York on August 10. This was practically from
our front door. The long trip from Nice to either Cherbourg or
Le Havre would be eliminated.

George Antheil decided to go with us. He and I planned to
work on a revision of a musical in the long leisurely hours
through the Mediterranean and on into the Atlantic.

But before we could close the house we received a visit from
Fanny Holtzmann, the theatrical attorney. She had written a
fan letter the year before about a *Variety* column. We had
received it in Bad Reichenhall and she hoped we could get together in Vienna. That didn't work out. So on her next visit to
Europe she wired from London and asked if we could receive
her. She arrived just as we were packing to leave. In fact we
left her and Thérèse to close the house.

Her coming set off a chain-reaction which is a good example
of how touch-and-go many of the big things in life are. It seems
Grand Duke Alexander, like Jimmy Walker, also had girl-
troubles. He had turned over certain literary rights to one of his
women.

After he died, those who had got hold of these rights kept
grinding out material in his name. This turned out to be most
embarrassing to his widow, the Grand Duchess Xenia, and his
children, because intimate matters, such as letters between the
Grand Duke and the then-reigning member of the Windsor
family in England, were published without even asking the
King's permission. As the Grand Duchess and her children put
up at Windsor Castle when she went to England, she was eager
to relieve all of them of this embarrassment.

I told her that the publishers would not continue the practice
if they knew the facts. Then I remembered that Fanny Holtzmann had quite a reputation in this field, so I said to the Grand
Duchess, "I have a friend who's coming to Nice next week and
I'm sure she will help you solve this vexing problem."

Out of this small acorn grew the oak of the famous libel
suit against the motion picture producers of *Rasputin*, a picture which featured Lionel, John, and Ethel Barrymore, but
became better known because of an alleged assault Rasputin
made on one of the ladies-in-waiting to the *Czarina*.

Like all pictures of this sort, *Rasputin* began on a supposedly

historical note and then went off into the blue. Had it started
with a supposedly *fictional* character, it could have used facts
freely thereafter and not have got into trouble. Had the Mad
Monk been called "Pinkovitch," nothing might have come of
this suit. But since he was called "Rasputin," then the girl he
allegedly attacked was Princess Irina Youssopoff, the daughter
of Grand Duke Alexander and Grand Duchess Xenia. (Irina's
husband was one of the group of young Russian nobles who
actually killed Rasputin.)

The producers' general attitude was: "Let them sue. It will
be good publicity." And while that might have been true in
America, it would not be true in England where libel laws are
rigged to favor the favored. If a witness gave her residence
as Windsor Castle, that would about settle the case in the minds
of British jurors.

This was a little thing we got Fanny Holtzmann into, having
no idea that Princess Irina's grievance against Hollywood would
so overshadow her mother's case against the ghostly practices
of the New York publishing world.

Though parting is supposed to be such sweet sorrow, in our
case it was downright melancholy. We had sent Skip off to
Norway, accompanied by a Norwegian nurse, and with his
departure. Thérèse sorrowed so she practically went on a hunger
strike. Alice tried everything, but to no avail.

We talked her into bringing Joseph from the orphanage. This
she finally did.

When we left to board the *Rex*, Fanny, Thérèse, and Joseph
were the only ones to see us off. Alice, Thérèse, and Joseph embraced and wept. It was a touching scene. Fanny called to us
that she would meet us on the dock in New York.

It was Fanny's intention to hop immediately to Cherbourg
and take the *Bremen* to New York while we moseyed across in
a slow Italian liner. As it turned out, she didn't get back to

New York for *seven months,* while we crossed the Atlantic so fast the Bremen was an also-ran.

We had most luxurious second-class accommodations, but unfortunately our huge stateroom was directly above the propellers. The *Rex* was a modern liner equipped with stabilizers. If the stabilizers were used, it slowed down the speed of the ship; and if they weren't used, the ship rolled like a barrel.

From Villefranche to Gibraltar the trip was leisurely enough. We stayed about a half-hour there. Walker had once said that if he ever saw a Prudential calendar again, with a trade mark of the Rock of Gibraltar, he'd jump from the top of the office building he saw it in. I sent him a postcard from there, telling him the rock was nothing really and hoping he was on the ground floor when he received it.

Immediately on leaving Gibraltar, the tempo of our ship changed. Four swimming pools were emptied. The stabilizers were cut off. The ship began to pick up speed. It also began to rock and shake as if it had the ague.

We raced along as if chased by devils. We began to get some hint as to what we were in for when we passed the *Bremen's* record for a twenty-four hour run. People were complaining on all sides, but Captain Commander Francesco Tarabotto was taking his orders from Il Duce, not from the paying customers.

Mussolini had ordered him to smash that transatlantic record, or else. One couple told us they had come down from Paris to the Riviera to take the *Rex* because they wanted plenty of sun and swimming. We took the *Rex* to eliminate all the shaking and vibrations of a train ride, since Alice was expecting her second baby in six weeks.

Our stateroom vibrated so that every few hours plumbers had to come in and tighten up all the fixtures. Between times we used all sorts of devices to quiet the thousand and one rattles. The ship began by averaging 28 knots on Saturday and by Sunday had averaged 28.40. By Monday noon it had averaged 28.70, making 719 knots in twenty-four hours.

The only quiet place in the ship, significantly, was the chapel. It was in the center of the ship. There everything was beautifully cool and quiet. It was decorated in a soft color. Mass was said there every morning, and though the swimming pools were closed, the chapel remained open for smart peasants like us who were looking for peace and quiet, not transatlantic records.

For those who would like to see what the chapel looked like, it is now Our Lady's Chapel, right behind the main altar in St. Patrick's Cathedral in New York, having been removed from the *Rex* when the ship was converted to wartime use.

Despite bad weather we tore through fog for thirty-six hours, the fog whistle blowing every other minute. Everybody was talking about the *Titanic* disaster, fearing history was about to repeat itself, but Commander Tarabotto had his orders. If we had hit an iceberg at the speed we were going, it is quite possible we would have split it in two and still smashed the transatlantic record. We averaged 29.61 knots between noon Monday and noon Tuesday. The total day's run was 736 knots.

We ran into Irving Mills, the music publisher of *Stormy Weather,* aboard ship and I induced him to listen to some of George Antheil's songs from *Candide.* It was the most laughable audition possible. The quaking ship had the piano bouncing around like mad; between Antheil's playing, keys would play of their own accord, as if it were a mechanical piano. Alice held down one end of the piano while Mills held down the other. I rather think that was the day the rhumba was born. Anyway it didn't sell Antheil's *I Am a Baroness.*

Mills obviously couldn't hear the music. In fact nobody could hear anything above the rattle of that ship. Except me.

I could hear what people were shouting across the table even when our table was the full length of the dining room away. The vibration of the ship and the rattle of the dishes, knives, and forks canceled out all the habitual noises in my head (I was 50 per cent off in my hearing) and made it possible for me to hear other people's conversations. The same is true, of course, in a plane or an automobile, but it seemed truer aboard the *Rex* because the shouting was louder.

Our chief worry, aside from possibly hitting an iceberg, or arriving in New York in a shell-shocked condition, was that our baby, if born at sea, would be considered an Italian subject. This was Italian law. The mere idea took the joy out of the fact that we were on a liner that was breaking all records for ocean travel between Europe and America.

By the time we reached Ambrose Light we had covered the 3180 miles between Gibraltar and New York in four days, thirteen hours, and fifty-eight minutes, breaking the record of the *Europa* by three hours. The Statue of Liberty was a blur. It looked as a referee must look to a punch-drunk fighter.

In the cold gray dawn, not due to dock till 9 A.M., we were suddenly roused out of the only restful sleep we had had on the entire trip by the shouts and cries of old friends who had apparently boarded the ship with the customs officers and reporters at Quarantine. Don Stern, Max Schuster, and Si Seadler were among them.

What a homecoming after sixteen years! Behind them came reporters, photographers, and baffled onlookers. They couldn't make out what all the fuss was about. Neither could we.

We were very second-class passengers, but apparently to New York we were returning natives with a great story to tell. All the reporters wanted to know about Jimmy and what he was drinking. When I told them tea, that he actually drank as many as four cups of tea in an afternoon, they thought I was the greatest clown since Grimaldi. No wonder *Fun in Bed* was such a success, edited as it was by a guy who could think up gags like that! It became the streamer-headline of the day:

WALKER HAS DROPPED HIGHBALLS FOR TEA,
SAYS FRANK SCULLY, HIS BIOGRAPHER.

It was amazing how hungry reporters were for news of their deposed playboy-mayor. Apparently they missed him, and the town seemed duller for his going.

Even the customs inspectors treated us as if we were from the diplomatic corps. On hearing we had spent the winter with Jimmy Walker and were Irish ourselves, they passed our fifteen bundles, battered old trunks, and generally dismal looking baggage as if they had been the Secretary of State's confidential diplomatic pouches.

I had a new artificial leg. It hurt and threw me on occasion. I didn't want to wear it until I could get it adjusted in New York. But I wore it from ship to shore to avoid the customs duty and promptly took it off, once we had been passed.

Alice (who always reads the fine print and obeys instructions to the letter, remember?) had failed to declare a small bottle of Napoleon brandy which I was bringing over for H. L. Mencken. She had read that anything over a hundred years old could be considered an antique and therefore did not have to be declared.

"Isn't this brandy over a hundred years old?" she wanted to know.

Prohibition, on its last legs, hadn't quite been counted out. But the customs officers were determined to pass us along with a minimum of inconvenience. They ignored the Napoleon Brandy as the Riviera customs officer had ignored the Vino Santo.

Cleared of customs in a matter of minutes, we were whisked

off to the Hotel St. Moritz and installed in, we were told, the Greta Garbo suite. High on the twenty-fourth floor, it overlooked Central Park. It was a green-carpeted gorgeous suite and it was filled with flowers.

In the lobby Lee Mishkin had introduced us to Walter Winchell, but in our dazed state I didn't realize it until after I had been called to a telephone and he had gone on about his business. It was a good thing for us we were really nobodies or that affront might have had international repercussions!

All I can remember of that day is that either the tempo of New York had increased to the breaking point or that we lacked the kind of help we gave Walker on the Riviera. We sat for everybody and anybody, accepted all kinds of interruptions, and kept whirling around from the awful beating we had taken on the ship. In fact we didn't get over that vertigo completely for months. Often we would wake up in the middle of the night and would grab each other's hand to steady ourselves as if still on that shaking crate.

Friends felt we ought to slap a good suit on the Italian Line, and if we were the sort who believed in going backward we certainly would have. But we weren't, so we kept weaving our way forward as best we could.

By the afternoon of our first day we found ourselves immortalized in six-column streamers, sharing photographic layouts with Desur Arjan Dangar from Lathi, India, who was importing a seventy-eight-inch moustache on which there was no duty because it grew out of his person. Also mentioned were Principessa del Vivaro Borghese, Prince Domenico Orsini, and Princess Laura Orsini, described as "members of two of Rome's oldest patrician families." Princess Domenico Orsini turned out to be the former Mrs. Robert Rowan of California.

Though we were brigaded with these people in the layout of photographs, we knew none of them socially, as obviously they had traveled first-class. (We had traveled second-class because there were no more accommodations in third.)

Our suite at the St. Moritz was crowded with callers, all of whom insisted we should take a rest. There was a dinner scheduled for us that night on the St. Moritz roof. All the old gang were to be there.

George E. Sokolsky, whom I had last seen in 1917 as an emaciated radical with a mop of wavy hair, had now returned from China with close-cropped hair and as fat as a Mandarin of the Fourth Order. Being the Sok of old, he naturally assumed the party was for him and the gang spent most of the evening trying to put him in his place—a practically impossible thing to do.

He had just come back from Washington. He didn't like the way things were going down there. "I'm going to have Moley fired," he said.

Within a week Moley was out as Under-Secretary of State. That was our Sok of old. Sixteen years hadn't changed him. The only change was that, like me, he now had a wife. She was Chinese, beautiful, charming. She certainly changed him for the better.

As the dinner was breaking up, the gang instinctively felt that it wasn't safe for any one member to leave and have his reputation torn to shreds by the rest of them, so they all agreed, at a given signal, to break ranks and scurry for home, leaving no one behind to bend my ear. It was a laughable finish to a wonderful evening.

To impress me with the changes time had wrought, Sok invited us to go with Rosalind and him to the new Music Hall in Rockefeller Center. By the time we could get together I had been loaned the Number One Gold Pass to Radio City. It was issued in the name of Sime Silverman, publisher of *Variety*. When Sok headed for the box office to buy tickets, I signaled him to follow us. We went in a private entrance and immediately, after we had flashed the pass, attention centered on us from all sides. Sok took all this big. Finally I had done something that impressed him.

Like the hero in Leonard Merrick's *Conrad in Quest of His Youth,* I wanted above all things to recapture the pleasures and scenes of my childhood. I wanted to show Alice the old home town. We headed for Steinway, but the intervening sixteen years had destroyed all proof that the place ever existed. Chinese farms had become suburbs. North Beach was no more. Where I promised we would see a lovely swimming beach and a sort of Coney Island, junior grade, we found an enormous dump. Huge trucks and tractors were pushing debris all over the place. Swamps were being filled in. It turned out to be La Guardia Field in the making.

"If I could only find a little Dutch graveyard, I could get my bearings," I said. "With that I could reconstruct the whole scene for you. The graveyard was behind the scenic railway. In fact the switchback was built around the tiny cemetery. If an amusement park would show such respect for the dead, I doubt that a city department would desecrate it."

After some search we did find the graves, and holding on to one of the gravestones I pointed out where we used to swim in Bowery Bay. I located Riker's Island, which first became a city dump and then a *prison.* This may represent some progress to a city overpopulated with juvenile delinquents, but not enough to impress a returning landsman.

I could not find Berrian's Island where my father had immortalized "Burke's Wooden Castle." On further inquiry it developed that the channel between the mainland and the island had been filled in and the island, as such, was no more.

The changes weren't so much a cause for disappointment as a source of baffling bewilderment. I couldn't make out what had happened. In Europe they still remedy and repair old things; in America, in the name of progress, they throw even whole towns on the scrapheap so that people may drive faster on "freeways" and get killed sooner. New York had become Moses Mazes. One wrong turn and you couldn't right yourself for miles.

It was not much easier to find Calvary Cemetery—at least not the first part of it where my father, mother, and eight sisters and brothers were buried. Celtic Park, the playground of the Irish-American Athletic Club in the neighborhood of the cemetery, was no more. It had become a real estate subdivision. But we did find the Scully headstone and the plot looked lovingly well kept. This of course was the saddest part of our homecoming.

One night we went from a dinner with Sid Silverman to see *Let 'Em Eat Cake*, the sequel to *Of Thee I sing*. *Let 'Em Eat Cake* enjoyed the same cast as the prize-winning play. The stars were William Gaxton, Victor Moore, and Lois Moran. We particularly wanted to see Gaxton. He was supposed to resemble Walker, and his imitations of him had made Jimmy writhe. They certainly did look alike.

This must have been the play that convinced George Kaufman that satire is something that closes on Saturday night, for it was loaded with satire and it didn't last long. In one scene two youths walked past the Union League Club whistling and were stopped by a cop. He admonished them to be quiet and then allowed them to tiptoe past the Club.

I saw that same scene played straight in *Cavalcade* in London when a boy whistling in a park was stopped by a bobby because Queen Victoria had died a few days before and the whole town was still in mourning.

In *Let 'Em Eat Cake* two agitators fought for a soapbox, neither being able to speak without it. An international issue was settled by killing the umpire. Seven cabinet members were in jail. One of them kept yelling for Max Steuer, a lawyer renowned for springing notables in that era.

But the play didn't go over. This may have been strictly a matter of timing. *Of Thee I Sing* found audiences responsive to kicking the teeth out of a discredited federal administration. But by 1933 the Roosevelt Revolution had begun to rehabilitate a badly battered people. I had left New York when the town was suffering from the worst grippe epidemic in history and had come back to find everybody suffering from the NRA and a code in the head. In that respect it didn't seem like much of an improvement.

Through Barry Fox (who later married Dr. A. M. Stevens) we booked ourselves into New York Hospital, Alice in the Lying-In wing for a sixty-five-dollar baby in October and I in Surgery for a re-take on a tonsillectomy and anything that might be done to relieve the chronic pains in my stump. I had decided after my experience in Paris to get any backlog of repair work done whenever Alice was having a baby. There is precious little work a father can do while his wife is delivering a baby and why not get himself fixed up so he will be better able to increase his earning capacity later?

Meanwhile we made the rounds of all our friends, and Alice, I could see, was impressed with the degree of solvency they enjoyed, though the country as a whole was presumably broke. Most of them had apartments in town, though Howard Dietz owned a house in Greenwich Village and Merryle Rukeyser had one in New Rochelle and Jae Greenberg was summering in Cedarhurst. We dined at all these places as well as with Elliott and Eleanor Sanger and Si and Dodo Seadler in town.

At Seadler's where we went for dinner on a Friday night the cook was in a dither on seeing who we were. It seemed we were the self-same people whose picture was in the paper the market had wrapped the fish in for dinner.

Dodo Seadler, whose cooking many years before had pulled Si from being a pretty sick kid to where he had become the indefatigable dancing master of stage, screen, and radio in his off-hours from his post as advertising manager of Metro Goldwyn Mayer, was mighty pleased to have a cook who not only served her guests but could distinguish them from Columbia River salmon.

One day we were going to have a late afternoon picnic in Central Park. We had bought everything for it, but we had forgotten that New York might have sudden rains in summertime. By the time we planned to move from the St. Moritz suite to the park, the town was being drenched in a thunderstorm. So we spread our picnic on the green carpet of the hotel suite and had our picnic supper there. We looked across to the park and congratulated ourselves. In a hotel room sort of picnic one suffered no bites from ants, no sand in the food, no bruises from wildly thrown baseballs.

One night Alice and I left the St. Moritz and went slumming up and down Broadway. It was the first time she had ever seen it, but it didn't seem to me it had changed much in sixteen years. It did seem brighter, like an electric light bulb just before its filament breaks and all goes black.

The general effect around Times Square was a bit more like Coney Island. Traffic was better regulated but hardly moved at all. Instead of snarling and honking as in the old days, cars crawled along in fits and starts between traffic lights. Smart people got around faster on foot, even with the red lights against them most of the time. As a matter of fact, pedestrians seemed to ignore the lights, yet few of them were killed and none got tickets for crossing when the light was against them.

The buildings of Rockefeller Center towered above St. Patrick's Cathedral. Both gave organ recitals, which did much to soothe the nerves of a town running on tensions. Soft coal had made the town more sooty and less snooty than it was in days of old.

But the dirt did not seem confined to window sills. It seemed to have got into the language, particularly into the conversations of women. How these washroom recitals got into New York drawing rooms really puzzled me.

The kind of stories I liked were of the era. When I was riding one afternoon with Ed Anthony and Max Schuster, an armored car passed us. Max leaned over to Ed and whispered "A payroll wagon—remember?" It was a depression joke shared by fourteen million jobless people.

In other respects Ballyhoo Boulevard showed changes in degree but not in kind. Metro-Goldwyn Mayer was still experimenting with lights projected on other people's buildings. Earlier, Howard Dietz had used the wall of the Paramount to tell people to go to the Capitol. But now he was using a rotating light that tossed off colors. It was ballyhooing *Dinner at Eight* to millions who hadn't even had a breakfast for days.

When I left New York, the best remembered marquee was a chaste announcement of Ina Claire in *Polly with a Past*. When I returned, a billboard of Marlene Dietrich's breasts were covering Broadway from 44th to 45th Street. This block-long vulgarity was advertising a movie of *The Song of Songs*.

As we wandered up Broadway, we discovered that 57th Street was still 'way uptown and Columbus Circle the end. The Cosmopolitan Theatre was dark and mangy, unable or too tired to erase its shame. Anyway, there it stood with Zit's name above it on the roof as proof it had lived and died and was no more. Columbia burlesque was having an equally hard time of it. The clean shows of Miners and Barney Gerard had been replaced by Minsky's obscenities. But Radio City, which was off Broadway but of it, was a beautiful monument to show business.

Though this was in the depth of depression, everybody who could afford it went out of town weekends. Many owned a peak in Darien and profaned the silence by dragging guests out there over the weekend, though all of them had bought their country homes in the first place to get away from it all.

J. P. McEvoy was lining up a party for us over Labor Day at his sixty-acre place in Woodstock, New York. He had invited us to his place in the Catskill Mountains for an indefinite stay, giving rise to a story that after one week of Manhattan we were willing to flee to the hills forever. It turned out that way, but we didn't plan it that way.

Max Schuster told us that perhaps two hundred of our friends would be at the McEvoy party.

"Do we have that many between us?" I asked, bewildered.

"If we haven't, Mac has," said Schuster. "He serves apple-jack in the barn."

I long ago had discovered that the peace and quiet people craved could best be experienced on a Sunday morning in almost any big city in the world. We received many invitations to go out of town for our first weekend, but Alice and I wanted to go to St. Patrick's Cathedral for the eleven-o'clock High Mass. At Christmas or Easter we would not have had a chance on our own, though I do recall, through the influence of Jewish friends, that we were invited by a distinguished family to use their pew for the High Mass at Easter. It happened to be so close to the altar rail that we practically rubbed shoulders with Al Smith and Jim Farley. But on the occasion of our first Sunday in town the Cathedral was only half-filled, and after Mass we were privileged to study at leisure this finest example of Gothic architecture in America.

Another reason for our staying in town that first weekend was that we had been informed that Sime Silverman was coming down from Canada and would be at his desk Sunday afternoon. Fanny Holtzmann had put a new car and a uniformed chauffeur completely at our disposition for a week. So after Mass we drove over from Fifth Avenue and 50th Street to the *Variety* office at 154 West 46th Street. It was right next to the stage door of Loew's State. We climbed a short flight of stairs and met an old friend for the first and last time. In a press interview only a few days before, I had been asked what paper I thought had taken the place of the old *Sun* in modern journalism.

"*Variety*," I replied.

When we arrived, Sime was being interviewed by Arthur Ungar who had once been on his staff in Hollywood and had resigned to become a producer at Universal. Failing in that, he was trying to talk Sime into starting a daily in Hollywood. Sime obviously didn't want to do it and kept mumbling, "We get out a flop once a week, and now he wants us to get out another one *five times* a week."

Ungar looked pretty disconsolate, but it was obvious that Sime was going to give in.

So much had passed between us since 1927 that we really felt we were old friends. That peculiar news angle that he developed, the inside story for insiders, written in a gay vernacular peculiar to show business, had become a *Variety* tradition long before I joined its staff. Sime wrote like a man thinking out loud, trying to hit the bull's-eye and keeping at it till he did. When he did, that was it. He stopped cold. His critical opinions were honest and complete. He took no dictation from the front office. He *was* the front office. He called his staff his "muggs." They wrote as they saw things. If there were sacred cows, I never heard who they were. He had no use for dirt in show business and believed that it was economically as well as morally poor business.

He developed such short-cuts in writing that columns were compressed into paragraphs and paragraphs into lines. His news sense was terrific, and in the daily field this would have made him the best editor in the world, which, in my opinion, he was anyway.

While we were talking, Sime kept letting out bronchial whoops that left me white with fright. I used to have hemorrhages after coughs like that. He assured me it was nothing and that I ought to hear him when he was really warmed up to it. (One of them, a month later, actually did give Sime a terminal hemorrhage.)

Noting the galley proofs piled up before him as *Variety* was getting ready to go to press and realizing what a narrow margin of physical energy he had to work on, I felt that any further idle chatter was certainly doing him a disservice. We got up to go and he got up to walk down the steps of the old *Variety* office with us to where our borrowed car and chauffeur were parked.

Sime took the scene big. For the first time since our meeting he looked worried. In show business people put on fronts like this because they were broke. He feared we had rented this ensemble to impress a hard-boiled town where even knife-throwers supposedly practiced on their young.

As we neared the car and the chauffeur standing at attention, Sime leaned over and whispered, "Everything okay? Need any money?"

I assured him we didn't, that everything was fine. Nevertheless as we drove away he repeated, "Don't forget, if you need any money . . ."

We were home at last.

Postscript

•

For the benefit of those who must have their vitamin pills after a full and well-balanced meal, perhaps it would be nice to give a concentrate of what happened to the Scully Circus after the native returned and found that a few whiffs of his home town's air did not kill him.

We spent the winter of 1933-34 in the Catskills. Our first-born and his grandmother came from Norway to join us. Sylvia, our first daughter, born in New York in October, was there to greet them. The next spring we left in style for Hollywood by way of the Panama Canal, financed by a motion picture contract.

Arrived at our destination, we took the money we hadn't wasted impressing others and built a home above Hollywood and Vine, modeling it after Villa Variety in Nice. We called it Bedside Manor. We could look down into the school yard of Blessed Sacrament School, making it rather difficult for our kids to play hookey.

We made it a home for babies, pets, and callers who were between jobs. It was during the depression, remember, and we were singularly lucky; so we shared the wealth in a way perhaps more personal than Huey Long or Upton Sinclair proposed.

Up to then, I had been a one-suitcase political economist who

368

didn't want to be caught with much else when the whole thing blew up. But I changed to a do-gooder, and it did me more good than the people I helped. I entered politics, running for the lowest office in the lowest deliberative body in the world, and I was just low enough to make it.

Inspired by papal encyclicals on labor and social justice, I got in deeper and deeper. I ran into an alliance between the law enforcement arm and the underworld and was told if I didn't like the place to go back where I came from. My answer was, "You go back where I came from. I'm staying."

About seven of us decided to delouse "The City of Fallen Angels," as I called Los Angeles, and the cops started bombing our homes, wiretapping our private conversations, and otherwise acting like lawless goons. Our bodyguard, a former chief of detectives, stepped on his starter one morning and was dragged to the hospital with 186 shrapnel slugs in his body. Hard as it may be to believe, he lived, and the man who wired the bomb and fastened it to our bodyguard's self-starter, a cop and the acting captain of a squad whose job it was to intimidate private citizens possessed of some civic virtue, got a jail sentence of twenty years. We had the mayor recalled (he wasn't even a citizen) and in time got rid of others as well.

Eight assemblymen came and asked me to run for governor. I had picked another man, but they assured me he would not work out. Nevertheless, we elected him—the first time a man of the party I favored had been elected governor in forty-four years. They were right. He didn't work out.

Still fighting like Don Quixote, I got slapped with a political indictment a few weeks before an election and while I was on a visit to New York. I forced a trial before the election. The jury was out only twenty minutes and returned a verdict of not guilty. But having only a week to campaign for the assembly, I was defeated by a narrow margin. I didn't spend any time on my campaign. I spent it on fighting the D.A. who had thrown the mud at me. He went down to defeat.

On my one lung, one leg, and one idea, I got back to writing to keep doctors off the dole. My many ailments took their places in line and the only fear I had was that they might all attack at once someday. If so, I would be one of the best-known names in Calvary Cemetery.

Still, I kept my hand in things politically and every four years got elected to the County Central Committee, a sort of Tammany that had been cleaned up. I am still in there at this writing. I don't campaign anymore. I am a sort of left-wing Coolidge. I do better by shutting my mouth and letting my deeds talk for me.

With the introduction of smog, however, I felt I was being gassed out of the community. By this time we had five children, a beautiful home (all paid for), two cars (all paid for), and every reason to grow old gracefully. But my lungs would not take these new-found poisons. Alice developed sinus trouble. Our Whitley Heights became Mount Sinus. So we retreated to the desert. We bought a ranch eighty miles from Hollywood and the first improvement we made was to build a chapel in one of the bunkhouses. It was the first house of worship in the community and as of this writing (June 10, 1955) is still the only one in Desert Springs.

From the hands of Monsignor Charles E. Hagearty as emissary of the Bishop of Jaro, the Philippines, I received a papal knighthood in the Order of St. Elizabeth, which was founded by Queen Isabella of Spain. Ann Blyth, the actress, was the witness to the ceremony. I also was received in the Third Order of St. Francis. I even got elected president of a chamber of commerce, which was as unbelievable to me as it will be to most readers.

Our children, of course, are growing up. Two have graduated

from college. One is a lieutenant in the Air Force and the father at this writing of one-year-old male twins. A third child of our own, Patricia Ann, graduated in 1955 from high school and is now studying nursing with the hope of getting a Bachelor of Science degree as well. A fourth, whose name is Marguerite Alice (if I remember correctly), has never been known by any name but "Nonny." We called her that after Anon, the most prolific poet in literature. A fifth child, named Moreen Theresa and known as "Little Mo," was five in the summer of 1955. Whether there will be any more is in the hands of God.

He has been good to us and our gratitude has increased with the years. We have found that He gave us what we wanted if we wanted it long enough, but perhaps not at the time we wanted it most.

Where we will go from here is in His hands. We hope, of course, it will be up.

Index

•